Dance and Gender

UNIVERSITY PRESS OF FLORIDA

Florida A&M University, Tallahassee
Florida Atlantic University, Boca Raton
Florida Gulf Coast University, Ft. Myers
Florida International University, Miami
Florida State University, Tallahassee
New College of Florida, Sarasota
University of Central Florida, Orlando
University of Florida, Gainesville
University of North Florida, Jacksonville
University of South Florida, Tampa
University of West Florida, Pensacola

DANCE AND GENDER

An Evidence-Based Approach

Edited by Wendy Oliver and Doug Risner

University Press of Florida
Gainesville · Tallahassee · Tampa · Boca Raton
Pensacola · Orlando · Miami · Jacksonville · Ft. Myers · Sarasota

Copyright 2017 by Wendy Oliver and Doug Risner
All rights reserved
Printed in the United States of America on acid-free paper

This book may be available in an electronic edition.

First cloth printing, 2017
First paperback printing, 2018

23 22 21 20 19 18   6 5 4 3 2 1

A record of cataloging-in-publication data is available from the Library of Congress.
ISBN 978-0-8130-6266-2 (cloth)
ISBN 978-0-8130-6468-0 (pbk.)

The University Press of Florida is the scholarly publishing agency for the State University System of Florida, comprising Florida A&M University, Florida Atlantic University, Florida Gulf Coast University, Florida International University, Florida State University, New College of Florida, University of Central Florida, University of Florida, University of North Florida, University of South Florida, and University of West Florida.

University Press of Florida
15 Northwest 15th Street
Gainesville, FL 32611-2079
http://upress.ufl.edu

To our friend and colleague Jan Van Dyke: feminist, scholar, choreographer, dancer, and teacher

1941–2015

Contents

List of Tables ix
Preface xi

1. An Introduction to Dance and Gender 1
   Wendy Oliver and Doug Risner

2. Dance in America: Gender and Success 20
   Jan Van Dyke

3. Behind the Curtain: Exploring Gender Equity in Dance among Choreographers and Artistic Directors 39
   Eliza Larson

4. Engendered: An Exploratory Study of Regendering Contemporary Ballet 60
   Gareth Belling

5. Sassy Girls and Hard-Hitting Boys: Dance Competition Culture and Gender 76
   Karen Schupp

6. Boys Only! Gender-Based Pedagogical Practices in a Commercial Dance Studio 97
   Carolyn Hebert

7. Friendship Formation among Professional Male Dancers 115
   Katherine Polasek and Emily Roper

8. "Boys are Morons" . . . "Girls are Gross": Let's Dance! 135
   Karen E. Bond

9. Leadership and Gender in Postsecondary Dance: An Exploratory
   Survey of Dance Administrators in the United States   158
   Doug Risner and Pamela S. Musil

   References   185
   List of Contributors   205
   Index   209

Tables

2.1. Gender Ratio at ADF Six-Week School 25
2.2. Gender Ratio of Major U.S. Concert Companies, 2014 26
2.3. NEA Award Figures, 1994–1995 30
3.1. Ted Shawn Theatre, Jacob's Pillow Dance Festival 49
3.2. Doris Duke Theatre, Jacob's Pillow Dance Festival 50
3.3. Durham Performing Arts Center, American Dance Festival 53
3.4. Reynolds Industries Theater, American Dance Festival 54
4.1. Marriage of Choice? Perceptions of Normative and Regendered Casts on the Type of Marriage in *Les Noces* 72
4.2. Emotional Relationship between the "Bride" and "Groom": Shifting Perceptions 73
5.1. Appearance Norms 84
5.2. Movement Expectations 86
5.3. Female and Male Interactions 88
5.4. The Specialness of Boys 91
9.1. Position Title by Gender 163
9.2. Rank and Tenure Status by Gender 164
9.3. Workload as Percent Time by Gender 165
9.4. Average Salary by Rank, Annual Appointment, and Gender 166
9.5. Support Satisfaction by Gender 167
9.6. Most Influential Experiences and Persons by Gender 168
9.7. Primary Challenges by Gender 170
9.8. Participant Responses by Gender, Ability to Maintain Teaching 171
9.9. Participant Responses by Gender, Perception of Others 172

Preface

This book was created out of our mutual interest in dance and gender. Doug Risner has a long history of published articles on boys and men in dance, and his book *Stigma and Perseverance in the Lives of Boys Who Dance: An Empirical Study of Male Identities in Western Theatrical Dance Training* (2009a) delves into the problems and concerns of male dancers. Wendy Oliver helped found the women's studies program at Providence College in 1994, and since then she has been combining her interests in dance and women's studies, including publishing articles on the body image of female dancers (2005, 2008) and co-editing *Women Making Art: Women in the Visual, Literary, and Performing Arts since 1960* (2000).

As editors at the *Journal of Dance Education* from 2009 to 2012, we had the opportunity to read countless articles on the innovative ways in which dance educators are striving to move the field forward with research or best practices in the classroom. We sensed from some of these readings as well as other research that perhaps the field of dance is slowly changing and becoming more open and less discriminatory with regard to gender. When Jan Van Dyke published her gender equity dance research in 1992, 1993, and 1996, she showed unequivocally that female choreographers lagged far behind males in funding, compensation, and institutional support. We wondered if that had changed in the past twenty years, and if so, were women now just as likely as men to earn a living wage through dance? We also pondered the impact of Ramsay Burt's book *The Male Dancer: Bodies, Spectacle, Sexualities* (1995), one of the first to consider issues of homophobia and discrimination against males in the field of dance. Were men making gains in terms of acceptance of dance as a socially legitimate profession for males? We hoped to find the answers to these questions by creating this book.

In addition to the two questions posed above about gender equity and men in dance, we had some broad questions driving the creation of the book: What issues around dance and gender have been topics of study over the past twenty years? How have women's and gender studies, queer studies, and other critical studies areas informed the development of dance research in recent decades? And how could we contribute something unique to the conversation as well as advance new research in dance and dance education? This last question we answered after conducting a thorough review of literature on dance and gender.

Although a great deal has been written and theorized in the vein of performance analysis through a gendered lens (i.e., examining particular dance works, companies, dance forms, and styles including popular dance), not much empirical research dealing with gender in dance has been conducted or published. We believed that a book of empirical studies would make a unique contribution to the field and provide a much-needed update on the "state of gender" in the dance world.

Through a call for papers, we were able to identify several researchers from the United States, Australia, and Canada who had ideas for or were already working on studies relevant to this topic. We were delighted to read about the type of work these scholars were engaged in. The range of topics and variety of research methods gave an overall breadth to our project, while individual articles mined the depths of particular areas. A substantial period of writing and revision allowed authors to fully develop their studies.

This book provides a snapshot of dance and gender in the early twenty-first century. It is our hope that this research will lead to greater understanding of how the dance world, like the larger world we inhabit, is often constricted by dominant notions of gender. Yet along with this realization, we can appreciate that dance inquiry has profited from feminist, queer, and other critical outlooks and has moved toward greater self-awareness as a field.

We are indebted to the authors for their dedication to their projects that made this volume possible. We are also indebted to our colleague Sherrie Barr for her assistance with reviewing some of the chapters and giving invaluable feedback. Her thoughtful observations and willingness to contribute to the project were very much appreciated.

1

An Introduction to Dance and Gender

WENDY OLIVER AND DOUG RISNER

The fact that dance reflects gendered sociocultural patterns comes as no surprise to any who have studied dance history, attended a dance performance, or participated in a dance class. Choreographers, dancers, dance teachers, critics, and all those who are part of the dance world are first and foremost individuals who were shaped by the culture in which they grew and developed. When that culture tends to assign identities on the basis of gender, it is logical that creative expression in that culture may follow suit, albeit sometimes countered by the voices of artists who critique the status quo. The fields of gender studies, women's studies, queer studies, as well as the sciences and social sciences, have all investigated the concept and physical expression of gender "difference."

Psychologist and researcher Cordelia Fine (2010) uses the term "neurosexism" to describe the explanations that various experts have created to describe differences between men's and women's behavior that are thought to be "brain-based." The sexes are thought to have differences that are hardwired to the point where, for instance, men are at a disadvantage where intuition is concerned and where women are at a disadvantage in mathematics. Fine investigates the studies that have been done on the brain relating to gender difference and reveals how flawed many of them are. A typical problem is the jump from brain structure to psychological function: physical differences in men's and women's brains—such as the amount of white matter, specialization, and size of the corpus callosum— do not necessarily correlate to difference in behavior. Although Fine does believe that there are sex differences in the brain, she finds that "neither structural nor functional imaging can currently tell us much about differences between male and female minds" (154). She deconstructs popular ideas of natural differences by pointing to the ways in which people are conditioned from birth to be different on the basis of assigned gender, including those raised by parents who attempt "gender-neutral" households.

What are the implications of this type of research for dancers and the field of dance studies? In dance and other physical activities, men and women are often thought to move differently due to innate differences in body structure. For instance, men generally have more upper-body strength than women (Jensen et al. 2000), and women often have more hip flexibility than men (Etnyre and Lee 1988). These differences, along with a cultural tendency to highlight stylistic elements perceived as either masculine or feminine, have produced some distinctly gendered styles of dance, with masculine styles often emphasizing leaps, jumps, power, and upper-body strength and feminine styles focused upon flexibility, fluidity, and emotion (see Bond and Schupp chapters in this book).

Of course, many contemporary choreographers realize that women and men need not be restricted by these movement stereotypes. Instead of emphasizing "difference" in their choreography, they find ways of keeping the choreography neutral by ignoring gender (for instance, giving all dancers the same movement regardless of gender). Another option is to undercut or transform gender roles in some way (Alterowitz 2014; Belling, this volume; Boccadoro 2006), for instance using role reversal or regendering.

While physical factors certainly play a role in how people move, dance is about more than body construction, and the psyche of those in the field is also important in how they approach their work as dancers, choreographers, directors, and teachers. By the time dancers develop into artists, often in their late teen years, they have already participated in shaping themselves into gendered beings. Gender studies scholar Robert Connell (2002) notes, "People growing up in a gendered society unavoidably encounter gender relations, and actively participate in them . . . Young people learn how to negotiate the gender order. They learn how to adopt a certain gender identity and produce a certain gender performance" (79–81). The messages that dancers receive and respond to regarding gender are deeply ingrained and affect their psyches, behavior, and creative output. Dancers and choreographers adapt to the "gender order" mentioned above by finding their own ways of being male, female, or "other."

Although the professional dance world is often more tolerant than mainstream society when it comes to gender or sexual identities that fall outside of a strict binary (Polasek and Roper, this volume), this does not preclude daily (mostly unconscious) negotiations to maintain one's gender status, whatever that may be. And in cases where dance gender roles are strictly defined as masculine or feminine, such as in dance competitions (Broomfield 2011; Picart 2006; Schupp, this volume) or in a classical ballet, dancers must literally "perform gender" onstage, in a heightened form of the performance of gender that scholar Judith Butler discusses in her book *Gender Trouble* (1990/1999). Violations of these roles can lead to censure and can affect the outcome of competitions (Broomfield 2011).

Gender roles onstage are only the tip of the iceberg where gender and dance are concerned. There are other venues where gender comes into play, including children's and teenagers' dance classes, dance rehearsals, leadership within dance companies and university dance departments, and choreographer funding and prestige, to name a few. Some of the overarching questions prompting the writing of this book include: In what ways is dance gendered in Western society today? What is significant about these findings? How does gendering affect the agency of those within the dance world? Are there specific problems that can be addressed—and if so, how?

This book aims to show how notions of gender operate within the dance world in the early twenty-first century, based on empirical research focused on a variety of dance-related topics. The editors hope to fill a gap in the dance literature by providing concrete evidence about how gender impacts the everyday lives of those in the dance world through surveys, interviews, analysis of data from institutional sources, and action research. This book builds on the work of previous research done on the topic of dance and gender, an area of study that developed as an outgrowth of feminist theory and gender studies beginning in the 1980s. Before discussing the contents of *Dance and Gender* more specifically, it is important to understand the scope of the relevant scholarly literature in order to provide a context for discussion.

Review of Literature

This review includes sources positioned primarily from a Western perspective that are concerned with concert dance, dance education, and cultural and recreational dance forms found primarily in North America and Europe. The authors acknowledge that this leaves some areas of the literature untouched, such as gender roles in dance within anthropological studies, as well as non-Western literature (Reed 1998).

The consideration of race as it intersects with gender is another area that is not addressed in depth in the book. Although the crossover between race and gender is discussed in the literature review in this chapter, as well as in Risner and Musil's chapter in this volume, none of the other chapters in the book focus upon this important issue. This topic needs more attention in order to fully understand how racism and sexism coexist within the dance world, especially in the realms of professional ballet and postsecondary dance. Another important consideration that was not explored in depth is the consideration of gender beyond the binary of male and female. Although discussed in the introduction, gender diversity in all its dimensions within the world of dance is worthy of further investigation.

This review of the literature looks to contextualize the chapters within the book, which are written by authors from Canada, Australia, and the United States concerning dance within the authors' own countries. Therefore, the sources presented here are those most relevant to the framing of this book and are not meant to represent the sum total of available literature on dance and gender throughout the world. The sources searched include books, articles, dissertations, and theses, and they pull from many areas of research, including dance and dance education; gender, women's, and men's studies; queer theory and gay, lesbian, bisexual, and transgendered studies; black studies; and cultural and popular culture studies.

Feminist Perspectives

Feminist theory has influenced many fields since the 1980s, and among them is dance research (Daly 1991; Adair 1992; Oliver 1994; Marques 1998; Shapiro 1998; Stinson 1998b; Green 1999; Thomas 2003). Ann Daly (1991) noted, "The inquiries that feminist analysis makes into the ways that the body is shaped and comes to have meaning are directly and immediately applicable to the study of dance, which is after all, a kind of living laboratory of the study of the body—its training, its stories, its way of being and being seen in the world" (2).

Male gaze theory (Mulvey 1975) was originally developed as an explanation for how men viewed women in a filmic context; Daly extended this Freudian semiotic theory to include the viewing of dancers onstage. Laura Mulvey posited that women in cinema are represented for the pleasure of the heterosexual male viewer and thus become the object of the male gaze. The woman as object is then made passive by the male gaze, mirroring the asymmetrical power relationships in everyday life. Daly argues that dance holds the potential to disrupt the male gaze and that women could resist "being co-opted by the conventions and expectations of the male gaze" (1991, 3). This theory was widely embraced by feminist scholars in the 1990s; the tendency has been to view ballet and traditional concert dance training as vehicles for patriarchal oppression (Marques 1998; Stinson 1998a, 1998b; Shapiro 1998). However, others protested this view (Novack 1990; Banes 1998; Feurer 2001; Thomas 2003), criticizing feminists "who held ballet responsible for all that's bad for women in dance" (Banes 1998, 4), noting the limitations of gaze theory. For instance, it assumes "an ahistorical universal structure of male, heterosexual looking for presuming that men, unlike women, are not objectified through the gaze and for not taking account of difference, except along the lines of Freudian male/female binary divide" (Thomas 2003, 159).

Feminist pedagogy recommends that teaching be inclusive, nonhierarchical, and maintain a multicultural, multiclass, and multiage perspective. Embracing the body within a view of mind and body as a whole, and incorporating questioning of gender stereotypes were also recommended (Oliver 1994). Dance educators have proposed pedagogies incorporating gender issues; for instance, Sherry Shapiro (1998) proposes a theoretical framework for liberatory pedagogy that emerges from feminist and critical perspectives involving self-exploration by both teacher and students. Shapiro argues for greater attention to social justice in arts education, especially concerning how the body is valued, and developed a pedagogy of embodiment in dance (2004). Daly (1994) considers how gender issues can shape dance history pedagogy and provide a rich basis for discussion.

The issue of race as it intersects gender is also important to consider in dance education (West 2005). Educators must resist and transform gendered and hypersexualized assumptions and attitudes that devalue readings of black and brown bodies. Ananya Chatterjea (2004) examines the role of race, gender, and cross-cultural aesthetics in dance through the lens of choreography by Zawole Willa Jo Zollar and Chandralekha, claiming that their works "redefine notions of beauty and empowerment . . ." (xiv). "Womb Wars" by Zollar focuses on the body as the site of oppression and violence. "Yantra" by Chandralekha focuses on sexuality and its political implications. Looking at the Latina dancer in Hollywood film, Priscilla Ovalle (2006) finds intersecting tropes of race and gender that stereotype the abilities of these performers.

The concept of gender and sexuality as a performed identity is another theme in the literature. Judith Butler (1990) famously presented the idea that males and females learn to perform the behaviors and appearances that culture deems appropriate for each gender. Bodies are considered not as objects with inherent boundaries and properties but as material-discursive phenomena (Allegranti 2011). Continuing the theme of women's bodies, scholars have attended to the idea of perfection and how dancers strive to achieve it. Some writers are critical of this perfection-oriented mindset (Heiland, Murray, and Edley 2008), while others accept it, within limits (Grigner, et al. 2006).

Body image is a common concern for female dancers, and quantitative and qualitative research points to the need for a focus on wellness to better support girls and women in the dance studio (Heiland, et al. 2008; Oliver 2008; O'Flynn, et al. 2013). Pregnancy and dance is also considered (Schaumann 2010). Other articles look at body image and training issues specifically within ballet (Aalten 2005; Oliver 2005; Pickard 2013; Pickard 2015). Finally, the *Encyclopedia of Body Image and Human Appearance* (Cash 2012) gives a comprehensive view from experts in the social, behavioral, and biomedical sciences, demonstrating that body image is an important topic throughout the scholarly community. Since the 1990s, dance scholarship has been strongly influenced by feminist scholarship, which has led to inquiry around the agency of the female dancing body both in the dance studio and on stage.

Social Construction of Gender

The social construction of gender is a concept from feminist theory and posits that nurture rather than nature plays the primary role in developing feminine and masculine traits throughout infancy and childhood. Within dance education, the social construction of gender is significant in forming student and parent attitudes toward dance. (Stinson, et al. 1990;

Flintoff 1991; Van Dyke 1992; Cushway 1996; Sanderson 2001; Stinson 1998a, 1998b, 2001; Gard 2001, 2003a; Green 2001, 2002–2003, 2004; Risner 2002a, 2002b, 2004). In middle-class U.S. culture, dance is often assumed to be a natural part of a young girl's activities. Beginning as young as three years old, girls may grow up taking classes on a regular basis, adopting values "which teach that it is good to be obedient and silent, good not to question authority or to have ideas which might conflict with what one is being asked to do" (Van Dyke 1992, 120). The typical dance class experience revolves around the teacher talking and demonstrating, with students replicating the movement presented, rather than discussing, questioning, or creating. This hidden curriculum in dance reinforces traditional gender expectations for girls including passivity, obedience, and escapism (Stinson, et al. 1990; Van Dyke 1992; Smith 1998; Stinson 1998b, 2005). This type of learning tends to produce passive followers rather than active leaders (Stinson, et al. 1990; Van Dyke 1992) and may also contribute to further gender bias in dance. Some suggestions have been made about how to approach these problems (Warburton 2009), however, there has yet to be an organized effort in the dance education community where teachers commit to adjusting their curricula to address gender bias (Oliver 1994; Kahlich 2001). Gender is a topic that should be addressed in teaching in order to make it visible within the curriculum (Ferdun 1994; Risner 2006, 2008; Stinson 2005).

Research in dance education has drawn from social foundations in education, particularly regarding schooling and its effect upon gender identity (Risner and Barr 2015). In tandem with theory in areas such as feminism, gender studies, critical theory and pedagogy, and men's studies, dance research in the twenty-first century now discusses issues of social justice including gender stereotyping (Risner and Stinson 2010; Barr and Risner 2014). Cultural assumptions about gender and dominant power relationships produce unjust educational and sociocultural outcomes (Clark 1994; Horwitz 1995; Marques 1998; Shapiro 1998, 2004; Smith 1998; Green 2000, 2001, 2002–2003, 2004; Schaffman 2001; Keyworth 2001; Risner 2002a, 2002b, 2004, 2005; Blume 2003; Letts and Nobles 2003; Gard 2003a, 2003b).

Some research analyzes differences between the movement tendencies of boys and girls. One 1995 study of eight hundred elementary school children found significant differences between boys and girls in dance classes. Boys covered large amounts of space, used more physical energy, moved quickly, took physical risks, and approached their own presentations with confidence. Girls worked in limited space, moved at slow to moderate tempos, did not take physical risks, spent considerable time standing still, and apprehensively showed their presentations. When working in mixed gender groups, boys assumed leadership positions frequently; girls often complained that boys would not cooperate because they separated themselves from the group (Willis 1995). Karen Bond (1994) found that although a group of children initially moved in gender-differentiated ways, with the use of masks and multisensory ritual, gender roles seemed to disappear.

Another study examined the extent to which personal interest accounted for boys' and girls' learning outcomes in a middle school dance unit within a physical education class, finding that situational interest may motivate all students, but the greater personal interest on the part of the girls was correlated to higher skill/knowledge outcomes (Shen, et al. 2003). A study on intergenerational dance looked at a father-son dance class where participants ranged in age from five to forty-five years old; they created an aesthetic community with a group style (Richard 2009).

Contact improvisation offers an alternative to traditional gender roles through weight sharing, lifts, and falls that are not prescribed by gender. This dance form challenges sexism, homophobia, elitism, and power relations, and possibilities for more meaningful human interactions are broadened (Horwitz 1995). Karen Schaffman (2001) claims that contact improvisation has contributed to postmodern dance by offering partnering skills, exploring gender identities, and performing varied representations of touch and weight. As performed by a range of bodies (trained, untrained, differently abled, differently sized), contact improvisation allows for issues of gender, sexuality, ethnicity, and difference to be exposed more candidly. This egalitarian attitude is possible largely due to the acceptance of the idea that gender is socially constructed, and as such, can be socially "unconstructed." Overall, the research on the social construction of gender within dance contexts focuses strongly on dance training and how it can either participate in or resist gender stereotyping.

Gender Equity

Dance has commonly been considered a "woman's world," yet this has not necessarily translated to equity between the sexes. Data from the United States has shown that men have an advantage over women when it comes to employment, income, scholarships, and grants. (Van Dyke 1996; McGuire 1999; Samuels 2001). Male-headed dance companies also receive more invitations to perform at prestigious U.S. venues such as Jacob's Pillow, the American Dance Festival, and the Spoleto Dance Festival (Van Dyke 1996). Additionally, men head a proportion of dance companies far greater than their numbers within the dance world would suggest. (Adair 1992; Hanna 1988; Van Dyke 1996). In the ballet world, female choreographers are a rarity, even in the twenty-first century (Meglin and Brooks 2012).

Within higher education dance departments, women again far outnumber men, but males tend to hold more leadership positions; women also have less career mobility (Stinson, et al. 1990; Clark 1994; Van Dyke 1996; Lodge 2001; Samuels 2001). Sue Stinson (1998a) notes that female and male responsibilities in higher education tend to divide along gender lines, with females in "housekeeping" or care-giving roles relative to students, staff, and faculty, and males in managerial roles with decision-making capabilities. Women in dance administration often spend large amounts of time doing service and caretaking work within departments—to the detriment of their own scholarly and creative work. A 2004 study found the typical faculty profile to be a "49-year-old female, part-time, non-tenure-track instructor teaching up to six classes per semester, reporting no creative activity over the past two years" (Risner and Prioleau 2004, 350). Research in gender equity in dance has shown that differences between the career status of men and women in various areas of dance are real and significant.

Men in Dance

The topic of masculinity in dance is key to work by scholars Michael Gard (2006), Doug Risner (2007c, 2009a,b), and Mark Broomfield (2011). The authors point out that dance both contradicts and plays into culturally mandated versions of masculinity, in dance studios, performances, and popular television dance shows. Author Maxine Leeds Craig (2014) posits that in the Swing Era, men of all races participated in popular dance, but in the 1960s, white men left the dance floor due to suburbanization, homophobia, and fragmentation of music cultures; changing beliefs concerning race, class, and sexuality have redefined what it means to be a man in American culture.

Usually when male dancers do not fit the masculine stereotype, they are criticized and made to feel inferior. Bullying of young male dancers is common (Risner 2014a) and should be addressed in a supportive environment by educators. Male teachers of dance within physical education also experience prejudice (Keyworth 2001). Gender and gay male stereotypes are revealed as problems stemming from societal attitudes that manifest themselves within the dance world (Warburton 2009; Polasek and Roper 2011; Risner 2014b). However, the subculture of ballet can offer an alternative form of masculinity that allows for expression and exploration (Berger 2003).

Dance teachers often mention the need to create a comfortable environment for boys and men in the dance studio by inviting them to contribute ideas for movement, music, costumes, and themes (Risner, et al. 2004). Strategies for cultivating a more robust male participation in dance include using famous heterosexual male dancers as role models (Hanna 1988), masculinist comparisons between dance and sport (Crawford 1994), and minimizing the significant gay male population (Spurgeon 1999). In Western culture, male participation in dance is generally frowned upon (Sanderson 2001; Stinson 2001; Risner 2002a, 2002b; Gard 2003b), largely due to the fact that dance is viewed as a feminine activity. Strategies for combatting these prejudiced attitudes include positioning the social construction of gender as a conscious aspect in dance education and training as well as validating and affirming individual differences in gender and culture (Bond 1994; Kerr-Berry 1994).

Working to counter the idea that dance is not for boys, projects such as "Boys Dancing" in Warwick, UK, have successfully challenged common ideas about dance and gender (Holdsworth 2013). Jennifer Fisher and Anthony Shay (2009) look across cultural borders in their study of masculinity in dance and offer discussion of "choreophobia," "homophobia," and "effeminophobia" as well as descriptions of dance from a variety of world regions and time periods. In the United States, the men of early modern dance broke away from the founding women to create their own styles of expression (Guo 2014). The American male dancer of the twentieth century had varied expressions of masculinity, with more ready acceptance in tap dance than in modern and ballet (Jowitt 2010). Research on boys and men in dance has become much more prevalent in the twenty-first century than in earlier decades and has brought to light the deep discomfort that Western culture, and particularly the United States, has with males who dance.

Queer Theory and GLBT Studies

Queer theory and gay, lesbian, bisexual, and transgendered studies have also contributed to dance scholarship (Bristow 1988; Burt 1995; Foster 1997; Desmond 2001). Ramsay Burt (1995) charts the development of homophobia as a means for males to culturally rationalize their close attraction to one another. Although men might enjoy watching other men dance, in order to do so, males must profess a repulsion toward homosexual attraction. Burt argues that straddling this important boundary for men, acceptable homosocial bonding and repressed homosexual attraction, is the crux for the heterosexual male spectator watching men dance. When extrapolated societally, this is a key element in men's culturally prescribed anxiety toward gay men.

Dance literature has critically explored prejudice and homophobia directed toward both gay and straight men in dance. (Keyworth 2001; Sparling 2001; Risner 2002a, 2002b; Gard 2003a, 2003b; Risner and Thompson 2005). These scholars suggest that dance education may unwittingly reproduce asymmetrical power relationships, social inequities, and sexism by reaffirming the status quo. In doing so, the dance profession ignores opportunities for diminishing homophobia and antigay bias. The dance education profession might benefit from knowing more about its male students and their attitudes and experiences rather than trying to increase male numbers by making dance more traditionally masculine (i.e., dance as sport, competition, stunts).

Analysis of the work of queer, lesbian, and gay choreographers including Katie Pule, Deborah Lohse, Mark Morris, Matthew Bourne, Sean Dorsey, and Masaki Iwana has appeared in the conversation of scholarly dance criticism, focusing on the upending of traditional gender tropes in new works or the reimagining of classical and romantic ballets (Alterowitz 2014, Duerden and Rowell 2013, Jowitt 2010, Midgelow 2007, Tikkun 2010). Queer identity politics can also form the focus of concert dance (Hart 2014). Analysis extends into the realm of popular dance as well in an examination of gay male dance in clubs, positing that as homophobia has decreased, "Popular choreographies of gay men's dance have become more feminine in expression" (Peterson 2011, 608). An ethnography of the Detroit queer ballroom scene examines ballroom as a cultural phenomenon that undercuts traditional notions of gender and community (Bailey 2013). Queer and GLBT studies has contributed greatly to dance scholarship by pointing out how homophobia shapes attitudes through outside pressure to conform to preconceived notions of masculinity and also includes voices of choreographers, dancers, and scholars who are working against these restrictions.

Modern and Ballet

Some dance history scholars have taken a backward look at genres and artists, reinterpreting their work through the lens of gender. France in the eighteenth (Tomko 2007), nineteenth, (Lee 2014), and twentieth centuries (Karthas 2006), and 1930s America (Mozingo 2008), all serve as contexts for exploring dance and gender relations. Some research focuses on particular choreographers or performers. Vaslav Nijinsky is famous for his strength and agility but also presents a transgressive image related to his sexuality as a performer: a blend of feminine sensitivity and masculine virtuosity (Burt 2001). Graham's work provokes analysis on "how the body and the feminine are inscribed" (Dempster 2010, 225), invites reinterpretation focusing on gendered, feminist, and queer perspectives (Thoms 2013) and notes its affiliation with modernism (Richmond 2003). Two other authors also connect modernism and gender, one looking at Delsartism (2011) and the other at German choreographers including Lotte Goslar (Mozingo 2008).

Anna Pavlova, Albertina Rasch, and Rosina Galli are early twentieth-century choreographers whose artistry suggests a link between ballet and feminism (Casey 2009). Ruth Page is a rare phenomenon: a female ballet choreographer in the mid-twentieth century. Her work was deemed second-rate by critics who used gender as a focus (Harris 2012).

Examinations of more recent work include choreographer Siobhan Davies's *Rushes* (1982), which blends traditional and nontraditional gender roles (Jordan and Thomas 2010). A study of contemporary British dance theater shows how six artists deconstruct gender and heteronormativity (Sears 2002). Looking at contemporary ballet criticism, Clare Croft (2014) examines columns focused on NYCB ballerina Wendy Whelan, noting that reviews frequently focus on her onstage relationship to male partners, her relationship to choreographers, and her relationship to iconic figures of femininity in ballet, rather than on Whelan herself.

Study of the ballerina has been a popular theme in the last two decades. Anna Aalten (2005) did an ethnographic study of female ballet dancers, positing that each has two bodies: "the perceived and tangible body they feel and see in the mirror every day . . . [and] the ideal body that is presented to a dancer by her teachers . . . and choreographers" (60). A disjunction arises as the ballerina strives to make her body fit the ideal through pushing her own physical boundaries, sometimes to the detriment of her health. Heather Ritenburg (2010) makes a Foucauldian analysis of the problem of the ideal dancer's body and how this slim ideal has been normalized through popular magazines and children's books.

Jennifer Fisher (2007) interprets contemporary ballerinas in historical context by interviewing ten women (ages twenty-five to eighty-three) about their involvement with ballet. Internalized and conflicting narratives of beauty and power figure prominently; Fisher concludes, "Today, even the oft-neglected health of the ballerina is starting to be tended to, as draconian training procedures are increasingly being interrogated and revised. Ever so slowly, women have started to embrace their futures more positively, becoming choreographers, attending university while dancing, and continuing to invest even their princesses with no-nonsense force and exactitude" (14–15).

Amy Koritz (1995) contrasts ballet and modern dance through the idea of embodiment. Taking a cue from literary studies, Koritz looks at the symbolist tradition and how it necessitated the author standing apart from his or her creation. She posits that this attitude is also true for ballet but not for modern artists such as Isadora Duncan and Maude Allan, who so embodied their work that they could not be separated from it. Following the thread of embodiment, Lisa Arkin (1994) writes about using women's bodies and experiences as source material for choreography, with female bodies assumed as a source of positive rather than negative self-images. The pregnant body (Schuamann 2010) and Jewish identity (Rossen 2006) are also considered within the context of modern dance. Female identity in experimental Middle Eastern dance is explored in another study, showing how this new form reinterprets gender on the margins of traditional Middle Eastern dance (Osweiler 2011).

Adrienne McLean (2008) writes about ballet and the ways that audiences learn about it through film, noting that the complexities of the dancing body are typically subordinated to the necessity of plot which embraces the "natural order" of gendered roles in films such as *The Red Shoes* (1948) and more recently *Save the Last Dance* (2001) and *The Company* (2003). The dance film *Amelia* (2002) is discussed through the lens of feminist and poststructuralist perspectives, showing how choreographer

Eduoard Lock presents ambiguous gender identities that challenge balletic convention (Ireland 2009).

Within ballet and modern dance, historians have analyzed past eras through a contemporary gender lens, while other researchers have looked at training, embodiment, and identity. The twenty-first century has brought an increased awareness of the dangers of harsh ballet training and a better understanding of women's attitudes toward their own bodies.

Social, Religious, Popular, and Recreational Dance

In a historical vein, Linda Tomko (1999) focuses on dance as a vehicle for cultural intervention in Progressive-era United States, showing how middle-class women blended foreign and U.S. practices and negotiated gender issues in education, social work, dance-hall reforms, dance innovations, and dance patronage. Another historical study looks at the phenomenon of gender role-reversal in American dance since 1850, including practices such as the Sadie Hawkins Day dance (McKernan 2002), and Kathleen Casey studies cross-dressing and race-crossing in the era of vaudeville (2010). Also historical is a study on jazz, gender, and dance in postwar France (Carter 2004).

Moving into the twenty-first century, scholars have presented ideas on dance and gender within Reform Judaism (Newstadt 2007) and Matachine Mexican American dances in the US Midwest (Christ 2010). American vaudeville (Casey 2010), social dance in Chicago from 1910 to 1925 (Bryant 2003), and New Orleans carnival balls of 1870–1920 (Atkins 2008) are other sites of study.

The movie *Dirty Dancing* (1987) is the subject of a collection of essays (Tzioumakis and Lincoln 2013) focusing on symbolism within the narrative; the film is posited as a female coming-of-age tale with cross-class elements, and discussions often use gender as a category of analysis. Ballroom dance gets close scrutiny through the lenses of gender, race, class, and nationality (Angus 2010, McMains 2003, Picart 2006); scholars acknowledge the stylized gender roles that men and women must play, particularly in a competition situation. Ballroom is also the context for an analysis of soccer star Hope Solo on the reality TV show *Dancing with the Stars*. Within the competition, the show's producers create a mediated portrayal of Solo's gender roles, presenting clear lessons on the construction of gender and its narration (Butler, et al. 2014). Also within the realm of entertainment, the Broadway chorus is posited as the site of a particular construction of gender manifested in chorus "boys" and "girls" (Van Aken 2006).

Researcher Matthew Atencio (2008) studied minority adolescents who danced as a leisure activity, showing the intersection of race, ethnicity, gender, and class. His analysis focuses on how the women engaged with dance cultures that were underpinned by particular dance forms that reproduced versions of "normalized" femininity but also allowed the construction of multiple and shifting minority ethnic subjectivities. A follow-up article (Atencio and Wright 2009) examined a dance program at an inner-city high school that supported race and class hierarchies, along with dominant notions of femininity.

In contrast to the negative body image issues discussed in the ballet and modern dance literature, belly dancers seem to have avoided this problem. A study of 103 belly dancers showed broad and inclusive body image norms, lack of pressure for body image conformity, and high levels of body satisfaction (Downey, et al. 2010).

One researcher explored the gendered dynamics of "grinding," which refers to sexualized dancing common at college parties, drawing on the observations of student participant observers. This research found that men initiate this behavior more often and more directly than women (Ronen 2010). Within the strip-club scene, Mary Nell Trautner (2005) examined gender and class differences among four different clubs. Trautner found a distinction between middle-class and working-class strip clubs in the ways the women performed femininity, with physical presentation and movement style adjusted for the class of clientele at each location. A study of the self-concept of male strippers who dance for women found that participants reported a positive sense of self and an enhanced self-concept as a result of stripping (Scull 2013).

Dance scholarship now more than ever is attending to genres outside the canon of ballet and modern dance, including popular dance. This scholarship shows that gender roles are ubiquitous in dance, no matter the genre or style, and can be found in religious styles such as the Matachine dances, as well as the more plebian strip club scene.

Conclusion for Review of Literature

Perhaps the two most-researched themes within the area of dance and gender are: (1) women's bodies and how they are presented on stage, and (2) how male dancers disrupt traditional ideas of masculinity. These themes began appearing in the 1990s and have continued to be a source of scholarly interest. However, the output on dance and gender in the twenty-first century has grown tremendously and extended into many areas heretofore untouched including Reform Judaism, experimental Middle Eastern dance, and ballroom dance. It is evident that all areas in the arts and humanities have been influenced by discussions of gender, race, class, and sexual orientation, which trace their origins to women's, men's, black, Latino/Latina, and queer studies. It is logical that these discussions should extend into the dance world, since no aspect of life is untouched by gender and its social construction. Particularly since social dance has been used as a tool of acculturation for centuries, it is not surprising that learning dance of any kind teaches something about the nature of being male or female. This scholarship gives readers a window into the many ways that gender has been shaped and reshaped within the dance world, as well as the problems it has caused and efforts made to solve them.

Outside the Gender Binary

It is important to acknowledge that the conversation around gender extends beyond a discussion of male and female, as noted in the "Queer Theory/GLBT" section of the review of literature. Transgendered, intersex, androgynous, and genderqueer are all types of gender identities not covered by the normal binary of male and female. Transgendered individuals are those whose gender identity does not match the sex assigned to them at birth (112, Killerman). "Intersex" refers to those born with ambiguous genitalia; androgynous individuals are those whose physical characteristics are linked to both genders. Finally, genderqueer is an umbrella term referring to anyone outside the male/female norm and may refer to someone who considers himself or herself bigender (both male and female), genderless, moving between genders, or a third gender (220, Killerman).

These gender identities and expressions outside the norm are important to acknowledge because there are dancers, choreographers, dance educators, and others within the dance world who identify with them. And although some artists feel that their alternative gender identities are personal and so do not draw attention to them in their work, others organize dance companies around them. For instance, Sean Dorsey Dance has a show about LGBT lives: *Uncovered: The Diary Project*. Dorsey is a transgender artist who has won national acclaim: Dorsey's company was named "San Francisco's best dance company" by the *San Francisco Weekly*, and Dorsey was included in *Dance Magazine*'s (2010) "Top Twenty-five to Watch." The company toured the country in 2015 with a show about the impact of AIDS on the gay and transgender community, *The Missing Generation* (http://www.seandorseydance.com/).

Another transgender artist, Niv Acosta, participated in a 2011 NYC panel on transgender dance where he noted that he binds his chest to make himself appear more male, and he spoke of the problem of being assumed to be female. He also cautions dance teachers not to assume the genders of their students, asking them to use gender-neutral terms such as "dancers" rather than gender-linked terms such as "ladies." Acosta feels that performance is an opportunity to transcend gender and that the stage is a powerful place to be (NY Live Arts 2011). He says about his work *I Shot Denzel*: "[It] has represented black masculine identity in performance, as seen from my perspective as a queer trans-masculine identified young black person. I'm working with many ideas that continue to interest me such as, death, grieving through sound experiences, original philosophical text, voguing, and fear . . . How do I navigate being transgender in dance? Identifying as black in dance? Identifying as queer in dance? And not always be defiant or 'challenging?'" (https://www.kickstarter.com/projects/nivacosta/niv-acostas-world-premiere-of-i-shot-denzel).

Since discrimination against transgender people is common in Western culture, being "out" in public is an act of personal courage. Dancers including Dorsey and Acosta who proclaim their transgender identities, as well as those who choose to keep them private, are part of the evolving conversation on dance and gender.

Overview of Book

Dance and Gender is organized around three general subject areas: equity in concert dance, gender in the dance studio, and gender in higher education. Each chapter discusses a unique empirical study giving evidence of some aspect of gender within the field of dance. Equity within the concert dance world is discussed by authors Jan Van Dyke, Eliza Larson, and Gareth Belling in their chapters. Van Dyke and Larson particularly focus on material success in the concert dance arena. Van Dyke's "Dance in America: Gender and Success" reports on grants and awards from organizations such as the National Endowment for the Arts, as well as other private, federal, state, and local funding sources. These grants are often major means of support for nonprofit dance companies, and thus who gets these grants may determine which companies survive and thrive. Larson examines equity in the nonprofit world from the perspective of performance venues and choreographic opportunities in "Behind the Curtain: Exploring Gender Equity in Dance among Choreographers and Artistic Directors." She presents data from the 2012–2014 seasons at Jacob's Pillow Dance Festival, the American Dance Festival, and the Brooklyn Academy of Music, three of the most prestigious U.S. concert dance presenters.

Also exploring concert dance, but from a different vantage point, is Gareth Belling's chapter on his own experiences choreographing gender within contemporary ballet. Belling details his action research in his chapter "Engendered: An Exploratory Study of Regendering Contemporary Ballet." Belling choreographed various duets that were outside the heteronormative male-female partnering. There was a range of combinations, including male/male, female/female, male/female with the female in the typically male role and vice versa, as well as traditional role playing, followed by short audience questionnaires focused on interpretation of the duets.

The next grouping of articles explores the idea of gender in the dance studio setting within both adolescent and adult populations. There is evidence supporting the idea that girls and boys, as well as men and women, experience dance class and rehearsal differently. Karen Schupp's "Sassy Girls and Hard-Hitting Boys: Dance Competition Culture and Gender" focuses on adolescent dancers and training that they undergo in order to succeed in this world. She points out that competitions "encode implicit and explicit messages about gender" (79), requiring girls to appear seductive and emotionally demonstrative and boys to be assertive and in control of their female partners. In her chapter "Boys Only! Gender-Based Pedagogical Practices in a Commercial Dance Studio," Carolyn Hebert discusses the pros and cons of placing boys in a separate class. She reveals the approaches that studios feel they must use to bring boys in the door, offering boys-only classes that emphasize athleticism in order to counter homophobia. Also focusing upon male dancers, "Friendship Formation among Professional Male Dancers" by Kate Polasek and Emily Roper uses the lens of relational-cultural theory as the basis for conversations with adult professional males. Their interviews explore the nature of friendship relationships between these dancers and other men and women in their dance companies.

The final theme of the book is higher education, reflected in articles by Karen Bond, Doug Risner, and Pam Musil. Bond's "'Boys are Morons' . . . 'Girls are Gross': Let's Dance!" looks at college students' reflections on their own experiences of gender in childhood, as well as their responses to an article that chronicled a children's dance program that successfully avoided gendered movement. The study analyzed 267 written responses to the prompt: "What messages about gender did you receive as a child?" teasing out themes such as "the gender binary," "dance and the family," "dance and/as the feminine," and "gender trials." Moving out of the classroom and into dance administration, Risner and Musil's "Leadership and Gender in Postsecondary Dance: An Exploratory Survey of Dance Administrators in the United States" shows gender shifts beginning in the 1990s, when more men began to be hired in higher education dance. The analysis looks at gender representation, equity, workplace issues, professional motivations, and career choices of dance administrators, using both quantitative and qualitative data.

Each author follows a different path of inquiry and develops conclusions based on the data gathered. Taken together, these chapters show how gender influences dance as a field. Gender plays a significant role in shaping physical expression, classroom experiences, performance opportunities, and other aspects of the field; while this is not always perceived as problematic, it can be. These findings show how some of the practices within the field, as well as societal pressures in general, can create environments that are not conducive to the health, happiness, and success of those in the dance world. However, they also show ways that dancers, choreographers, and teachers are working to free this art form and its supporting structures from restrictions associated with gender stereotyping.

The dance community can strive to eliminate discrimination and open up new possibilities for expression and achievement in studios, choreography, performance venues, and institutions of higher education. The first step toward doing that is to understand the status quo regarding gender in the dance world. As these authors have so ably demonstrated, gender matters in the world of dance, and now we must decide how to respond. The new knowledge presented in the following chapters provides ample opportunity for responses and further investigations.

2

Dance in America

Gender and Success

JAN VAN DYKE

Dance occupies a strange and not always comfortable position in American culture that is marginal and yet compelling. It is a field largely populated by women, which partially accounts for its marginalization (Alksnis, et al. 2008). Although information about opportunity and recognition can never be fully known, figures cited throughout this chapter from a variety of sources do seem consistent with the notion that men now lead the concert dance field in the United States. The number of men who hold jobs as performers and choreographers is disproportionate to their representation as dance students; they also more readily achieve acclaim and financial security.

This reflects an ongoing cycle mirroring trends within the culture at large regarding salaries (AAUW 2015) and will probably be self-perpetuating until a conscious and sustained effort can be made to break it. One bias comes from within the field itself. For years, choreographers and teachers, struggling against the marginalization of dance, have encouraged boys and men to enter the profession, hoping both to legitimize the field by equalizing the numbers and to have the opportunity of working with male dancers. Males have been offered opportunities and attention that, in many respects, has given them a privileged position. This is evident in the statistics cited in this paper. The men who were invited into the profession have gained employment and honors that are disproportionate to their numbers.

Gender and Success in the American Dance World (Van Dyke 1996) was primarily concerned with exploring the effects of gender within American dance, using the distribution of funding, employment, and awards to gauge opportunity and satisfaction. Although recent figures seem to indicate that times may be changing, it continues to be an intriguing issue on many levels. In 2004 Jennifer Dunning published a piece headlined "Has Dance Evolved into a Man's World?" (*New York Times*, June 25, 2004), commenting on the number of male choreographers presenting their work on that particular weekend in New York City. Some of the men involved voiced their own thoughts regarding the influence of gender on success in dance, and opinions were as mixed as the work they were presenting. All agreed, however, that men stand out among dance artists because there is a paucity of them, giving them a professional advantage. In 2014, in describing the four new works being commissioned by the New York City Ballet that season, Marina Harss commented on a very similar situation: "Yes, they are all by men" (*New York Times*, September 21, 2014), she concluded.

This chapter will explore the most current figures on many of the same issues studied in 1996, seeking to determine trends in concert dance over the past twenty years and whether gender equity is evolving. My research methodology for this paper involved background reading on the political, economic, and social activity in the dance world (Steiner 1995; Heilbrun and Gray 2001; Brustein 2000; Campbell 2000; Munson 2000); reading about artistic activity (including reviews) and checking current websites, counting names, and figuring numbers and ratios of men to women. Additionally, staff members at various institutions were contacted to find names and numerical information not immediately available in print. Special attention has been paid to funding policies and procedures because it is the granting process that fuels the engine of the concert field: access to funding determines whose work will be seen, whose dancers will be paid, and who will attract additional funding.

A Historical Perspective

Looking back more than twenty years, the NEA publication *Dancemakers* (Netzer and Parker 1993) provides perspective on the situation for dance artists and gender. Published in 1993, it is a comprehensive study of choreographers working in the United States. Dick Netzer and Ellen Parker drew data from a questionnaire sent out in 1989 to 1,444 choreographers in four cities: New York, Chicago, San Francisco, and Washington, DC. Because the response rate was low in 1991 (35.7 percent), a briefer telephone survey was made to enable a comparison of the characteristics of choreographers who had responded to the mail survey with those who had not. More than 80 percent of choreographers contacted by telephone responded. Taken as a whole, the report provided a bleak picture of the lives of choreographers in this country at the end of the twentieth century, especially in terms of economic status as compared to the high levels of education many received.

Findings reveal that choreographers had one of the highest college completion rates of all professions for which there is no formal certification or licensing requirement: at the time, among those in the study, 77 percent were college graduates and many had advanced professional degrees, compared to 21 percent of the US population over age twenty-five (Netzer and Parker 1993, 40–41). In spite of this, the median total income for all choreographers in 1989 ($18,500) was only two-thirds of the median earnings for all American women professionals ($27,900). When income from choreography alone was considered, on average, female respondents earned only $6,000 including grants.

For men, average income from choreography including grants was twice that for women (table 4; Netzer and Parker 1993, 59). Survey data show that, at the time, grants to men averaged about 50 percent more than grants to women (59). There is no obvious explanation for this; the female respondents were more highly educated than the males and almost as experienced. Statistical analysis shows that when all differences in the characteristics of the surveyed men and women were considered, being a woman resulted in $3,804 less income from choreography (59).

In terms of how choreographers viewed the situation, the authors wrote that although 40–50 percent of respondents sometimes felt discriminated against because of the style of their work, and 18 percent perceived a racial bias, only 13 percent reported feeling excluded on the basis of gender. The report continued: "Men and women did not differ much in their perceptions of gender discrimination in the funding process, despite the study findings of substantial differences in grant amounts and incomes" (Netzer and Parker 1993, 68). It seems that choreographers may have had a blind spot regarding gender bias in this study.

Other more recent research includes a 2001 report by the Gender Project, a New York–based group led by JoAnna Mendl Shaw and Janis Brenner that looked at careers in dance. Despite the fact that women make up the vast majority of the dance community, the Gender Project found that at that time in New York City, men were much more likely to get dance jobs, including such major roles as artistic directors, teachers, and choreographers. The authors drew on data that included class schedules, programs from various theaters, and interviews with members of the dance community. It was found that during the fall 2000 season at the Joyce Theater, New York's primary modern dance venue, only one of the twelve companies presented was run by a woman: Ballet Hispanico.

Moving forward to 2014, there are similar patterns. At the American Dance Festival in 2014, only two of the eleven repertory classes offered were of women's repertoire. In the 2014 season performances by top African American companies, including Philadanco, Dayton Contemporary Dance Company, Dance Theatre of Harlem, Alvin Ailey American Dance Theater, and Dallas Black Theater, just nine of the forty-six choreographers were women.

Why is this the case? There are multiple reasons, including that the dearth of men in the dance world means less competition for openings for male dancers. Women often take time off at mid-career to have children or care for aging parents, and there is a lifelong socialization process that teaches men to be aggressive self-promoters and women to be self-sacrificing and apologetic.

Eliza Larson (this volume) cites the *2007 Dance/NYC's Census of New York City Dancemakers* as the study that, while not providing the figures on gender nationwide, gives reason to look at New York City as a microcosm through which to explore gender in dance on a broad scale. She states that the 2007 U.S. Census backs up and supports what is anecdotally known: that women outnumber men in dance with a ratio of two to one. She goes on to state that the report "recognizes it is appropriate to test artistic directors for the degree to which they parallel or deviate from the gender distribution of dancers overall. For example, if two thirds of dancers are female, it could be deemed equitable if two thirds of artistic directors are also female" (41). The study finds an equitable distribution does exist overall: for artistic directors, the ratio is 63 percent female to 37 percent male, a percentage that can be used as a baseline by which to analyze equity across the field.

However, major differences between male and female artistic directors emerge when considering budget and audience size, touring opportunities, and the salaries for dancers and staff. For instance, the median budget for companies run by female artistic directors is $19,600, while the median for those run by men is $72,350 (42).

Gender and Professional Dance in America

In the United States, dancers and choreographers represent only a small percentage of working artists. In 2000, 26,129 dancers and choreographers were listed as working in the United States out of a total of 1,999,474 employed and self-employed artists. Most work for private, for-profit organizations and among artists, they are the youngest (with 80 percent under the age of thirty-five), the least educated (only 14 percent hold an undergraduate degree), the most diverse racially and ethnically, and the most likely to be women (Gaquin 2008, 27). This study differs from the earlier one by Netzer and Parker in terms of the education level of those surveyed. Among the choreographers surveyed by Netzer and Parker, there was a high proportion of college graduates, but in this study there was not. The Gaquin study mentions that most of the dancers in the study worked for private, for-profit institutions, which suggests they worked for dance studios and the commercial dance industry. Whereas the first study only looked at choreographers, the second looked at dancers more broadly; therefore, one can deduce that choreographers in 1993 were better educated than the general population of dancers in 2008. As a form, dance intrigues people, but the art itself is not widely followed or understood. In spite of that—or perhaps because of it—young women from a broad socioeconomic spectrum are drawn to train and dream of one day "making it." Most girls begin training as children and are brought to classes by their parents. Dance classes for little girls have long been considered part of growing up in many American families. This results in a dancing population that is overwhelmingly female. In training situations, girls and women have historically outnumbered boys and men in virtually every traditional dance school and studio, whether modern, ballet, tap, or jazz. For example, describing a small, community-based school in an e-mail on December 11, 2014, Lauren Joyner at the Dance Project in Greensboro, NC, provided the following figures: among 120 registered students under the age of eighteen, six were male, or 5 percent.

Table 2.1. Gender Ratio at ADF Six-Week School

Year	Men	Women	% Males
1989	32	168	16
1993	58	219	21
1994	57	215	21
~			
2014	60	251	19

A more detailed analysis of enrollment at a public university reveals that in December 2014, the dance department at the University of North Carolina at Greensboro had 211 undergraduate dance majors and minors registered, of which 24 were male and 187 were female: males made up 11 percent of this college-aged group. Among 23 graduate students, (on-campus and distance learning), 2 were male (approximately 9 percent) (Jeff Aguiar, pers. comm. 12/13/2014). At another North Carolina training center, the Six Week School of the American Dance Festival in North Carolina, it is evident that the percentage of male to female students has not changed much over the past twenty or so years. In 1994, out of 272 full-time students, 21 percent were men. In 2014 the percentage of men dropped slightly to 19% (Nicolle Greenhood, pers. comm. 12/8/14).

In the beginning days of modern dance in the early to mid-twentieth century, women were dominant on the concert dance stage. In 1961, however, critic John Martin, writing in the *New York Times*, noted a trend: that year, for the first time, the bulk of the New York season was produced by male choreographers (Hanna 1987). Since then, we have seen the emergence of male leadership in the field, as reflected in awards, recognition, and employment. As cited by Judith Lynn Hanna (1987), a 1976 study by Wendy Perron and Stephanie Woodward illustrates the situation. Perron and Woodward gathered data from the 1900 students and company members of six New York City modern dance and ballet companies with affiliated schools and found that 32 percent of the students were male. Although that figure is high in comparison with the typical community-based studio or university dance program, even here male students were found to succeed out of proportion to their numbers: although 32 percent of the students were male, scholarship students were 38 percent male, and 45 percent of dance company members were men.

Male dancers complain of hearing things like, "Oh, you're a guy, you don't have to worry about anything, there are plenty of jobs for you"

Table 2.2. Gender Ratio of Major U.S. Concert Companies, 2014

Company	Women	Men
Martha Graham Dance Company	10	8
Paul Taylor Dance Company	8	8
Philadanco	9	5
Koresh	6	4
Alvin Ailey American Dance Co.	16	17
Hubbard Street Dance Chicago	8	10
New York City Ballet	51	42
San Francisco Ballet (principals)	8	10

(Dalzell 2014). However, because there are fewer male than female dance students, and most companies would like an approximately equal number of men and women, it is clear that young women do not have the same access to performing jobs as their male peers. For example, a look at websites of some of the well-known and financially stable U.S. concert companies in December 2014 indicates the figures on hiring dancers. Even those with more women than men on the roster do not come close to matching the representation of females among the general population of dancers.

More examples of career success in which men and women are different can be seen in the national honors and awards given to dance artists:

1. Established in 1952, the Capezio Dance Award is presented annually in recognition of significant contributions to dance in the United States. Initially presented to individual dancers, choreographers, critics, teachers, producers, and administrators, and as selected by an independent committee, the program was restructured and broadened in 1992 to include companies and institutions as well. Over the sixty-two years between 1952 and 2014, the award has gone to forty-four men, twenty-four women, and five dance organizations (Capezio Dance Foundation n.d.).
2. The Kennedy Center of the Performing Arts in Washington, DC, holds an annual celebration honoring American performing artists for lifetime achievement. Of the eighty-five men and women honored between 1978 and 1993, sixteen have been dance artists, eleven men and five women. More recently, the figures have favored women more. From 1994 through 2014, nine awards have gone to dance artists, three to men and six to women, bringing

the totals to fourteen men and eleven women ("Kennedy Center Honors" 2014).
3. According to the 1994 award ceremony program, the Samuel H. Scripps American Dance Festival Award was "established to honor those great choreographers who have dedicated their lives and talent to the creation of our modern dance heritage." Instituted in 1981, this award has, through 2014, been given to twenty men and seventeen women, and Pilobolus Dance Theatre (Dean Jeffrey, pers. comm., 2014).
4. The Dance Magazine Awards are given to "the outstanding men and women whose contributions have left a lasting impact on the dance world." From 1954 through 1994, these awards were divided among sixty-eight men and fifty-four women. During the twenty years from 1995 through 2014, one organization was given the award, along with forty-four men and forty-three women. The ratio is improving, but the overall total is 112 men honored and ninety-seven women (http://dancemagazine.com/dance-magazine-awards).
5. The National Medal of the Arts is the highest honor given by the US government to artists and arts patrons who have significantly enriched the cultural life of the nation. From 1985 to 2013, of the fourteen dancers and choreographers honored with this award, eight have been women, and six have been men—a rare example where women lead, though not by a percentage proportionate to their representation in the dance population (National Endowment for the Arts, Annual reports).

Statistics in this section show the contrast between the high proportions of women training to become dancers (anywhere from 68 to 95 percent, depending upon the studio or institution) versus the low percentages of women "making it" as dancers in the professional concert dance world. The professional companies shown in table 2.2 tended toward an even balance of men and women, which must result in hiring a far greater proportion of available men than available women. The awards listed show a clear majority of men receiving them, with one exception: the National Medal of the Arts. If all the awards surveyed above are aggregated, men received 196 awards to women's 157, a five to four ratio. Keeping in mind that there are far greater numbers of women in the field than men, it is men who receive an outsized share of awards. However, the numbers do show that women have been receiving more awards in the past decade than previously.

Gender and Teaching

Many dance artists depend on guest teaching and choreographic opportunities to round out their yearly income. More important than a mere job, these positions are seen as occasions to show work, build reputation, express points of view, recruit dancers, and broaden one's audience. Guest-artist jobs are highly sought after and are, in a sense, another kind of professional award; here, in recent years, women have fared better.

Dance festivals in the United States draw heavily on performers and choreographers for their faculties and guests, making use of well-known names and company affiliations as a means of advertising quality and excitement. Here, men are represented in strength even though, as noted above, student attendance is largely female. Of late, however, representation of the two genders is seeing a shift. In 1994 the ADF program listed thirty-five faculty names for the Six Week School: twenty-one men and fourteen women. In December 2014 the website's register of faculty showed a change, listing twenty-nine faculty names: thirteen men and sixteen women, a definite movement toward equity (American Dance Festival).

A slightly different kind of opportunity is put forward by the Bates Dance Festival in Maine. Every summer since 1993, Bates has hosted the Emerging Choreographers Program for invited U.S.-based artists. Participants are offered a three-week creative residency that includes daily classes and studio time, access to the BDF Archive, Bates College Library and other college facilities, housing, meals, and an honorarium. The Emerging Choreographers Program develops a new work that is featured on the Different Voices Concert each year. Since its inception, this residency has been offered to fifty-one different choreographers: twenty men and thirty-one women. This ratio reflects an unusually high ratio of women receiving the honor, with three women for every two men.

A year-round program is open to applicants at the Maggie Allesee National Center for Choreography, a process-oriented center for choreographic work located within the School of Dance at Florida State University in Tallahassee. Providing residencies for invited choreographers and their collaborators for development of new work, the center actively supports artists at all career stages. The website (www.mancc.org) lists the names of six companies and sixty-three dance artists who have participated in the center's programs since its inception in 2004: twenty-six men and thirty-seven women. This represents almost 60 percent of opportunities going to women, which is good but still somewhat under the proportion of women in the choreographer population.

Overall, women have the most career opportunities in the category of guest teacher/choreographer residencies as represented by the three programs profiled above. The American Dance Festival, Bates Dance Festival, and Maggie Allesee National Center for Choreography have all given a majority of their teaching and residency spots to women, with ADF showing a distinct change over the past decade from a male majority to a female majority of teachers.

Gender and Funding at the National Level

Since its founding in 1965, despite periods of intense political disfavor, the National Endowment for the Arts (NEA) has taken on a leadership role in defining art in America. Through the distribution of its own funds and, more importantly, through its influence on other funding agencies, private foundations, corporations, and individual donors, the agency has become a major force.

NEA policies have profoundly affected the organization of the American professional dance world, with wide-ranging impact on the lives of dance artists and their work. Since 1965 the profession has been changed from a disorganized group of predominantly small, loosely structured dance companies to a more uniform national field of nonprofit, tax-exempt corporations with boards of directors.

In promoting its goals, the NEA has used funding guidelines to reshape the dance world, requiring compliance for eligibility. It has had additional influence through the creation of funding categories, effectively stimulating interest in government goals by making money available to carry them out. For example, by making funding available for professional management and then requiring evidence of management staff as a credential of artistic professionalism for certain grants, the NEA has directed dance companies toward a business model based on the not-for-profit corporation.

Table 2.3. NEA Award Figures, 1994–1995

Grant Cycle	Awards to Men	Awards to Women
1994	22	27
1995	28	22

Grant giving at the federal level showed a gender bias early on. When the agency began operations in 1965, choreographers were the first individual artists recommended for grants by the National Council on the Arts; however, of the eight grants awarded, six went to men (Bauerlein and Grantham 2009, 174). Since then, the agency has moved toward distributing funds to choreographers more equitably, although men have traditionally had more success than women in the area of funding, and have, over the years, been awarded more grant money. Again, Perron and Woodward's early study (Hanna 1987) speaks to the situation. They surveyed recipients of 316 dance grants given by the National Endowment for the Arts during 1974 and 1975 and by the New York State Council on the Arts during 1971–1974. Data showed that although 55 percent of company members were female at that time, 73 percent of grant recipients were male. Of grantees receiving $70,000 or more, 100% were male. By 1994–1995, the statistics had changed considerably. Women received 55 percent of grants in 1994, and 44 percent of grants in 1995. This shows a great deal of improvement over the figures from the 1970s. Because the NEA no longer gives grants to individual dance artists, no comparison data is available for recent years.

Among the most intriguing and prestigious grants in the United States are those offered by the John D. and Catherine T. MacArthur Foundation through the MacArthur Fellows Program—the so-called genius grants. Since the program began in 1981, among the hundreds of Fellows who have been named, twenty have been dance artists. Individuals cannot apply for these grants; instead they are selected annually by anonymous nominators. No conditions are placed on use of funds, which currently amount to $625,000 paid to each recipient over five years in quarterly installments. There is no annual quota of Fellows and no predetermined time for naming them. Among the twenty dance artists selected thus far, nine have been women, nine have been men, and two are a husband-and-wife team ("MacArthur Fellows Program" 2015). The women include

Martha Clarke (1990), Yvonne Rainer (1990), Trisha Brown (1991), Twyla Tharp (1994), Jeraldyne Blunden (1994), Elizabeth Streb (1997), Susan Marshall (2000), Liz Lerman (2002), and Michelle Dorrance (2015). Although there was a long gap between Lerman and Dorrance, the count is currently evenly balanced by gender.

Application is made for Guggenheim Fellowships, which are mid-career awards, intended for men and women who have already demonstrated exceptional capacity for productive scholarship or exceptional creative ability in the arts. Fellowships are awarded through two annual competitions: one open to citizens and permanent residents of the United States and Canada and the other open to citizens and permanent residents of Latin America and the Caribbean. Candidates must apply to the Guggenheim Foundation in order to be considered in either of these competitions. The foundation receives between 3,500 and 4,000 applications each year, and approximately two hundred fellowships are awarded annually. Although the foundation does not provide information on gender in its report, a little digging reveals that between the years 2000 and 2014, among the fellowships awarded to dance artists, thirty-four went to women and eighteen to men, possibly reflecting proportions within the applicant pool (Gf.org).

The MacArthur and Guggenheim grants to individuals in the late twentieth and early twenty-first century represent an improvement from the earlier days of the NEA grants of the 1960s and 1970s. Female choreographers have received half of MacArthur grants, while they have received almost two-thirds of Guggenheim grants, which is nicely in proportion with the gender balance within the field.

At the State Level

State and local arts agencies, as opposed to the NEA, are often more responsive to the field as it exists in their areas, perhaps because they are smaller and closer to their constituencies. This has proved true in the case of North Carolina. Between 1981 and 1994, North Carolina offered choreographer's fellowships every other year, and over that thirteen-year period made nine awards. Five of these went to women, or 55 percent. Andrea Lawson, current dance program director for the state arts agency, writes that since 1994 the ratio of women to men has vastly improved for these grants, which are still awarded every other year. As of 2014 twenty-three women have been honored along with seven men (pers. comm. Andrea Lawson, 10/29/14). It would be interesting to look at state funding within several different states to see if this is a trend or an anomaly.

A Cultural Perspective

The finding that in this country men succeed more readily than women in dance should not be surprising. The United States is rated twentieth among nations in all-around gender equity (*News and Record,* October 29, 2014). Although dance is often considered a woman's field, and dancers may think of themselves as enlightened about gender equity, the annual Gender Gap Index by the Geneva-based World Economic Forum shows that success figures for dance are in line with the general culture. American women have made real gains, now earning more college and graduate degrees than men, according to the National Women's Law Center (2015); however, women who work full time, year-round are paid only seventy-eight cents for every dollar paid to their male counterparts, and two-thirds of minimum wage workers are women (National Women's Law Center).

Dance is just one area where gender differences are evident in society, both in terms of recognition and money received. As recently as October 4, 2013–July 13, 2014, the National Portrait Gallery, part of the Smithsonian Institute in Washington, D.C., hung a show entitled "Dancing the Dream." According to the brochure, the exhibit was designed to show how "dance conveys the dynamism and innovation that has fueled the personality of American culture in the past 100 years." Portraits of ballet and modern dancers were combined with dancing film and Broadway stars, from Isadora Duncan to Beyoncé, and overall, images of thirty-three men and thirty-one women were included. The dance artist-in-residence selected for the show was a male modern dance choreographer. While this ratio may seem good at first glance, once again, the proportion of women in the field must be ignored in order for these numbers to be interpreted as "fair."

Although we tend to think of artists and art lovers as progressive thinkers in this country, on May 1, 2005, Greg Allen published an article in the *New York Times* titled "Is the Art Market Rational or Biased?" He noted that although female abstract expressionist painters such as Lee Kramer were overlooked in their youth, curators and historians now recognize them as being nearly as important as male contemporaries like Willem de Kooning and Franz Kline. However, he writes, at auction their paintings still sell for a fraction of what male artists command—often by millions of dollars. This disparity is no lingering relic of less enlightened times, says Allen, as he goes on to cite differences in selling prices for male and female artists into the twenty-first century. Interestingly, during the last half of the 1960s, several up-and-coming women artists chose to withdraw from the market when they found that success was dependent on networking in heavily male-dominated cliques, possibly because they did not want that kind of life.

Although the visual art field is a bit more level now, the scarcity of women whose work has been sold for over a million dollars is clear. Allen quotes Amy Cappellazzo, director of Christie's contemporary art department, who wonders if some women are, "'by their very nature, less'—here she searches for a word—'Machiavellian about their careers.'" Whatever the cause, it seems, as in almost every other field where money changes hands, women's production continues to be valued below that of men, and for all the explanations offered in this article, the primary conclusion seems to be that art by women sells for less because it is made by women.

Research reveals that this kind of bias exists broadly in both the perceiver and the perceived. "Women are just 2% of the CEOs of the nation's Fortune 500 companies. In the political realm, they make up just 17% of all members of the U.S. House of Representatives; 16% of all U.S. senators; 16% of all governors; and 24% of all state legislators. Internationally, the U.S. ranks in the middle range—85th in the world—in its share of women in the lower house of its national legislative body" (Pew Research Center 2008).

This slant on male leadership is reiterated in academia as many professors worry that students automatically rate male professors as smarter, more authoritative, and better overall just because they are men. Studies have borne this out, showing that students give online professors they think are male much higher evaluations across the board than those they think are female, regardless of actual gender (Marcotte 2014).

There is evidence that brain structure and hormonal influences on cognition and behavior play a significant role in the differences between men and women. Estrogen, the hormonal driver for women, supports the part of the brain involved in social skills while discouraging conflict and risk taking. On the other hand, men have ten times the level of testosterone in their systems as women do, which creates a competitive instinct and an appetite for risk taking and helps to fuel male confidence (Kay and Shipman 2014).

Our brains and hormone levels may be more changeable than we have known, however, and there is evidence that we do experience change in response to our environment. For instance, researchers have found that testosterone levels in men decline when they spend more time with children. On the other hand, sports may be an area that can help women become more competitive. Here, failure and loss are accepted as part of the game—very different from dance, which holds perfection as the ideal. There is a direct link between playing sports in high school and earning a bigger salary as an adult. It has been found that girls who play team sports are more likely to graduate from college, find a job, and work in male-dominated industries. However, fewer girls than boys participate in athletics, and those who do, often quit early. According to the Centers for Disease Control and Prevention, girls are six times more likely than boys to quit sports teams, with the steepest drop occurring during adolescence. Because of their genetic structure, most girls are easily socialized to the demands of what brings them praise, which is usually being obedient, neat, quiet, and perfect. As a result, they tend to avoid taking risks and making mistakes. They follow rules. Boys, meanwhile, by involving themselves with slamming around, roughhousing, teasing, and calling each other morons and dweebs, frequently absorb more scolding and criticism and learn to take failure in stride, becoming more resilient (Kay and Shipman 2014).

Along this same line, Doug Risner (2009a, 5), points to the pressures on young dancing males that girls do not experience in this country. Significant cultural stresses, including social stigmatization, social isolation, heterocentric bias, and often, homophobia, make boys' preparations for a career in dance a difficult path to follow. Because of the challenges they face, perhaps most boys who make the decision to train for the dance profession are determined to make a success of it from the beginning. Or perhaps they are made resilient by the social stigma that usually accompanies such a decision. On the other hand, often they start training later than girls and, it might be argued, do not absorb as much of what Risner calls the "hidden curriculum" in traditional dance classes, teaching passivity and taking direction along with building strength and grace.

School, and classes in general, can be seen as reinforcing this kind of learning. School (and dance class) is often where many girls are first rewarded for being quiet and "good." Girls then leave school determined to please, proud of their ability to work hard and get the best grades, only to find that in the passage from classroom to job, the rules have changed: assertiveness, ability to absorb criticism, and willingness to make mistakes without becoming discouraged are the more rewarded attributes in the adult world. According to Katty Kay and Claire Shipman (2014), writing in the *Atlantic*, success correlates just as closely with confidence as it does with competence, and that it is in self-assurance where women lose ground. This is true in dance as well as in the general culture. Their research shows that men initiate salary negotiations four times as often as women and that when women do negotiate, they ask for 30 percent less money than men do. In studies, men overestimate abilities and performance, while women underestimate both, although performances do not differ in quality. There seems to be a natural feeling among women that they will not get a prestigious job and therefore trying is not worthwhile. They often opt out, going into less competitive fields. Kay and Shipman call men's self-assurance "honest overconfidence" and note that men consistently rate their general performance level as better than it is, because this is what they actually believe. Researchers have found that, regardless of how good they really are, people who think they are good at something display confident verbal and nonverbal behavior, such as expansive body language, a lower vocal tone, and a tendency to speak early and often in a relaxed manner. This makes them look confident to others and whether they are actually competent is "kind of irrelevant." True overconfidence does not seem to alienate others, because the self-belief is what communicates. Apparently, having talent is more than being competent; for success, confidence is a necessary part of talent. Kay and Shipman (2014) suggest that confidence can be increased by turning thought into action, (which may also require courage, intelligence, anger, a strong will to persist, and creativity). They report that just taking action bolsters belief in one's ability, so confidence grows through hard work, success, and even failure. It is when women do not act at all, when they hesitate because they are not sure, that they hold themselves back. When they do act, even if it is because they are required to, they tend to perform as well as men. Researcher and Harvard professor Amy Cuddy asserts another possible response: she holds that humans create their own sense of personal ability and confidence through bodily postures and posits that some of the feelings that hold women back can be changed by altering the physical. According to Cuddy, women often literally shrink in public settings, and perhaps the feminine ways girls are trained to move help to cause this. She notes that the men in her classes shoot their arms straight up to answer questions, while the women tend toward a bent-elbow wave. Touching the face or neck or crossing the ankles tightly while sitting are other self-restricting positions often displayed by women: "These postures are associated with powerlessness and intimidation and keep people back from expressing who they really are." She advocates power posing, stating that "making yourself big" for just two minutes before a meeting changes the brain in ways that build courage, reduce anxiety, and inspire leadership. "We tested it in the lab—it really works," she says (Hochman 2014). The articles cited above suggest that women can change their own possibilities for success, but one very real question about social limitations has not yet been asked: if young women behaved just like young men, with that kind of confidence, would they be rewarded? Women do suffer from lack of confidence, but when they act assertively, they may suffer another set of consequences that men don't typically experience: social disapproval and criticism of character—being labeled as a "bitch"—in exchange for success. Biology, upbringing and society all seem to conspire against female confidence.

Final Thoughts

The opinions cited throughout this article reinforce a subtle lesson about corollaries between the American culture generally and the American dance world: the population ratio between women and men throughout the dance world (two or three women to one man) is mirrored in the proportion of female to male dance company leaders. However, the earning power of the female directors is far lower, on average, than that of the male directors (Larsen, this volume). According to a report by the American Association of University Women in 2015, women in the general population earned 78 percent of what men earned nationwide. If we compare this ratio to the salaries of women versus men who direct dance companies according to Larson's figures (this volume), the dance field is significantly behind the U.S. working population: the average budget for dance companies run by female artistic directors was $19,600 in 2007, while the budget for companies run by men was $72,350 (42). This means that female artistic directors on average earn only 27 percent of what male directors earn. Given these figures, perhaps it can be said that, even more than the lack of opportunity, it is the lack of financial reward that holds women back. In a culture with capitalist values, packaging becomes increasingly important to symbolizing success. When one group has money to spend on advertising, costuming, dancers' salaries and production, regardless of the quality of the work, a group spending less will begin to look less successful. Less opportunity in the studio and onstage for women than for men, in addition to less visibility in the media, despite the numbers, underlines the traditional gender roles and translates into a loss of confidence and lowered expectations for young female dancers. "'What girls see is a very powerful force in motivating and shaping their behavior,' says Ruby Takanishi, executive director of the Carnegie Council on Adolescent Development" (Golden 1994, 53). The evidence in this chapter suggests that funding and other opportunities for women have increased over the past decade. In areas such as jobs as guest teachers and choreographers, women are offered positions just as often (or sometimes more often) than men. Women have done increasingly well as grant recipients over the past decade, with the Guggenheim Foundation in particular awarding grants to a much larger proportion of women than men. However, awards in general have gone to more men than women, with the Capezio, Kennedy Center, Scripps, and Dance Magazine award count all balanced significantly toward men. In addition, women are not competitive at all when it comes to the very important area of financial support for women-led companies, as their income as artistic directors is far lower than men's. Since this study examines the field of concert dance as a whole, further insights might be gained by studying the statistics around individual dance genres.

These figures have a strong parallel in the visual art world, where paintings by women tend to command far less than works by men, even when all are established artists. Finally, there is also evidence that women are at a disadvantage in the dancer hiring process, since there are more women than men competing for fewer spots in well-paid, established dance companies.

It will be up to those in the field to look within, questioning not only the role of dance in the United States but also how those employed in the dance profession are managing their careers. How we teach, as well as what we teach, should be brought more clearly into view. The strong numerical presence of women in the field clearly has not been sufficient to ensure that women maintain equal representation in professional leadership and financial success. Thought and work are needed now for application to policies and practices that lead to success for both genders. For women's perspectives to be positively established and visible, women must aspire to positions of power and decision making as choreographers, administrators, presenters, and professors. This is perhaps most important for the long term. Strong and capable women in leadership roles speak to an art that utilizes all its talent to engage the surrounding society and establish a place for itself by emphasizing possibilities for both women and men. A thriving field today will provide models for all the young students who fill the studios and have future aspirations in the profession.

Note

Thanks to Wendy Oliver for significant contributions during the editing and revision process.

3

Behind the Curtain

Exploring Gender Equity in Dance among Choreographers and Artistic Directors

ELIZA LARSON

It should come as no surprise that women outnumber men in the field of dance. However, though dance classrooms and studios are filled with women, the following empirical study indicates that a majority of the most visible and well-funded choreographers in this country are men. Men receive prestigious choreographic opportunities at a rate disproportionate to their numeric minority in the field. These choreographic opportunities represent positions of leadership and power in the field of dance, further exacerbating this imbalance of gender.

The conversation of gender inequity in dance is certainly not new. Writing in 1992, Jan Van Dyke ascertained, "Economics seems to be the dominant value system in dance, determining what is done, how to train for it, who will do it, and how it will be produced" (19). Initiatives such as the Gender Project, a short-lived undertaking started in 1998 designed to bring a discussion of gender in dance to a national level, and a more recent Philadelphia-centric study by dance artist Nicole Bindler, have continually found gender disparity at the top echelon of dance presenters.[1] The Gender Project co-founder JoAnna Mendl Shaw explained that the "people who are making major decisions about both the presenting and the creation of the art are men. And yet the women in numbers dominate the lower echelons of the field" (JoAnna Mendl Shaw: The Gender Project

2004). In a field numerically dominated by women, do women today face a glass ceiling as choreographers and artistic directors in receiving funding as well as national attention and acclaim?

This chapter seeks to assemble data and render visible the gender divide in dance today. Recent statistics in the field are first explored in order to establish a baseline for understanding gender in dance on a broader scale. An analysis of gender disparities in dance is then presented through an examination of the 2012, 2013, and 2014 performance seasons at Jacob's Pillow Dance Festival, the American Dance Festival (ADF), and the Brooklyn Academy of Music (BAM), creating a foundation for further discussion of gender in dance. This chapter offers a feminist perspective as a way to decenter gender hierarchies among choreographers in concert dance in the United States.

Dance/NYC

Dance/NYC and its parent organization Dance/USA (the national service organization for professional dance) have led a recent movement to gather data and shed light on the landscape of dance, particularly in New York City, the epicenter of dance in the United States. In 2007 Dance/NYC's *A Census of New York City Dancemakers* was published, a groundbreaking study that was the first of its kind to systematically examine the field of dance. This study offers analysis and data for "an art form in this time and place that heretofore was the subject of anecdotes, best guesses and conjecture" (Munger 2007, 2). This study focuses directly on the people who comprise the field, providing statistically accurate information to give the dance scene in New York a "sense of self, a sense of who we are" (2).

Recent years have seen the publication of several additional studies that all work toward disseminating the economics of dance in New York, including Dance/NYC's *State of NYC Dance* (2011) and *State of NYC Dance* (2013), based on the New York State Cultural Data Project (CDP) regarding nonprofit dance organizations with budgets of more than $25,000; Dance/NYC Junior Committee's *Dance Workforce Census: Earnings Among Individuals, Ages 21–35;* and *Discovering Fiscally Sponsored NYC Dancemakers*. As New York City Council speaker Christine C. Quinn affirmed, "Dance/NYC is creating a model for discipline-specific arts research, and helping to guide policy, funding, and management practice" (Moss, et al. 2012,

4). Though these surveys are geared toward understanding the financial implications of the dance workforce in New York City, the reports also reveal information about the gender of dancers working there. Understanding dance in New York City helps us comprehend the broader situation of dance in the United States; data collected by Dance/USA describes almost identical statistics in Chicago and Washington, D.C., particularly with regard to gender distribution, thereby rendering New York City a microcosm through which to explore gender in dance on a broader scale (Munger 2007, 7).

Of the studies named above, the 2007 Dance/NYC's *A Census of New York City Dancemakers* study most clearly investigates and notes variations with regard to gender. The 2007 census study backs up and supports what is anecdotally known: that women outnumber men in dance. Specifically, the ratio of dancers is two women for every one man (7). The study recognizes that "it is appropriate to test artistic directors for the degree to which they parallel or deviate from the gender distribution of dancers overall. For example, if two-thirds of dancers are female, it could be deemed equitable if two-thirds of artistic directors are also female" (27). The study finds an equitable distribution does exist overall; for artistic directors, the ratio is 63 percent female to 37 percent male (28). These foundational numbers are especially important here; this percentage represents a baseline with which to analyze equity across the field.

Major differences between female and male artistic directors become apparent when considering budget size, audience size, touring opportunities, and salaries of dancers and staff. As the study describes, the ability to present works in larger venues, gather audiences through national rather than regional venues, and pay dancers are all a reflection of budget, which serves as a proxy of value (33). With more money, companies can reach larger audiences, thereby increasing their revenue and visibility. The study demonstrated small or nonexistent differences in the areas of artist roles, longevity in the field, ensemble structure, and genre(s) of dance (30).

Of the top fifteen companies—specifically, those with annual budgets of over one million dollars—six are led by a female artistic director, and nine are led by a male artistic director. Moreover, "There is clear factual evidence that larger ensembles are more likely to have male ADs than female, and that small companies are more likely to have female ADs than male" (29). Of all female-led companies, only 44 percent have budgets over $25,000. For male-led ensembles, 68 percent have budgets that exceed $25,000. The 2007 study establishes the following data:

- The average budget for female-led ensembles is $143,490. The average budget for male-led ensembles is greater than ten times that at $1,703,000.
- The median budget for female artistic directors is $19,600; for male artistic directors, the median is $72,350.
- Of the largest companies—those with budgets exceeding $500,000—over 60 percent are led by a male.

Of the thirty-four companies that reported offering salaries to dancers (as opposed to rehearsal and performance stipends or nonmonetary exchanges), the majority, twenty-one out of thirty-four, have male artistic directors. Likewise, companies with male artistic directors are more likely to have paid staff, highlighting that "prevalence of male ADs in larger companies matters because the presence of salaries is directly related to budget size" (33).

The data are clear: men are more likely to lead larger companies with larger budgets. On the whole, women lead smaller companies, with fewer dancers and smaller budgets. Interestingly, though the overall distribution of dancers in the field remains 67 percent female to 33 percent male, companies with larger budgets are more likely to employ female and male dancers in equal numbers. As the study explains, "Males are relatively scarce and therefore can command bargaining power. They are more likely to end up in better-compensated situations" (34). The same fifteen companies with the largest budgets account for 87 percent of the expenses for the total field of dance in New York City. With companies in this bracket led by a male artistic director 60 percent of the time, it means that men control an overwhelming majority of the New York City dance budget.

Study

The following study adds to the existing gender analysis in the field of dance by elucidating contemporary findings on the gender of top-tier choreographers in concert dance presented in various American performing arts venues. Specifically, this study analyzes performances between January 1, 2012, and September 1, 2014, at Jacob's Pillow (MA), the American Dance Festival (NC), and the Brooklyn Academy of Music (NY). This data relies on physical and digital program archives from each of the three venues. Archives from physical programs were used for Jacob's Pillow and BAM, and electronic PDF archives were used for ADF. All three institutions' program data were verified against performance season promotional brochures and publicized listings.

These three venues were chosen for their importance and renown in the dance world and also because they represent three separate regions in the United States: New England, mid-Atlantic, and the southeast. Additionally, all three venues present performances on at least two stages. This additional element allows for distinctions to be made regarding ticket prices and the gender of the choreographers whose work is presented across tiered programming. The following section first examines the methodologies employed by this study before presenting the data collected at each venue, leading to comparative and in-depth analysis.

Methodologies

Dance is a complex field, without clear delineations of genres such as ballet or modern and without obvious hierarchies or institutionalized structures. Because dance companies form for unique reasons, company organizations vary immensely. Some companies consist of one person who functions as artistic director, choreographer, and performer, whereas other companies are collectives with multiple artistic directors, dancers, and choreographers. Frequently, two people create companies, with one as artistic director and the other as executive director. Where choreographers are concerned, some are hired to choreograph as guest artists, and some perform with a company, invited from within to create a specific piece. Often, the artistic director is the sole choreographer for the company. In working to examine gender differences among companies, the process is often like comparing apples to oranges. For the purposes of this study and in order to gather the clearest and most direct data for the work analyzed here, each company has been considered by the gender of the presenting choreographers rather than by the gender of any nonchoreographer artistic director. For the purpose of this research, the term "choreographer" refers to the movement maker of each piece, regardless of any self-selected title.

Genre Distinction

Genre is another variable affecting analysis, especially because different genres have historically dealt with unique issues of representation and gender roles. Considering all concert dance equally, without regard to gender, might blur gender bias present in one genre and not another. Complicating this issue is the difficulty and inherent subjectivity of identifying a choreographic work within a specific genre. Many companies and choreographers exist at the intersection of multiple genres of dance. Often choreographers train in several movement forms, which may influence their choreography in subtle or even unconscious ways. Other artists decline to identify their work with a particular genre. In ballet, for instance, contemporary ballet companies and artists that are rooted in ballet vernacular often do not align themselves with traditional ballet company models. Two choreographers included in this study, Jessica Lang and Trey McIntyre, exemplify choreographers who work outside of genre labels. Both artists come from ballet backgrounds and work exclusively with classically trained ballet dancers, but both shun the ballet title. Jessica Lang in particular has said that she considers her work neither ballet nor modern, but just dance (Lang 2012).

Likewise, two of the venues here, Jacob's Pillow and BAM, do not seek or claim to present a singular style of dance. Though Jacob's Pillow has strong ties to the modern dance world through its founder and modern dance pioneer, Ted Shawn, the most recent performance season brought styles ranging from Bharatanatyam to classical ballet to contemporary. BAM, too, invites dance explorations across genres. In a 2012 website press release for the opening of BAM Fisher, which houses BAM's secondary dance stage, Executive Producer Joseph V. Melillo explained that "the vision of BAM Fisher was to create an open space to permit adventurous exploration into new approaches to visual imagery, movement, technology, and storytelling." This also implies freedom of genre. ADF alone of the three exclusively presents modern dance. However, because many of the choreographers who present at each venue decline to identify their work within a specific genre, and because of the broad nature of concert dance presented across the venues, all work has been considered equally and without bias to genre.

In considering performances at BAM, which presents across an array of artistic mediums in addition to dance genres, BAM's own classification system was used for distinguishing a performance as dance rather than theater, circus, or music. This categorization was not necessary for programing at Jacob's Pillow or ADF, which are both dance festivals and present programming exclusive to the genre. Also excluded are ADF student showcases and Jacob's Pillow School student performances, which list program directors, not choreographic information.

Performance Practices

Just as each dance is unique and singular, so too are the performance events each company curates. Often a company presents a single, evening-length dance performance. Other companies present two or more separate, shorter dance works, all by a single choreographer. Some companies showcase the work of several choreographers in a single evening—a practice often seen in ballet and repertory companies. Additionally, the presenting festivals may curate evenings of mixed-choreographic works, sometimes bringing two or more choreographers together for a collaborative experiment or placing diverse choreographic voices alongside one another for an evening of assembled performance. In response to these variables, individual choreographers are counted once per performance event, which is defined here as a single performance or series of consecutive performances (for example, a three-night performance run). Analyzing by performance event, rather than each performance night, ensures companies with a five-night performance run are given the same statistical value as companies who only perform for a single evening. This also means a choreographer has equal weight, whether she or he presents a single work in an evening or six different works. For example, Paul Taylor typically presents three or more shorter pieces in each performance, whereas Noa Wertheim usually presents a single, evening-length piece. In the case of a repertory company or mixed-choreographic evening where two or more choreographers present their work alongside one another during a single show, individual choreographers are counted once per performance event. Lastly, analyzing by performance event does not differentiate among companies that present the same program several nights in a row, and companies that present a mixed program of different works each night: each choreographer is counted once per performance event.

This methodology raises questions of how to differentiate dance works created by a single choreographer versus a choreographic duo or team. Just as each choreographer is counted the same whether they present a single dance in an evening or multiple pieces, choreographic duos or groups have been counted once per performance event. For dances created by an all-female team of dance makers, they have been counted as a single female choreographer; likewise dances created by all-male teams are counted as one male. For any dance created by a male/female choreographic duo, or for dances created by a group or collective comprising both male and female choreographers, these mixed-gender choreographic teams were counted a single time; this applies regardless of the number of choreographers of each gender in the team. The exception is Pilobolus, which embraces collaboration in how they give credit to the choreographic team of each work. For simplicity, and to honor their collaborative spirit, Pilobolus has been counted as one mixed-gender choreographic team per performance event, though the collaborators may differ for each specific piece they present.

Limitations

It is of note that a critique of this nature places a binary on gender in order to document how gender inequality is represented in dance. For the purposes of this study, the evidence produced here addresses the specific variable of gender with the goal of granting more visibility and providing insight to critique a gendered form of inequality. Yet because gender is also constituted by myriad other processes, intersectionality and queer studies would inform further investigation of the role of trans and intersexuality, as well as race and class inequalities in the dance world.[2] While the editors of this volume believe that an understanding of gender would be well informed by a complex analysis of race and ethnicity, this is beyond the purview of this study and will not be addressed in this chapter.

Furthermore, it is of additional import that specific transgender and nonbinary-identifying choreographers did not come up during this investigation. To identify gender, the pronoun used in each program's biography section has been employed by this study. For choreographers without program biographies, a simple Internet search revealed the pronoun used for their website, Facebook profile, or other relevant biography or profile. It is likely that among the selection of choreographers, one or more may identify as transgender or nonbinary; if so, this identification was not mentioned or highlighted in any biographical information. To that end, it is hoped that using the same pronouns as listed in these choreographers' biographies serves to identify them as they wish.

Finally, another complication is the nationality of companies and artists. Jacob's Pillow, ADF, and BAM are all international festivals, presenting companies from around the globe. However, any numerical data available has been collected with an eye on a single country or continent. The New York City Dance Committee limited its research to dancers working within the New York City boroughs, and it is impossible to compare a location-based study to an international performance series. To that effect, the information gathered in this study serves to strengthen the purview of understanding gender bias in concert dance today.

Jacob's Pillow Dance Festival

Jacob's Pillow brings in artists and companies from around the world and the United States. As a case study, the festival offers a broad scope of the current state of dance beyond any regional trends. Likewise, the festival brings in artists of all genres, including ballet, modern, tap, hip-hop, and world dance. Founded in 1930 by Ted Shawn, the Pillow served as a home for Shawn and his Men Dancers, an all-male dance company that performed from 1933 to 1940. The festival is also the home of the first theater in the United States specifically designed for dance, the Ted Shawn Theater. Women have directed the institution since the 1990s, and it brings in thousands of audience members and visitors each year. Though Shawn's own artistic legacy is within modern dance, the festival's reach is far broader, representing all dance forms. As the longest-running international dance festival in America, the *New York Times* describes Jacob's Pillow as "the dance center of the nation and possibly the world" (Jacob's Pillow).

In analyzing the Jacob's Pillow performances, this survey was limited to the Ted Shawn Theatre, the Doris Duke Theatre, and the Henry Lier Inside/Out performance series, considering the genders of choreographers to see what, if any, patterns were discernible. The two primary stages, the Ted Shawn Theatre and the Doris Duke Theatre, invite established companies and choreographers to present evening-length concerts. The Inside/Out Series is the only performance space of the three that actively invites choreographers to apply to present choreography. The Jacob's Pillow website (www.jacobspillow.org) solicits applications, and the selected choreographers, usually emerging artists, present one night of choreography (as opposed to the typical three-night performance run of the other venues). The artists and companies who present at the Pillow are both established and emerging choreographers.

During the 2012, 2013, and 2014 performance seasons, Jacob's Pillow presented 147 performance events across their three stages. The Ted Shawn Theatre is considered the most prestigious of the three, with the largest seating capacity and most expensive ticket prices. The Doris Duke Theatre has a smaller seating capacity and also commands high-ticket prices, though less expensive than those of the Ted Shawn Theatre. The Inside/Out series is free and open to the public and presents work outside with informal seating (audience members may bring their own blankets and lawn chairs).

The overall breakdown of gender among Jacob's Pillow performances does not accurately represent the field at large. The 147 performance events at Jacob's Pillow were given by 128 total companies, with nineteen companies returning for multiple performance events over the course of the three summers. Of the 379 works presented in total, there were ninety-one female choreographers, 119 male choreographers, and seventeen mixed-gender choreographic teams. Thus, women choreographed only 40 percent of the works presented at Jacob's Pillow, despite comprising 63 percent of choreographers in the field.

Breaking down the festival by performance space paints an even more imbalanced picture. Twenty-five unique companies presented work at the Ted Shawn Theatre; five of those companies returned over several summers, which totals thirty performance events at the most prestigious of the Pillow's three theaters, representing the work of sixty-five choreographers. Of these thirty events, twelve choreographers were female, fifty-two were male, and one was a mixed-female/male choreographic team. Of particular note was the 2012 season where only one company, Vertigo Dance Company, credited a female choreographer, though the Bill T Jones/Arnie Zane Dance Company did credit a female assistant director. Over the three years of this study, only 18 percent of performances at the Ted Shawn Theatre featured works choreographed by women.

At the Jacob's Pillow secondary stage, the Doris Duke Theatre, the percentage of female choreographers rises slightly, though the balance is still far from equitable. The Doris Duke Theatre saw twenty-nine performance events, which featured twenty-four unique companies (again, five companies returned to the stage over several seasons), presenting the work

Table 3.1. Ted Shawn Theatre, Jacob's Pillow Dance Festival

Year	Companies at the Ted Shawn Theatre	Number of Pieces[a]	Female	Male	Mixed
2014	Aspen Santa Fe Ballet	3		3	
2014	Circa	1		1	
2014	Companhia Urbana de Dança	2	1		
2014	Dance Theatre of Harlem	3		2	1
2014	Daniel Ulbricht/*BALLET 2014*	6	1	5	
2014	The Hong Kong Ballet	3		3	
2014	Hubbard Street Dance Chicago	4		3	
2014	Mark Morris Dance Group and Music Ensemble	4		1	
2014	Pacific Northwest Ballet	4	2	2	
2014	Trey McIntyre Project	2		1	
2013	3rd Étage: Soloists of the Paris Opera Ballet	1		1	
2013	Ballet BC	3	1	2	
2013	Cedar Lake Contemporary Ballet	3	1	2	
2013	Compagnie Käfig	2		1	
2013	Companhia Urbana de Dança	2	1		
2013	Dance Theatre of Harlem	5	1	4	
2013	L-E-V	1	1		
2013	Martha Graham Dance Company	4	1	2	
2013	O Vertigo Danse	1	1		
2013	Wendy Whelan/*Restless Creature*	4		4	
2012	Bill T. Jones/Arnie Zane Dance Company	1		1	
2012	*Borrowed Light* by Tero Saarinen	1		1	
2012	Canada's Royal Winnipeg Ballet	3		3	
2012	Compagnie Käfig	2		1	
2012	Hong Kong Ballet	3		3	
2012	The Joffrey Ballet	3		3	
2012	Mimulus	1		1	
2012	Morphoses	2		1	
2012	Trey McIntyre Project	3		1	
2012	Vertigo Dance Company	1	1		
	Totals:		12	52	1

Note: a. Numbers may not add up properly when there is more than one work in a performance event created by the same choreographer.

Table 3.2. Doris Duke Theatre, Jacob's Pillow Dance Festival

Year	Companies at the Doris Duke Theatre	Number of Pieces	Female	Male	Mixed
2014	Carmen De Lavallade	1	1		
2014	Compagnia T.P.O.	1	1		
2014	Dance Heginbotham and Brooklyn Rider	1		1	
2014	David Rousséve/REALITY	1		1	
2014	Dorrance Dance	1			1
2014	Doug Elkins choreography, etc.	2		1	
2014	LeeSaar The Company	1			1
2014	Reggie Wilson/Fist & Heel Performance Group	1		1	
2014	Unreal Hip-Hop	4	2	1	
2013	Abraham.in.Motion	1		1	
2013	BODYTRAFFIC	3		3	
2013	Brian Brooks Moving Company	4		1	
2013	Dorrance Dance	1			1
2013	Jessica Lang Dance	5	1		
2013	La Otra Orilla	1	1		
2013	LEO	1		1	
2013	Shantala Shivalingappa	5	1	1	
2013	Tere O'Connor Dance	1		1	
2012	CIRCA	1		1	
2012	Dance Heginbotham	2		1	
2012	Doug Elkins and Friends' *Fräulein Maria*	1		1	
2012	Jessica Lang Dance	5	1		
2012	The Joffrey Ballet	3		3	
2012	Jonah Bokaer and David Hallberg, with Daniel Arsham	3		1	
2012	Kidd Pivot Frankfurt RM	1	1		
2012	LeeSaar The Company	1			1
2012	Liz Gerring Dance Company	1	1		
2012	Luna Negra Dance Theater	3	1	2	
2012	The Men Dancers: *From the Horse's Mouth*	1			1
	Totals:		11	22	5

of thirty-eight choreographers. Of these choreographers, eleven were female, twenty-two were male, and five were mixed-gender choreographic teams.

The third and most informal performance space, the Inside/Out Stage, presented by far the most works by female choreographers. The Inside/Out Stage presented eighty-nine performance events, or eighty unique companies, with nine companies returning over consecutive summers. Not only did the Inside/Out Stage present far more works that the other two stages, but these performances represented a broader array of the dance population. These performance events included the work of seventy-one female choreographers, fifty-six male choreographers, and twelve mixed-gender choreographic teams. In sum, women choreographed 51 percent of the works shown on the Inside/Out Stage.

The Jacob's Pillow Dance Festival illustrates the census's conclusion: women are underrepresented in larger performance spaces. Likewise, the analysis of the tiered programming follows suit with the trends outlined by the census. Jacob Pillow's tertiary stage comes closest to representing equity but still falls short of the 63 percent necessary for balance. As the theater prestige increases, the percentage of female choreographers decreases, marking a disparity in levels of representation within the field.

American Dance Festival

ADF is perhaps the best-known dance festival in the United States and possibly the world. ADF comes out of the same era as Jacob's Pillow; its roots lie in the historic experiment of the Bennington School of the Dance of the mid-1930s. In 1978 ADF moved to the Duke University campus in Durham, North Carolina, where it currently resides. ADF particularly prides itself on being a home for and incubator of new choreographic works. As explained on its website (www.americandancefestival.org), "One of the most important functions of ADF throughout its history has been to provide choreographers with the opportunity to produce and present new works, many of which are especially commissioned by ADF. ADF has played a critical role in increasing the repertoires of our country's modern dance companies . . ." In evidence, the festival has seen over 650 premieres, 350 commissions, and 50 reconstructions. As a consistent and celebrated home for dance, ADF is inseparable from the history of modern dance in the United States. Writing of the festival in 1987, dance critic Jack Anderson asserted that "throughout its history, [ADF] has been a microcosm of American modern dance as a whole, and both its achievements and its problems have been symptomatic of those of modern dance across the nation" (236). ADF's strong voice in providing commissions and a performance space for new and established choreographers makes it an especially important touchstone for understanding gender representation in the field.

ADF presents dance in two theaters, with the exception of the 2014 season, which included two site-specific creations. These two theaters represent different stratums. The Durham Performing Arts Center (DPAC) in downtown Durham is considered ADF's premier theater with a seating capacity of 2,700. As demonstrated by ADF's website, ticket prices vary, but they can be as much as three times the price for the other ADF stage, the mid-sized Reynolds Industries Theater, located on the Duke University campus. Similar to Jacob's Pillow, here the price differentiation between performance spaces also suggests a stratified approach to programming: the festival invites to DPAC only those companies that can command higher ticket prices. Companies are chosen to perform and scheduled years in advance, and are either specifically invited or selected from performance applications solicited through the ADF website.

Unique to ADF programming is the inclusion of two annual curated mixed-choreographic evenings: *Footprints,* which commissions major choreographers to create work while at ADF and *NC Dances,* a celebration of regional choreographers from North Carolina. *On Their Bodies* is the newest ADF commission from 2014, featuring solos created and performed by four choreographers. In addition to these ADF-commissioned programs, the festival presented thirty companies for a total of forty-two performance events over the study's sample.

This selection of ADF choreographers spans continents and also represents a broad range of dance styles, including aerial dance and ballet, while still primarily focusing on modern dance. The distribution of gender across the stages of the festival is as follows: twenty-eight female choreographers, thirty-five male choreographers, and six mixed-gender choreographic groups. Thus, women choreographed 41 percent of the works. Though roughly equivalent to Jacob Pillow's 40 percent, this 41 percent again falls short of the 63 percent that would represent equity in the field at large. Of the two site-based works not included in the theater-specific analysis below, one work was choreographed by a male/male duo, Nov

Table 3.3. Durham Performing Arts Center, American Dance Festival

Year	Companies presented at the Durham Performing Arts Center	Number of Pieces	Female	Male	Mixed
2014	Ballet Hispanico	4	2	2	
2014	Ballet Preljocaj	1		1	
2014	Cedar Lake Contemporary Ballet	3	1	2	
2014	On Their Bodies	4		4	
2014	Paul Taylor Dance Company	3		1	
2014	Pilobolus	5			1
2014	Vertigo Dance Company	1	1		
2013	Brenda Angiel Aerial Dance Company	1	1		
2013	Forces of Dance	4	2	2	
2013	Kyle Abraham/Abraham.In.Motion	1		1	
2013	Paul Taylor Dance Company	3		1	
2013	Pilobolus	5			1
2013	Shen Wei Dance Arts	2		1	
2013	Trisha Brown Dance Company	3	1		
2012	Doug Elkins and Friends	1		1	
2012	Hubbard Street Dance Chicago	3	1	2	
2012	Mark Morris Dance Group	4		1	
2012	Paul Taylor Dance Company	4		1	
2012	Pilobolus	5			1
2012	Scottish Dance Theatre	3	1	2	
2012	Stephen Petronio Company	1		1	
2012	Vertigo Dance Company	1	1		
	Totals:		11	23	3

Sheinfeld & Oren Laor at the Nasher Museum of Art at Duke University, and another by a male/female duo, Ishmael Houston-Jones and Emily Wexler at the PSI Theatre at the Durham Arts Council.

Again, analyzing by performance space elucidates specific trends in gender representation. DPAC follows suit with the bias of other institutions illustrated here. At DPAC, eleven female choreographers showed work, compared to twenty-three male choreographers and three mixed-gender groups. Thus, choreographers were 30 percent female, 62 percent male, and 8 percent mixed-gender.

ADF's case confirms this study's finding that female choreographers tend to be better represented in less prestigious theaters even within one institution. The Reynolds Industries Theater is ADF's secondary theater,

Table 3.4. Reynolds Industries Theater, American Dance Festival

Year	Companies presented at the Reynolds Industries Theater	Number of Pieces	Female	Male	Mixed
2014	Adele Myers and Dancers	1	1		
2014	Footprints	3	2	1	
2014	Gregory Maqoma/Vuyani Dance Theater	1		1	
2014	Here and Now: NC Dances	4	2	2	
2014	John Jasperse Projects	1		1	
2014	Tere O'Connor Dance *also presented work in an informal venue, the Ark	3		1	
2013	The 605 Collective	1			1
2013	Camille A. Brown & Dancers	1	1		
2013	Faye Driscoll	1	1		
2013	Footprints	3	3		
2013	LeeSaar The Company	1			1
2013	North Carolina Dance Festival	4	3	1	
2012	Brian Brooks Moving Company	4		1	
2012	Footprints	3	2	1	
2012	Keigwin + Company	5		1	
2012	Kyle Abraham/Abraham.In.Motion	1		1	
2012	Monica Bill Barnes & Company	3	1		
2012	Ragamala Dance	1	1		
		Totals:	17	11	2

with lower overall ticket prices and smaller seating capacity. At Reynolds, women choreographed 57 percent of works, marking the highest percentage of female choreographers at any theater included in this study. Of the remaining works at this theater, men choreographed 37 percent, and mixed-gender groups choreographed 6 percent. Interestingly, both *Footprints* and the North Carolina–centric performances presented an overwhelming majority of female-choreographed works, demonstrating the prevalence of women at a regional level. Though the percentage of women choreographing 57 percent of the works is a dramatic improvement over the 30 percent seen at DPAC, both venues fall short of the 63 percent that would represent gender parity.

Brooklyn Academy of Music

The third venue of this study, BAM, represents the smallest selection of performance events included here, with thirty-two performance events across two stages between January 1, 2012, and September 1, 2014. A multiarts center centrally located in Brooklyn, New York, BAM is the only venue of the three that presents nondance performance events. Because of this, they present fewer dance events than the other two organizations. However, this does not diminish the importance of BAM as a major hub for concert dance within New York City, which is known as the dance epicenter of the United States and one of the country's most important venues for concert dance.

BAM currently presents dance concerts in only two spaces. As with Jacob's Pillow and ADF, BAM's two theaters represent different levels of prestige, as illustrated by seating capacity and ticket prices. The Howard Gilman Opera House seats 2,090 and commands ticket prices ranging from equal to three times higher than ticket prices at the Fishman Space, a 250-seat flexible theater space that opened in 2012. As explained in BAM's 2012 press release (available at www.bam.org), the consistent and modest price of Fishman Space performances seeks to "encourage risk-taking and to cultivate a new generation of live performance devotees."

Though the selection of choreographers at BAM is comparatively small, BAM's gender distribution parallels the other venues in this survey. During the 2012, 2013, and 2014 seasons (through September 1, 2014, only), BAM presented thirty-two performance events, representing the work of fifty-six choreographers. Of the twenty-one performance events at Howard Gilman, women choreographed thirteen works, men choreographed twenty-seven, and mixed-gender groups choreographed three. Again, the Howard Gilman follows suit with the other venues included here, featuring female choreographers 30 percent of the time.

BAM's secondary theater, the Fishman Space, presented eleven works, the smallest collection in the survey. Five female and eight male choreographers presented works in this theater. Despite the small selection, the Fishman Space corroborates data gathered at the secondary theaters of the other venues here. BAM's two performance spaces confirm that fewer female choreographers present at top-tier theaters: while women comprised 30 percent of the Howard Gilman choreographic pool, females represented 38 percent of choreographers at the Fishman Space.

Of special note is DanceAfrica, which according to the festival's 2013 program notes, is the longest-running African dance festival in the world. DanceAfrica brings together African dance performers and companies from across the globe and was directed by Baba Chuck Davis during the seasons included in this survey. In 2012 DanceAfrica celebrated the thirty-fifth year of its annual festival and celebration, bringing in thirteen companies from around the world, with eleven separate credited choreographers (three companies did not list a choreographer). Alongside DanceAfrica, six additional companies presented on the Howard Gilman Opera House stage that year. Of these additional six, only one company, Tanztheater Wuppertal, presented work by a female choreographer: that work was by Pina Bausch (the group's founder). It is striking that without the inclusion of the DanceAfrica festivals, the number of female choreographers at the Howard Gilman Opera House drops from 30 percent to 23 percent for the three years studied. The disparity in gender inequality in concert dance at large points to the need for further study of gender parity in specific genres of dance, including ballet and African dance.[3]

Comparative Analysis

Because each venue studied here uses a tiered programming structure, it is possible to conduct a side-by-side comparison of gender representation overall.

Looking across the study, the data can be corroborated among venues. At the primary theater of each venue, the female choreographic representation was 18 percent, 30 percent, and 30 percent, marking the lack of female choreographers as particularly conspicuous at the top echelon of concert dance. At the secondary theater, the percentages of female choreographers increased to 29 percent, 57 percent, and 38 percent. No primary or secondary theater matched the average of 63 percent female choreographers demonstrated by the census, though ADF stands out as coming close to an equitable presentation of choreographers at their secondary theater.

The pool of data gathered here allows for further analysis of the specific artists whose work was seen across these venues. It is striking that many of the same choreographers reappear time and again over the course of this study, marking them as significant to the purview of this analysis. The work of thirty-seven choreographers appears in two of the three venues, counted here as separate performance events. These thirty-seven choreographers may be considered to be more distinguished, having presented their work across multiple venues and to a multitude of audiences in different regions. Of these standout artists, ten are female, sixteen are male, and one is a male/female choreographic duo.

Additionally, only six choreographers stand out as having their work performed across all three venues during the scope of this survey. This marks these artists among the most highly sought-after choreographers. Here, the gender disparity is striking: five of these six regularly programmed choreographers are men. Crystal Pite is the only female to have her work appear across all three venues.

The data show a clear imbalance in the number of choreographers of each gender presented in these three institutions. The gender gap at the top echelon of choreographers is exemplified by the fact that of the 145 choreographers whose work was shown in a premier theater, only thirty-six were women, bringing the total percentage of female choreographers presenting at the highest level to only 25 percent. Though, no doubt, programming decisions are the result of numerous factors (including schedules and availability) the pricing of tickets through stratified programming attaches a monetary value to each group. These organizations send a clear and direct signal to their audience and the general public by placing a very real dollar sign on the worth of the choreographers they present.

Conclusion

As evidenced by the forty-three choreographers mentioned in this study who presented across multiple venues, well-known choreographers tend to attract large audiences and work with larger budgets: these two factors lead to more prestigious performance opportunities. Is it possible to change the cycle? Is it possible to award more funding to women, who will in turn receive more performance opportunities? Is it possible to give more performance opportunities to female choreographers, who will then receive more funding? This simplified approach has complicated reactions. Jessica Lang objected in her 2012 "Jacob's Pillowtalk" interview that she does not want to get work because she's a woman, and she does not want what she calls a "pity commission." But as Nicholas Leichter explained, gender may never be fully separate from the calculus of who gets work and who does not: "I like to think that the work that I do has nothing to do with my gender, let alone my race or sexuality, and yet I'm sure it does. . . . Hell, my successes and failures could have something to do with all these issues. But I do believe that at the end of the day it's a struggle for all of us" (Dunning 2004). Lang and Leichter, like most choreographers whether male and female, want to be considered and rewarded for their work and choreographic ability. However, although the desire for gender-neutral meritocracy certainly exists, equitable selection practices remain the exception rather than the norm. Consequently, this study is not intended as condemnation or affirmation for the gender distribution of the festivals investigated here. Their choices largely reflect the current practices and standards in the field.

Gender imbalance reaches beyond presentation venues and impacts all levels of the dance field, from decisions about who performs when and where, to how much money a company receives, to critical reception of dances and dancers. This has long been known. Writing in 1992, author Christy Adair explained that gender imbalances in the dance world reflect society at large, and that "the power relations of the society within which dance is produced affect the work at the levels of economics and ideas" (23). Key decision makers for presenting bodies make choices that reflect the world they live in, thereby rendering decisions that reflect all aspects of society, including its inequities. That this has been an ongoing conversation in the dance world for over twenty years with little resulting change reflects a deeply embedded gender imbalance in the field as a whole.

The gender divide in dance is indicative of complex issues that reflect our society, our cultural norms and values, and the history of dance and dance training in this country and around the world. This imbalance is particularly disconcerting in dance, where women outnumber men in such great numbers. It is also significantly ironic that this disproportion occurs alongside the great legacy of the female founders of modern dance, such as Isadora Duncan, Ruth St. Denis, and Martha Graham. This chapter demonstrates the necessity for further discursive analysis of why women lack equitable representation in positions of power within the field of dance.

As Dance/NYC Director Robert Yesselman wrote in his introductions to the 2004 and 2007 census, "With knowledge comes power, with power comes influence, and with influence the dance capital of the nation will remain so, and leap into a future richer with possibility and resources and promise" (Munger 2004, 1). It is beyond the scope of this chapter to propose a plan of action to erase gender inequality in the dance world, and such an undertaking will require the effort of all levels of society where gender inequities are culturally embedded in ways intangible and emblematic of the world as a whole. It will take bold and forward-thinking steps to make headway toward gender equality in dance, steps that Jacob's Pillow, ADF, and BAM would be well situated to spearhead. However, with knowledge does come power, and power carries influence. This chapter hopes to encourage all of us—women and men, performers, presenters, and audience—to envision ways of achieving more equity in dance.

Notes

1. In 2003 Jacob's Pillow Dance Festival, one of the venues included in this chapter's study, hosted a two-day retreat for the Gender Project, which was designed to stimulate discussion about gender disparities in dance opportunities and funding.

2. Kimberlee Crenshaw's work comes to mind as she coined the term "intersectionality" (e.g., C. Sumi, K. W. Crenshaw, and L. McCall, 2013, "Toward a Field of Intersectionality Studies: Theory, Applications, and Praxis," *Signs: Journal of Women in Culture and Society*, 38[4]: 785–810). However, recent feminist studies work has also critiqued the potential rigidity of intersectionality as a paradigm (see for instance Helma Lutz, Maria Teresa Herrera Vivar, and Linda Supik, 2011, *Framing Intersectionality Debates on a Multi-faceted Concept in Gender Studies*, Farnham, UK: Ashgate). An intersectional perspective regarding power and economic inequalities in dance would require a complex and fluid deployment of this methodology, perhaps turning to Jasbir Puar's concept of "assemblage" to account for the formation of subjectivities based on myriad sex, gender, class, race, and sexuality processes, rather than on strict identities (Jasbir K. Puar, 2007, *Terrorist Assemblages: Homonationalism in Queer Times*, Durham, NC: Duke University Press).

3. This is, again, a dimension that would benefit from deploying the concepts of intersectionality or assemblage mentioned above (see note 1), particularly because gender is informed by other such processes including culture, race, class, sex, and sexuality among others.

4

Engendered

An Exploratory Study of Regendering Contemporary Ballet

GARETH BELLING

This practice-led research project investigated the choreographer's creative process for regendering contemporary ballet, the dancers' experiences of the rehearsal process and performance, and audience perception of meaning in the ballets. It sought to test the "inborn" and "natural" gender binaries of classical ballet and partly to answer Alastair Macaulay's question: "What future does ballet have as an art of modern expression?" (2010, 4).

This research operated within the scope of Ted Polhemus's definition of gender as the social and cultural construction of maleness and femaleness (1993, 14) and was framed within Helena Wulff's study of classical ballet as a transnational culture (2008). Feminist ballet critique (Daly 1987a; Copeland 1993; Anderson, 1997) established a method for looking at classical and contemporary ballets with reference to visual focus and performer agency. Sally Banes's analysis of feminine agency and the "marriage plot" in ballet (1998) was most influential to the project's choreographies, particularly to *Les Noces*, while Ramsay Burt's *The Male Dancer* (2005) challenged the sharing of visual focus between male and female dancers. Finally, recent critical discourse on gender in ballet (Macaulay 2010, 2013b; Jennings 2013, 2014) crystallized the project's areas of inquiry.

Contemporary ballet is defined here as dance works created within the foundations of the classical school (*danse d'ecole*) that apply a plastic sense to movement through academic steps and positions in what Brenda Way explains as "a more pluralistic aesthetic" that "resonates with the grounded authenticity of a regional dialect-real people, really moving" (Looseleaf 2012, 53). This lens restricts the scope of the research to a particular style of choreography, and to particular approaches to my own choreographic practice.

The project was carried out over three stages between February 2013 and December 2014 within the context of an MFA dance program at the Queensland University of Technology. Through two intermediary ballets to test themes and methods of research, the project culminated in the creation of an original contemporary ballet, *Les Noces* (2014), for the Queensland Ballet.

Regendering Ballet

Ballet has a long history of cross-gender performance: from the male-dominated court ballets of Louis XIV, to nineteenth-century romantic ballet where men all but disappeared from the stage. Twentieth-century classical choreographers continued to include roles *en travesti* as a comic device in their character-driven narrative ballets, most notably Fredrick Ashton (*Cinderella* [1948]; *La Fille mal Gardee* [1960]), rather than to explore or test gender roles. Peter Stoneley (2007) explores two queer revisions of classical ballet in John Neumeier's *Illusions like Swan Lake* (1976) and Matthew Bourne's *Swan Lake* (1995). Kent Drummond contends that Bourne's queering of the narrative challenges notions of "sex, gender, and sexual desire" (2003, 235). This regendering of a ballet text or narrative in an original choreographic work is echoed by David Dawson's male duet *Faun(e)* (2009)—a reworking of Fokine's *L'Après-midi d'un Faune*—and Pascal Touzeau's *Les Noces* (2013). Dawson's duet provides a framework for my own regendering of Nijinska's *Les Noces*.

Central to the project's conceptual framework is the possibility that original choreography may be regendered without significant change to the dance material. Created first for female soloist and male *corps de ballet*, Maurice Bejart's *Bolero* (1961) has been regendered twice since its creation: in 1979 for Bejart's muse Jorge Donn and a female *corps* and later in an all-male version (Boccadoro 2006) without change to the dance material. In Jiri Kylian's *Nomaden* (1981) the choreography is performed twice, swapping the roles of men and women for the entire cast when the choreography is repeated. Large sections of Nils Christe's ballet *SYNC* (1990) have been regendered in later restagings but never performed in the same evening as the original. While these ballets offer the choreography verbatim in the regendered versions, their movement vocabulary features little or no weight-bearing partnering, which became a feature of this project.

Two particularly enlightening papers were published in the final months of this project: Clare Croft's "Feminist Dance Criticism and Ballet" (2014, 195) opens new avenues for reading ballet in ways that permit a number of femininities, while Gretchen Alterowitz (2014) allows a broadening of the definition of contemporary ballet through analysis of Katy Pyle's *The Firebird, a Ballez* (2013), a textual regendering of Fokine's *The Firebird* for an all-female cast.

Chris Johnson presented her contemporary duet *Physical Manifestations of Assent* (2014) at the World Dance Alliance Forum in Angers, France, in which dance material was performed twice, swapped verbatim between the male and female dancers the second time. While it echoes the structure of Kylian's *Nomaden* by regendering and repeating the piece in the same performance, neither its movement vocabulary nor conceptual framework can be defined as contemporary ballet, and so it falls outside the scope of this project.

This growth in literature surrounding the applications of regendering contemporary ballet shows that, as a mode of expression, ballet can no longer ignore issues of gender and sexuality and that Macaulay is correct when he states that questioning ballet's form must come from the artists within (2013a, 10).

Research Design

Engendered was a practice-led research project incorporating a mixed methodology of studio-based action research and qualitative data collection. Practice-led research is defined as, "Firstly research which is initiated in practice, where questions, problems, challenges are identified and formed by the needs of practice and practitioners" (Gray in Haseman and Mafe 2009, 213). In the context of this research, practice was undertaken through studio-based action research as the creation and adaptation of original contemporary ballets through regendered movement. Regendered movement refers to a process where choreographic material is created or adapted with the intention that it may be performed by either male or female dancers with little or no change to the original steps.

The project was structured as a three-stage action research project. Action research is a method of inquiry "distinguished by a deliberate and planned intent to solve a particular problem (or set of problems)" (McMahon 1999, 167). Each stage followed a cycle of plan, act and observe, reflect, and revise plan (Kemmis and Wilkinson 1998, 22) with new areas of inquiry emerging from the preceding stage's outcomes. The cyclical form, where new information and outcomes were continually observed and reflected upon, benefited methodological rigor.

The creation, regendering, and performance of original dance works were the primary focus of each of the three stages. These ballets were performed at programs of contemporary and classical dance presented by Ausdance Queensland (*Intimate Distance,* three performances, 31 March–2 April, 2013), Queensland University of Technology Dance (*rebeginnings,* six performances, 5–9 November 2013) and Queensland Ballet (*Les Noces,* fourteen performances, 30 October–13 November, 2014). Only one cast of each ballet was presented at each of these performances. This was designed to focus audience responses on their perception of meaning in the ballets, rather than any differences in the performances of the individual casts.

Each of the three ballets included at least one role that was regendered. *Intimate Distance* was a duet for a male violinist and dancer, where one performance was given by a female dancer, while two performances were given by a male dancer. The ballet *rebeginnings* was adapted from a heteronormative *pas de deux* from one of my earlier ballets and performed by three combinations of four dancers. The versions were single-sex duets for two men (Michael and Zachary), two women (Chloe and Asher), and a reverse gender version where Chloe partnered Zachary. The third ballet was a revision of *Les Noces,* a ballet originally choreographed in 1923 by Bronislava Nijinska with music by Igor Stravinsky. The only roles to be regendered in *Les Noces* were the "Bride" and "Groom." Within the ballet for five couples, the "Bride" and "Groom" were performed as a heteronormative version by Lina and Vito, and there was a reverse gender version, where Alec danced Lina's role and Eleanor danced Vito's.

Phenomenology was introduced as a framework for the clarification of meaning in the choreography during the second stage of research. "Phenomenology is the study of the nature and meaning of things—a phenomenon's essence and essentials that determine what it is" (Saldana 2011, 7). My application of phenomenology focused on the meaning of gestures, particularly those that led to intimate touch between two dancers. It clarified the meaning of the ballets for the performers, so that gender might be isolated as the primary difference between each cast.

Qualitative data was gathered through the use of written audience questionnaires for all three stages of the project. The first two stages were used as trials to refine data collection methodology. The final stage of research saw a three-question anonymous questionnaire offered to audiences at six performances of *Les Noces*, with the majority of responses collected at the completion of each performance. Audiences were also given the option of e-mail submission, with only three responses returned in this way.

Regendering Dance—Addressing Concerns, Applying Theory

The greatest concern during the project was that regendering might limit my ability to create interesting, meaningful choreography. Regendered dance works must stay as close to the original choreography as possible to isolate the performer's gender as the primary site of variation between different casts. Additional research concerns such as communication of choreographic intention, partnered movement and intimate touch, and their impact on the choreography were also addressed through a gender lens.

Regendering acts as a method for decentering the visual focus of a dance work. In this project, visual focus particularly relates to how the dancers are displayed by the choreography and how they might be viewed relative to gaze theory. Regendering is an undoing of ballet's inherent gendering: a framework in which to question the classical traditions.

Ann Daly outlines classical ballet's inherent gender differences as being "inextricably rooted in the notion of 'inborn' or 'natural' gender differences" (1987b, 34). Helena Wulff goes on to write, "In the Romantic ballets, the male dancer is a strong support for the fragile woman" (2008, 526). Although contemporary ballet choreographers have largely moved away from the ideal of fragile women, the historical gender roles of the female being partnered, lifted, and supported by the male dancer remain entrenched. This has meant that a significant amount of coaching in partnering technique was required during the project in order to challenge these gender roles.

Clear communication of choreographic intent was essential to conveying meaning through each cast's performance. It was important to accurately measure differences in audience perception among varied casts. The need for clarity was framed by Maxine Sheets-Johnstone's idea that, "In art, each perceiver imaginatively grasps the symbolic abstraction that the artist puts forth" (1979, 30). By focusing on the phenomenological impact of gestures and touch in the choreography, I was better placed to communicate meaning clearly to an audience.

The process of regendering seeks to have the performer's gender as the only noticeable change between casts. During the adaptation of *rebeginnings,* Judith Butler's writing on gender performativity and undoing gender (1990, 2004) was increasingly vital to the regendering process. Butler states, "If gender is a kind of a doing, an incessant activity performed, in part, without one's knowing and without one's willing, it is not for that reason automatic or mechanical. On the contrary, it is a practice of improvisation within a scene of constraint" (2004, 1). The "scene of constraint" is then both classical ballet's traditional gender roles and the choreography itself. The dancers were being asked to perform the choreography as their own gender, thereby undoing the gender roles of the choreography specifically and classical ballet more broadly.

Intimate touch was an important signifier of gendered movement from the beginning of the Engendered project. Throughout the three cycles, an increasing emphasis was placed on how the dancers performed touch and weight-bearing partnering. It was assumed that learning "to partner" would be more difficult than learning "to be partnered," and as such, that female dancers would face a greater challenge than the male dancers with the regendered choreography. However, it was observed that the technique required to be partnered was a significant challenge for the male dancers to learn, and so dancers of both genders faced equal but different challenges with weight-bearing partnering. "Lifts are a matter of coordination; they do not occur solely from the strength of the cavalier to move the ballerina" (Cohen, et al. 2005, 133). This observation gives substance to Bane's reading of female agency in classical ballets as the technique of actively working the body while being partnered involves a coordination and agency with its own considerable challenges.

Coordination in classical ballet partnering is often built on a foundation of sexual dimorphism: the smaller woman being lifted by the larger man. The performance of new coordinations and techniques for the dancers, and the undoing of sexual dimorphism by regendering, proved the greatest difficulty in the research cycles but the most satisfying outcome of the performances.

Data Collection

Data collection methods were developed during the first two stages of the project, culminating in the use of an anonymous audience questionnaire in the third stage. This questionnaire was administered at six performances of *Les Noces*. The questionnaire consisted of three short questions about audience members' perception of meaning, relationships, and visual focus within the ballet. It was designed to evoke sentence-length answers from participants and was deliberately kept brief so as to attract the greatest number of responses from participants.

The three questions were:

1. "Did *Les Noces* tell a story? In a few short words, could you explain your interpretation of the piece?"
2. "How would you describe the relationship between the two dancers in *Les Noces*?"
3. "Did one dancer have a stronger presence or more control over the other dancers? If so, can you describe which dancer, and how it made you feel?"

Three performances of each cast were surveyed, making a total of six data sets. Audience members were offered questionnaires as they returned to the theater after intermission and asked to complete the form at the conclusion of the performance. Approximately a hundred audience members were offered forms each night, with a total of ninety-two responses across the six performances.

Questionnaire responses were initially coded with the date of the performance and cast that performed. This allowed for accurate separation of data sets between casts and their various performances. The second coding involved an *in vivo* schema that is "the practice of assigning a label to a section of data, such as an interview transcript, using a word or short phrase taken from that section of the data" (King 2008, 473).

Words or short phrases were taken verbatim from the participant's responses. The frequency with which these words appeared across the data set offered a clearer picture of the salient themes. Where responses were too varied to assign a common word or short phrase directly from the responses, a second round of coding was necessary. I developed simple one- or two-word codes for each of the answers to describe my understanding of the response's intent.

Creative Works: Descriptions and Research Outcomes

The three original dance works created during the research project, *Intimate Distance, rebeginnings,* and *Les Noces* were created within the style of contemporary ballet, which Wendy Perron describes as, "Anchored in the old, hungry for the new, contemporary ballet is a style that remains ambiguous" (2014, 34).

Intimate Distance

The first duet was created with the intention of gender neutrality from the outset. It began with the violinist caught in a circle of light surrounded by thirteen wire music stands. As the music started, the violinist began a series of walking patterns that were stopped, counter-balanced, and directed by the dancer, who used physical touch and the rearrangement of the music stands to guide the musician through the dance. Intimate touch was limited, as the violinist was not able to touch or partner the dancer, and the dancer was only able to have contact with the violinist's back, waist, and legs so as to avoid his instrument.

The dancer's movement was looped and stretched but cut by abrupt stillness in awkward positions. It showed the dancer waiting for direction from the musician and the music. The dancer's arms sliced wide circles from the shoulders, fidgeting or wrenching at one body part or another as if struggling with the absence of the violinist's touch. Toward the end of the piece a long diagonal of music stands echoed the arrangement of corps de ballet from *Giselle* or *Swan Lake*, which was the clearest statement of the choreography's underlying debt to the structuralism of the classical tradition.

An informal audience questionnaire was undertaken as a trial method of data collection. Feedback discussions with audience members were also used in reflection. Upon reflection, I feel that the restriction of touch made the choreography too neutral and was also lacking many of classical ballet's gender signposts such as partnering, pointe work, and virtuosic leaps.

rebeginnings

The second stage of this project was an adaptation of the first duet from *Sweet Beginnings*, a short ballet created for Queensland Ballet's *Elegance*, August 2013. The first duet from *Sweet Beginnings* was regendered and performed by three different casts as the duet *rebeginnings*.

The process of regendering in this cycle differed from the first cycle in that gender neutrality was never an intention of the original choreography. The original ballet's strongly gendered movement, partnering sections, increased intimate touch, and heteronormative theme made the adaptation of *rebeginnings* incredibly challenging.

During the rehearsal period, it was decided to code the dancers' roles with the first names of the original cast members. This personalized the roles for the *rebeginnings* dancers: they were no longer dancing "the boy" or "the girl." The codes used were "Lina," which was performed by Zachary and Asher (a female), and "Matthew," which was performed by Michael and Chloe. That they knew and admired the dancers from the original cast also helped make the dancers feel more comfortable performing these roles.

The duet begins with the couple separated across a long diagonal, both facing the back. Reaching, searching *port de bras* lead into unison movement. The first touch comes after a demonstrative solo by "Matthew" full of leaps and turns that "Lina" watches throughout, reacting to "Matthew's" display. Lifts are held close to the body, often emerging fluidly from the end of supported promenades. While the promenades and lifts display "Lina," she remains an active partner in their coordination.

The movements emphasize fluidity, with the weight being distributed so that lifts emerge and dissolve organically. "Lina" is lifted onto "Matthew's" shoulder in a variation of the "Bluebird" lift from *Sleeping Beauty*, before rolling into the next movement. Supported *jetés* curl around "Matthew's" body. Fluid *ports de bras* emphasize the complementary movement language of the two dancers. The "Bluebird" lift is restated before "Lina" rolls into a spinning lift, is flicked onto "Matthew's" back into a balanced high release and slides softly to the floor, ending the duet sitting facing away from the audience with "Matthew" lying curled behind her.

The most significant change to the choreography in *rebeginnings* was to have the role of "Lina" danced on *demi-pointe* rather than *en pointe*. It was agreed that dancing *en pointe* would add an unwanted element of "drag" to Zachary's performance and was not essential to the choreography. It is a credit to the talent and dedication of the dancers that all partnering and lifts were retained without significant change.

Close observation of gesture reshaped the relationship between the couple, the placement of weight, balance between the two bodies, and communication with the audience. It allowed "Lina" to retain agency during the partnered sequences and to never appear unequal to "Matthew." The original ballet's heterosexual love story became problematic during rehearsals though, and it became necessary to clarify how they might perform the ballet.

It was my intention that the dancers perform their own gender, rather than act feminine when dancing "Lina" or masculine while dancing "Matthew." Through Butler I was better able to understand how a movement or gesture could be performed with the original intention, without challenging the performer's gender identity. The original choreography acted as the culturally defined framework in which the individual dancers performed improvisations of their own gender. Our intention was to undo the perception that certain movements should only be done by certain genders rather than undoing the performer's gender.

Les Noces

Les Noces was commissioned by Queensland Ballet for *Dance Dialogues*, October 2014. This original contemporary ballet for five couples looks at the traditions of marriage. Within the frame of Banes's "marriage plot" (1998), it would be seen as an "endocentric" marriage, where the couple are members of the same culture or class system, and so ends happily. Cultural events and symbols, the undoing of ballet's gender roles, and sharing of visual focus were framed within three movements of Stravinsky's dance-cantata *Les Noces* (1923).

The creation of *Les Noces* began with research into Chinese traditional marriage practices (McLaren and Qinjian 2000; Mann 2002). It is framed within the context of Stravinsky's dance-cantata *Les Noces* (1923), as well as the ballets *Les Noces* by Bronislava Nijinska (1923) and *Svadebka* by Jiri Kylian (1982). I omitted the second movement of the score, as there were time constraints during the creation and rehearsal process and combined the dances for the women and men (originally separate in Nijinska and Kylian's ballets) into the first movement.

In Nijinska's *Les Noces*, the "Bride" and "Groom" appear as if "Byzantine icons" (Banes 1998, 111), removed from the action of the wedding festivities. They dance very little, remaining silently complicit with their fate. My "Bride" and "Groom" are more like Kylian's in *Svadebka*: they dance energetically but are also allowed moments of reflection. They each dance a solo and three duets together, which give insight into their characters and advance the narrative; however, while Kylian's couple seem very familiar (the "Groom-to-be" steals a kiss from his betrothed at the start of the ballet), my couple retain a formal separation in the first movement.

A "Maid of Honor" and "Best Man" act almost as the "Matchmakers" from Nijinska's version, while the parents who are present in both Nijinska and Kylian's ballets are omitted in my version. The "Maid of Honor" and "Best Man" are distinguished by short solos in the first and third movements and a small duet that acts as a climax to the "Best Man's" solo in the third movement. They lead the group dances, guide the proceedings throughout the ballet, and have the most interaction with the "Bride" and "Groom."

Partnering became a strong motif for the group, who retained their traditional gender roles. The use of intimate touch and partnering signified the marriage of the "Bride" and "Groom," who remain separate and do not touch until after the second movement wedding vows.

Chinese wedding traditions informed many of the opening gestures: rolling and folding gestures first seen in the bridal party's choreography echo the tradition of wrapping dowry gifts in rice paper. Translations of wedding lamentations from the Nanhui region described by McLaren and Qinjian (2000, 205–238) were the inspiration for the first movement solo of the "Bride."

The men and women share a gesture where they press the heel of the hand into the sternum, directly above the heart. The gesture is repeated throughout the ballet, and by varying the force it is performed with, it reflects either the weight of obligation or the couple's overwhelming love for one another. Prior to the premiere, Lina, who danced the role of the "Bride" in the normative cast, recalled me telling her that when seen in her first movement solo the gesture "was like you have doubt in your heart, but you push it away."

The roles of the "Bride" and "Groom" were choreographed to be regendered during the creation of the ballet in a similar process as *Intimate Distance*. This process initially limited the movement vocabulary of both couples, but as all four lead dancers were present at rehearsals, movements that one cast suggested were easily tested by the other cast.

The focus during the creative process shifted from collaborating with Lina on the solo material of the "bride" to working more closely with the reverse-gender couple of Eleanor and Alec on the partnering sections. The greatest problem in this research cycle was to create interesting choreography in which Eleanor could partner Alec, but that was still challenging enough for Vito and Lina to dance. I eventually found that compromises in the steps, partnering techniques, and movement dynamics gave us fertile material to explore new possibilities of movement, partnering, and expression. A vocabulary of supported balances, promenades, and unison steps, with a limit of lifts to small *soubresaut* and supported *grands jeté* gave enough choreographic scope and performer agency.

In *Les Noces* the women danced *en pointe*, while the men danced on *demi-pointe*, as is the classical tradition. This differed from *rebeginnings*, as Eleanor danced the steps of the "Groom" *en pointe*, and Alec adapted the steps of the "Bride" to be danced on *demi-pointe*.

Les Noces also differed from *rebeginnings* in that the choreography for the second movement duet was significantly different for the two casts. As the "Bride" and "Groom" were at the climax of their marriage vows, Vito tossed Lina into the air, catching her at the height of the lift in an *arabesque pressage*. This sequence would prove difficult for many dancers, and impossible to regender for Eleanor and Alec. It is a particular intersection of coordination, skill, and sexual dimorphism that enables such a dynamic display; and so I choreographed a completely different, grounded sequence for Eleanor and Alec, which emphasized her control and direction of Alec's movement. Other partnering in *Les Noces* was modified slightly to suit the comparative size differences between the two casts, always within the process of regendering.

The structure and form of *Les Noces* adheres strongly to neo-classical traditions. The "Bride" and "Groom" are presented as the lead couple. They are supported by a *corps de ballet*, who are not referenced as individuals and predominantly share unison steps. Two members of the group

Table 4.1. Marriage of Choice? Perceptions of Normative and Regendered Casts on the Type of Marriage in *Les Noces*

Date/Cast	Choice	Arranged	Unclear	Marriage	Gender	No story
Tues 4/11 B	10		1	3	1	
Wed 5/11 A	11	8	3	1	1	
Thurs 6/11 B	10	1	5			
Fri 7/11 A	5	3	1	1	1	1
Sat 8/11 A	10	6				
Tues 11/11 B	7			1		1—Conflict

are distinguished as the "Maid of Honor" and "Best Man" in the choreography and their prominence is reflected in the questionnaire data.

Responses to the *Les Noces* questionnaire were first coded with the performance date and cast (A or B). Responses to the *Les Noces* questionnaire were more detailed and varied than responses in either of the other two stages, and so a simple coding schema where words or phrases were taken verbatim from the response's text was not sufficient to determine recurring themes in the data. "Since statistical frequency of occurrence becomes one important measure of salient themes" (Saldana 2011, 10) a second round of coding was necessary to reduce the intent of these lengthy responses to one word codes such as "arranged," "choice," or "unsure." After developing a spreadsheet that listed each response and its coded intention, tables for each question were drawn up to show the number of responses per code for each performance.

The clearest indication that the performer's gender impacted the audience's perception of meaning in *Les Noces* was reflected in the participants' understanding of the type of marriage the lead couple was entering (see table 4.1). A clear majority of audience members that saw the performance of the regendered cast (Cast B) saw their marriage as a choice, while almost half the audience of the heteronormative couple felt Lina and Vito may have been part of an arranged marriage. The strength with which Eleanor danced the steps of the "Groom" and her direction of Alec's movements was read as self-determination and troubled the formal structure and gender binaries that the group's choreography exhibited.

The second question asked audience members about their understanding of the relationship between the "Bride" and "Groom" (see table 4.2). Responses were also coded through this two-round coding schema. The

Table 4.2. Emotional Relationship between the "Bride" and "Groom": Shifting Perceptions

Date/Cast	Love	Marriage (positive)	Marriage (negative)	Improving/ shifting	Gender	Misc
Tues 4/11 B	6	1		3	2	1—Expected
Wed 5/11 A	10	3	4		1	5
Thurs 6/11 B	9		1	2		2
Fri 7/11 A	3			5		
Sat 8/11 A	7		3	7	2—Hetero-normative	1—Dancing
Tues 11/11 B	6			2		1—Equal

first round took a word or short phrase directly from the response's text. Words and phrases of similar meaning were then assigned codes such as "love," "shifting-positive," and "shifting-negative," which were used to align common themes.

A primary element of classical ballet is the display of the female ballerina by her male partner (Copeland 1993, 141). The third question sought to measure the visual focus within the ballet and if it changed when the female dancer acted as the "cavalier" to her male partner. Responses were troubled by the number of dancers on stage: ten dancers in total. While the "Bride" and "Groom" were the most easily recognizable characters in the ballet, there were two other dancers who performed the uncredited roles of "Maid of Honor" and "Best Man," which were not regendered. There was no clear distinction or majority opinion between the casts on which dancer held the visual focus.

As *Les Noces* was performed by Queensland Ballet in their 2014 season, many dancers were also known to questionnaire participants by name and identified in responses as such. These responses were labeled with codes such as "Dancer's Name," specific character titles such as "Groom," "Bridesmaid," and "Equal." When participants named a specific dancer in their responses, it was most often accompanied by a comment on their physicality or facial features, such as "lovely smile."

Personal Reflection—Concluding Thoughts

As a contemporary ballet choreographer, I remain excited by the possibilities that the classical holds as a framework for new movement and modes of expression. Macaulay's vocal contention that sex, gender, and race are "not matters to which the art form can shut its doors" (2013a, 10) has spurred on this research as I broadened my choreographic practice in an attempt to answer his question, "How well equipped is this genre to speak to, or of, the world we know?" (2010, 4).

The phenomenon of intimate touch has been the greatest signifier of gendered movement in this project. Its absence in *Intimate Distances* resulted in choreography that was too neutral. Touch clarified the relationships in *rebeginnings* and *Les Noces* but allowed for ambiguity in the motivations for those relationships.

Within the *pas de deux*, that traditional symbol of heterosexual love (Novak 1993, 43), regendering has given new depth to existing relationships in my choreography. The regendered cast of *Les Noces* shared an equality that removed any perception of the arranged marriage perceived for the heteronormative cast: questionnaire data from three different audiences appear to indicate that participants clearly saw the marriage as a loving union. It was equally clear that the two men dancing together in *rebeginnings* were also in love, which is an interesting clarity when compared to the mixed audience responses for the other two casts.

The audience questionnaire for *Les Noces* was the most successful method of data collection during the project. Between eight and twenty-five survey forms were returned at each performance. I believe there were three factors that aided the likelihood of participation: performances were not overly long (1.5 hours) and consisted of only five short works, Queensland Ballet's artistic director spoke about the questionnaire in his introduction to the work, and the printed program mentioned that *Les Noces* was a research outcome of the Engendered research project. Drawing the audience's attention to the questionnaire in these three ways undoubtedly improved the likelihood of more audience participation.

It was a decision early in the research project for participants to remain completely anonymous. No information on participant demographics was collected during Engendered. Personal observation of audience members at *Dance13* and data obtained from Queensland Ballet (2014) show a stable demographic representation, with only small variations for matinee performances. Within the scope of this research it was preferred to capture the group's perception, rather than that of specific demographics. However, this choice limited the data analysis since participants were not asked to identify their gender. Knowledge of the questionnaire participants' gender would have better served my understanding of gendered gaze and its impact on the audience's perception.

The final limitation of this research was that it was only possible to present two casts of *Les Noces*. There was no chance to present at least one same-sex lead couple due to limited rehearsal time. It would clearly be the most obvious method of undoing the gendered traditions of classical ballet and marriage concurrently. Upon reflection, I would have focused less on the creation of group choreography, a very time-consuming part of the research cycle, and given more time to the rehearsal and regendering of the lead couple's choreography. This would be the focus for further research on this ballet in particular and this research question in general.

"The notion of 'inborn' or 'natural' gender differences" (Daly 1987b, 34) in the classical tradition will continue to present challenges for contemporary ballet. Macaulay weighs in, stating, "The future of the form is to be determined not by critics but by choreographers, artistic directors and, not least, by dancers, working together" (2013b, 10). The Engendered project has ignited a certain creative excitement for further collaboration—one that will allow my choreography to express something about today's world and to help develop a future for contemporary ballet.

5

Sassy Girls and Hard-Hitting Boys

Dance Competition Culture and Gender

KAREN SCHUPP

> Dance competitions are very competitive. Although they are stressful and have a few minor flaws, they are overall a great time. Girls shouldn't be discouraged simply because of the shape of their body or the color of their skin.
>
> Female competition participant, age 17

> What I like least about them is they are judged according to societal norms.
>
> Female competition participant, age 18

In the United States, dance competitions focusing on tap, jazz, contemporary or lyrical, hip-hop, and ballet have long served as venues for dance students and their studios to display their talents as teams and individuals. For most participants, who are predominantly adolescent girls, dance competitions are a way to share what they love with an audience and to learn more about themselves and dance. Furthermore, participants view dance competitions as an opportunity to feature the discipline, teamwork, technique, fitness, and grace under pressure that they have worked so hard to develop in the dance studio (Guarino 2014; LaRocco 2012; Schupp 2006; Wollins 2014). The chance to perform for an audience and learn more about dance at these events makes dance competitions highly appealing to adolescent dancers.

Through participating in dance competitions, adolescent dancers can potentially learn valuable lessons about responsibility, teamwork, dealing with criticism, and performing under pressure. At the same time, dance competitions can convey strong messages about how participants should look, move, act, as well as how gender should be performed. Although there has been some introductory research into the culture of dance competitions (Guarino 2014; Kinetz 2005; LaPoint-Crump 2007; LaRocco 2012; Schupp 2006; Weisbrod 2010), there has yet to be a full investigation of this cultural phenomenon that includes and contextualizes the voices of the adolescent dancers who compete in these events. This chapter establishes a broad understanding of gender in dance competitions by examining, articulating, and contextualizing the participants' experiences with and beliefs about gender in dance competitions. Analyzing adolescent dancers' perspectives about gender in this context provides insight into what makes dance competitions increasingly compelling to the general public as well as imparts valuable information about the expectations and attributes of dancers from this background.

Dance Competition Frameworks

Dance competitions, as they currently exist, emerged in the 1970s and rapidly increased in popularity in the late 1980s and early 1990s. The typical dance competition occurs over two to four full days in hotel ballrooms, high school auditoriums, or professional performance venues. On average, dance competition organizations host between twenty-two and twenty-five regional competitions and one to three national events per year (Guarino 2014; LaRocco 2012; Schupp 2006). Dance competitions can also be organized as dance conventions. In this scenario, master classes, including classes taught by judges, are offered for additional fees alongside the opportunity to perform in the dance competition portion of the event. Dance competition entry fees range from $30 to $60 to perform as a member of a group to over $100 to perform a solo. These fees are in addition to the costs of weekly lessons, required shoes, costumes, and related travel expenses. For competitors who are deeply involved, the costs can top $1,000 per month per dancer (LaRocco 2012).

Competitors, who are largely female, perform short choreographed dances called "routines" or "numbers." Dances are organized into different competitive categories based on the dance style, number, and average age of the performers (and in some cases, the intensity of the competitors' weekly training). For example, soloists aged ten to twelve performing jazz routines are placed in their own category and groups with an average age of thirteen to fifteen performing tap routines are placed in their own category. Unlike athletic events, male and female participants compete in the same category, with the exception of a few dance competitions that offer an all-male group category.

A panel of three to five judges, many of whom are former competition participants and have gone on to professional commercial dance careers, evaluates the dances. The judges provide each dance with a numerical score and often recorded performance critiques. Although the evaluation is subjective, judges are looking for "quality technique" (ballet informed), performance quality, clear lines, movement transitions, musicality, personal style, professional overall appearance, appropriate costume choices, and memorability (Wollins 2014) as epitomized in U.S. commercial dance venues. In many dance competitions, every dance receives an award based on a predetermined score rubric (i.e., a score of over ninety-five is a "high platinum"), and awards for the highest score may be offered for each individual category, age division, or dance style. Dances that achieve a certain minimum score are then invited to participate, for a fee, in the organization's national dance competition.

Dance Competitions and Gendered Bodies

This specific type of dance competition is a uniquely American phenomenon (LaRocco 2012; Schupp 2006); it can be argued that dance competition culture reinforces specific ideas about the social construction of gender in the United States. Beliefs about how the body should look and move and how genders should behave reflect the values of this specific cultural phenomenon.

Gender norms are reinforced and disciplined according to a given society's ideals to create specific "masculine" and "feminine" ways of looking, behaving, and moving in relationship to the society's values and norms (Bordo 1993, Butler 1999, Foucault 1990, Weitz 2010). Because dance genres and styles reflect the cultures in which they developed (Kealiinohomoku 1983), the social construction of gendered bodies can be reinforced in dance practices. For example, Cynthia Novack (1990) discusses how the emerging importance of egalitarianism in the 1970s is mirrored in the non-gendered partnering of contact improvisation. Additionally, Susan Leigh Foster (1997) addresses how dance training shapes bodily consciousness in relationship to two dancing bodies, one that is sensorially perceived and one that is based on the aesthetic archetypes of the dance style. The ideal dancing body, the body that many dancers continually strive to achieve, combines "fantasized visual or kinesthetic images of a body, images of other dancers' bodies," and the desire to expertly execute specific movements (Foster 1997, 237); each of these components reflect the gender expectations of the dance style.

Dance competitions encode implicit and explicit messages about gender. In her examination of televised dance competitions, Foster (2013) refers to the industrial body, the body that results from working in or the desire to work in "the industry" of commercial dance. The industrial body reveres the absorption of diverse types of dance into a uniform endorsement of youthfulness and heterosexuality and is primarily concerned with how it looks from the front, which is determined by the camera's location. In dance competitions, the importance of defining one's dancing from an external frontal perspective is further reinforced by the positioning of the judges, who are usually seated front and center. Another key attribute of the industrial body seen in televised dance competitions is that every movement attempts to demonstrate the dancers' heterosexual desirability as central to their identities and reasons for dancing (Foster 2013). In this context of gendered bodies, female dancers appear seductive and display a varied array of emotions, most often portraying the ups and downs of being in a heterosexual romantic relationship. And although they possess a great deal of athletic ability, the female dancers are expected to yield to their male partners' dominance. Male dancers portray moments of emotional sensitivity within an overarching narrative about heterosexual amorous pursuits and must come across as confident, authoritative, and in charge of female dancers (Foster 2013). Because a large number of competition dancers desire to work in "the industry" or are greatly influenced by televised dance competitions, Foster's ideas about gender and the industrial body provide a valuable framework for examining gendered bodies within dance competition culture.

Practices in the dance studio, where dance competition participants learn to dance and rehearse their competition routines, can further enforce attitudes about gender. The lion's share of dance competition participants and students who train in private dance studios are female. Sue Stinson (2005) critiques models of dance education where young girls, who can start studying dance at age three, implicitly learn that it is best to follow the teacher's instructions and to avoid voicing viewpoints that may conflict with the ideas of the teacher and the rest of the class. She explains how traditional dance pedagogy implicitly puts forth a "hidden curriculum" that reinforces traditional gender expectations for girls such as obedience and passivity. The fact that traditional dance pedagogy mirrors widely accepted gender-prescribed behaviors for girls is perhaps why it is thought to be "normal" for girls to want to dance. Boys who opt to study dance, however, are often invited to take leadership roles and to creatively contribute to the dance class and dance routines as a way to make them feel more comfortable (Risner 2009a, 27). Doug Risner (2009a) observes how this creates a paradox for boys who dance in that they are "at once devalued by the culture, yet prized by the [dance] field" (27). Additionally, dance competition students are subject to highly prescribed notions about what constitutes acceptable dance movement (Schupp 2011; Schwartz 1994), and teachers in this setting are usually seen to be authority figures, rather than facilitators of students' dance learning, which inhibits students from making personally relevant choices about dance (Smith 1998). While competitive dance training can lead to a high caliber of technique and artistry, it is achieved through teaching methods that implicitly reinforce specific ideas about gender with little room for critical examination of those constructs.

Outside of the dance studio, adolescents are constantly observing and assessing their own behavior in line with what is thought to be acceptable. Many adolescents are in what developmental psychologist Jane Loevinger (1976) refers to as the "Self-Aware," also known as the "Conformist-Conscientious" stage of ego development. In this transitional stage, the ego is characterized by greater self-awareness, enhanced ability to imagine multiple outcomes to a given scenario, and self-criticism of the self in relation to society's expectations (Loevinger 1976). As they move from the conformist stage to the conscientious stage of ego development, adolescents become more aware of interpersonal relationships and are better able to identify the welfare of others as they begin to reconcile their understanding of themselves and those around them. Michel Foucault (1979, 1990) in his work on the connections between power, the body, and sexuality, builds upon Jeremy Bentham's ([1787] 1995) panopticon prison model to suggest that individuals internalize a type of anonymous power that regulates their actions according to what they believe to be society's norms. For adolescent dance competition participants, this anonymous power is a combination of attitudes and messages from the larger culture, the dance culture in which they participate and or aspire to join, their dance teachers, and their families. The internalization and embodiment of these dominant messages create compliant adolescent dancing bodies that reflect regulated beliefs about gender in dance competition culture.

A full understanding of how this occurs in dance competition culture requires an investigation into the lived experiences of the actual participants. Through uncovering adolescent participants' motivations, perceptions of gender, and experiences with dance competitions, the construction of gender in this setting becomes more transparent. Revealing and contextualizing adolescent competition dancers' beliefs about what the dancing body should look like, how the dancing body should move, and the roles of boys and girls in dance competitions demonstrate how gender is constructed and embodied according to dance competition norms.

Methodology

The research aims to present an understanding of gender in dance competitions and provide portraits of the individuals who participate. A mixed-method research approach implementing a sequential explanatory strategy is used so that a general description of dance competition participants' beliefs and attitudes as well as more detailed illustrations of their experiences can be included. As is standard with a sequential explanatory strategy, the qualitative portion follows the collection and analysis of the quantitative data (Creswell 2009). Because there is very little research in this area, the data weighting favors the quantitative results to provide a broad summary of the participants' attitudes and beliefs.

The quantitative portion of the research consists of a survey using a cross-sectional design, a survey devised to collect data from a specific population at one point in time, (Edmonds and Kelly 2013, 108) and descriptive statistical analysis, an interpretation method that provides a description of the basic components of the survey data (Chambliss 2012, 159). Survey questions primarily address adolescent participants' perception of what a competition dancer should look like, how competition dancers should move, and the similarities and differences for male and female participants in dance competitions. One hundred eleven people participated in the survey with an average of sixty to seventy responses per question. Participants are female and male adolescents (ages thirteen to eighteen) who self-identify as dance competition participants in the United States, and the majority are female adolescents (only three survey participants identified as male).

Data gained from the quantitative portion informs the qualitative portion (Creswell 2009), which consists of interviews, primarily through shaping interview questions and determining participants. The purpose of the interviews is to elaborate on the findings of the quantitative survey. All survey participants had the opportunity to participate in an interview. Seven adolescent females participated in a thirty-minute interview conducted via video conferencing or in person. Interview questions centered on personal experiences with dance competitions around topics including what it feels like to participate in dance competitions, the role of dance competitions in their lives, and similarities and differences in the expectations for male and female competitors. Analysis of the interviews aims to describe, examine, and interpret the qualitative data in relationship to the quantitative findings (Creswell 2013). Coding initially focuses on three large areas: information that reinforced survey responses, emergent information that was unexpected based on survey responses, and information that was theoretically unusual (Creswell 2013, 195). The use of several codes in each of these larger areas permits the breadth and depth of the data to be fully analyzed before aggregating the data into larger themes (Creswell 2013).

Besides information regarding gender, information emerged from the qualitative research that chronicles the importance of dance in interviewees' lives, what it is like to perform, and what it takes to participate in dance competitions. Because this data does not directly address gender, it was eliminated from the data analysis for this chapter; however, it is used to contextualize the discussion of the results.

Analysis of Data

Both the quantitative and coded qualitative data were based on appearance norms, movement expectations, how genders interact, and the specialness of boys. Analysis of the qualitative data reinforced survey responses and is therefore reported in tandem with the quantitative data.

Appearance Norms

> I think . . . the competition dancer looks very tall and slim—for girls at least. And they usually—when they get up onstage—show a lot more skin, with like half-tops. That's what I see when I think of a competition dancer.
>
> Female competition participant, age 16

> And then, you know, they always have a big hairdo, and a bunch of make-up, and fake eyelashes, and the big earrings.
>
> Female competition participant, age 16

Survey respondents answered questions regarding the ideal body type for each gender, the importance of dancers' general appearance, and appropriate costuming choices. For female dance competition participants, the body is thought to be both "long and lean" and "athletic and solid." Slightly more than half of respondents described the ideal female dancing body as "long and lean" and the remaining survey respondents labeled it as "athletic and solid." An overwhelming majority of respondents reported that the ideal male dancing body is "athletic and solid." Bodies that are "round and full" did not fit into survey respondents' perceptions of the ideal dancing body for either gender. Interviewees echoed these ideals when explaining what competition dancers look like. Nicole[1] portrayed female competition dancers as "tall and slim," while Tanya noted, "Most have abs," whereas male competition dancers were depicted by Emma as "muscular [so] they can lift the girls." These descriptions reinforce the survey findings and are representative of general trends in the qualitative interviews. Some interviewees acknowledged that there is some room for a variety of body types in competition. However, their language indicated that dancers, specifically female dancers, who are not long, lean, athletic, and solid, are considered outside the cultural norm. This was illustrated by the use of wording such as "bigger girls" and the idea that dancers who are talented and have a "round and full" body type are the exception to the norm.

For both male and female dance competition participants, appearance contributes to their overall success. A large preponderance of respondents agreed or strongly agreed that overall appearance is an important factor for girls and boys in dance competitions. Vanessa, speaking from her own experience of listening to judges' audio critiques, mentioned the high frequency of comments about dancers' appearance. She discussed how "[judges] will comment on makeup [and] hair" before providing feedback

Table 5.1. Appearance Norms

THE IDEAL DANCING BODY IS:

	long and lean	athletic and solid	round and full
For girls (69 respondents)	38 (55%)	31 (45%)	0 (0%)
For boys (71 respondents)	6 (8%)	65 (92%)	0 (0%)

A DANCER'S OVERALL APPEARANCE IS AN IMPORTANT FACTOR IN DANCE COMPETITIONS.

	Strongly Agree	Agree	Neutral	Disagree	Strongly Disagree
For girls (71 respondents)	27 (38%)	28 (39%)	18 (18%)	2 (3%)	1 (1%)
For boys (71 respondents)	13 (18%)	31 (44%)	20 (28%)	5 (7%)	2 (3%)

COSTUMES HIGHLIGHT THE DANCERS': (*Survey respondents had the option to check all options that applied.*)

	legs, arms, and back	delicacy and prettiness	movement and choreography	musculality and physique	strength and aggressiveness
For girls (71 respondents)	43 (61%)	23 (32%)	62 (87%)	20 (28%)	10 (14%)
For boys (71 respondents)	23 (32%)	1 (1%)	61 (43%)	55 (77%)	28 (39%)

on the dancers' technique. Denise, Christy, Marie, Vanessa, and Tanya described typical hairstyles, such as "high buns" and "big hairdos," make-up norms for girls including "fake eyelashes" and "purple eye shadow [worn up to the ends of the eyebrows]," and feminine accents such as "big earrings" and "big . . . chokers" in their descriptions of female competition dancers. Male competition dancers were characterized typically as less made up and identifiably masculine.

Costumes choices help define gender in dance competitions. Although the predominance of respondents felt that girls' costumes should highlight the movement and choreography of a dance, slightly less than two-thirds thought that costumes should feature the dancers' bodies, and one-third believed that costumes should draw attention to their delicacy and prettiness. For more than three-quarters of respondents, featuring a boy's muscularity and physique was the top costuming concern; featuring the movement and choreography was the secondary concern. Marie, Tanya,

Denise, Christy, Emma, Nicole, and Vanessa took great joy in describing the costumes of their memorable competition dances: three wore a sleeveless, short dress; three wore short-shorts and a half top; and one wore pants and a shirt. When describing boys' costumes, they largely recounted costumes that consisted of pants and short sleeved or sleeveless shirts that were "less blingy" than girls' costumes. None of them discussed any discomfort, physically or psychologically, in wearing somewhat revealing and overtly feminine costumes.

Movement Expectations

> For the girls, they just have like a lot of grace and like beauty in their dancing. For boys, they like are very strong . . . They can be hard hitting, but they can also be flowy in their dancing.
>
> Female competition participant, age 13

Survey respondents were asked about what types of dance steps and movement qualities are most suitable for female and male dance competition participants. For both boys and girls, respondents believed that movement should be performed in "a way that best suits the dancer." This was the only option provided that does not describe a movement quality or performance intention and that recognizes the unique movement and performance capabilities of individual dancers. Nearly all respondents thought that a female competitor should perform in "a way that best suits the dancer." Three-quarters of respondents found this to be true for male competitors, while the remaining respondents thought that boys should perform in a "powerful and athletic way." Information gathered from the interviews indicates that there are some gray areas when determining what it means to perform in "a way that best suits the dancer." Interviewees readily articulated the differing movement qualities they believed male and female dancers should possess. Good male dancers were described as "hard hitting" and possessing the ability to "man-up" choreography, and good female dancers were often characterized as "flowy" or "fluid" movers.

Although respondents thought that both boys and girls should perform in "a way that best suits the dancer," there are delineations as to what constitutes appropriate movement vocabulary, or steps, for each gender. Almost half of respondents believed that choreography for girls should highlight their ability to control movement. One-third of respondents felt

Table 5.2. Movement Expectations

THE MOVEMENT SHOULD BE PERFORMED IN A:

	powerful and athletic way	flirty and fun way	delicate and detailed way	way that best suits the dancer
For girls (65 respondents)	1 (2%)	1 (2%)	4 (6%)	59 (91%)
For boys (66 respondents)	17 (26%)	0 (0%)	0 (0%)	49 (74%)

CHOREOGRAPHY SHOULD FEATURE STEPS THAT HIGHLIGHT:

	flexibility like battements or kicks and *développés* or extensions	upper body strength like push-ups and floor work	lower body strength like jumps, *tours*, leaps, and *grand jetés*	control, like turns or pirouettes and difficult balances
For girls (64 respondents)	21 (33%)	0 (0%)	13 (20%)	30 (47%)
For boys (64 respondents)	0 (0%)	18 (28%)	34 (53%)	12 (19%)

that showing girls' flexibility is choreographically important, and one-fifth of respondents believed choreography should accentuate girls' lower body strength. Featuring lower body strength was selected as the most critical aspect of boys' choreography by more than half of survey respondents, followed by emphasizing upper body strength, and lastly highlighting control. Although the movement vocabulary for boys and girls overlaps, it is evident that choreography for girls should feature control, flexibility, and some lower body strength, whereas choreography for boys should demonstrate muscular strength.

Data from the interviews reinforced this division in movement vocabulary and movement qualities. Interviewees had the opportunity to describe the best competition solos they had witnessed and their favorite dancers. They were impressed by female dancers' abilities to "hold [their] leg[s] up there," "humbleness and grace," "flowy lines," and "sassiness." Male dancers who made impressions on them had "a masculine flair," performed "a lot of floorwork . . . Russians . . . and [amazing] jumps," and "[made] it look easy." Interviewees also recognized the versatility, commitment, and presence that their favorite dancers possess and readily acknowledged that boys need flexibility and girls need strength in today's dance competition culture. Although there are defined ideas about how boys and girls should move, there is a recognition that really great competition dancers should be able to do all types of steps, regardless of their gender. Many felt that their favorite male and female dancers had the same technical ability and were capable of performing the same movements, although male dancers would perform these movements in a more "hard-hitting way" and women would bring a "flowy" quality to their dancing.

Male and Female Interactions

> A lot of people don't understand that boys and girls are pretty much the same, they just have different looks. A lot of girls dance like guys, and a lot of guys dance like girls. It doesn't really have to be girls dancing like girls, and guys dancing like guys.
>
> Female competition participant, age 15

After answering questions about how competition dancers look and move, survey respondents considered how dance competition participants should learn dance, how genders should choreographically interact, and appropriate choreographic content or intentions for dance routines. When asked if they agreed with the statement, "It is important for boys to learn dance from male teachers," most respondents were neutral. The bulk of respondents were neutral when the same statement was offered regarding girls and female teachers. Survey respondents were also prompted to contemplate the importance of boys learning masculine dance movement and girls learning feminine dance movement. The data suggests that it is slightly more important for girls to learn feminine movement than it is for boys to learn masculine movement. The majority of respondents felt that it was equally important for boys and girls to learn both masculine and feminine movement when learning to dance.

In dance competitions, choreographic content is largely based on portraying a story or evoking a feeling through featuring dancers' technique and highlighting or relating to a song's lyrics. Therefore, survey respondents were asked to determine the appropriateness of a boy dancing to a song performed by a woman and a girl dancing to a song performed by a man. For both scenarios, the data favored responses of "neutral" to "strongly agree" and suggest that it is slightly more appropriate for a girl to dance to a song performed by a man than for a boy to dance to a song performed by a woman. Survey respondents were also asked to consider

Table 5.3. Female and Male Interactions

	Strongly Agree	Agree	Neutral	Disagree	Strongly Disagree
IT IS IMPORTANT FOR BOYS TO LEARN DANCE FROM MALE TEACHERS.					
60 respondents	10 (17%)	9 (15%)	23 (38%)	10 (17%)	8 (13%)
IT IS IMPORTANT FOR GIRLS TO LEARN DANCE FROM FEMALE TEACHERS.					
61 respondents	8 (13%)	4 (7%)	28 (46%)	14 (23%)	7 (12%)
WHEN LEARNING TO DANCE, BOYS SHOULD FOCUS ON LEARNING MASCULINE DANCE MOVEMENT.					
61 respondents	8 (13%)	14 (23%)	26 (43%)	8 (13%)	4 (7%)
WHEN LEARNING TO DANCE, GIRLS SHOULD FOCUS ON LEARNING FEMININE DANCE MOVEMENT.					
61 respondents	6 (10%)	19 (31%)	23 (38%)	8 (13%)	5 (8%)
WHEN LEARNING TO DANCE, GIRLS AND BOYS SHOULD FOCUS ON LEARNING MASCULINE AND FEMININE DANCE MOVEMENT.					
61 respondents	21 (34%)	27 (44%)	12 (20%)	1 (1%)	0 (0%)
IT IS APPROPRIATE FOR A BOY TO DANCE TO A SONG BY A WOMAN.					
64 respondents	18 (28%)	17 (27%)	19 (30%)	7 (11%)	3 (5%)
IT IS APPROPRIATE FOR A GIRL TO DANCE TO A SONG BY A MAN.					
63 respondents	21 (33%)	21 (33%)	17 (27%)	2 (3%)	2 (3%)

WHEN BOYS AND GIRLS DANCE TOGETHER:

	the boys should primarily lift and support the girls	the girls should primarily lift and support the boys	boys and girls should lift and support each other
60 respondents	41 (68%)	0 (0%)	19 (32%)

WHEN A BOY AND GIRL PERFORM A DUET, THE IDEAL STORY FOR THE DANCE IS:

	about a relationship where the boy leads and the girl follows	about a relationship where the girl leads and the boy follows	about a relationship where the boy and girl take turns leading and following
63 respondents	13 (21%)	2 (3%)	48 (76%)

THE MOST MEMORABLE DANCES ARE ABOUT:

	his/her relationship with a girl/boy	a personal adventure	a personal point of view on a topic	his/her expression through the movement
For boys (63 respondents)	2 (3%)	10 (16%)	6 (10%)	45 (72%)
For girls (64 respondents)	2 (3%)	4 (6%)	10 (16%)	48 (75%)

how boys and girls should interact when performing together in terms of thematic and choreographic content. A larger part of respondents believed that the ideal story for a duet performed by a boy and girl is about a relationship where they take turns leading and following. Choreographically, in boy-girl duets, nearly two-thirds of respondents felt that the boys should primarily lift and support the girls. Almost one-third of respondents thought boys and girls should lift and support each other, but no one expected that girls should primarily lift and support the boys.

Survey respondents were asked to assess the thematic or expressive content of memorable dance competition solos. Overwhelmingly, according to respondents, a dancer's "expression through the movement" makes for the most memorable performances. Very few respondents felt that solos about romantic heterosexual relationships make for memorable dances. All interviewees echoed the significance of a dancer's personal expression through the movement in becoming a standout dancer. When asked to describe their favorite dancers, they discussed dancers from well-known ballet companies, *So You Think You Can Dance*, competitions and conventions, and from their own studios. Although their "favorite dancers" work in a variety of contexts and perform different genres, all mentioned the expressive capacity of each dancer as they explained how the dancers were "eye catching," "demanded your attention," had their "own system[s] of performing," and were "seriously perfect." Interviewees acknowledged that their favorite male and female dancers had numerous similarities, including impeccable technique, stage presence, and dedication.

The Specialness of Boys

> Well, it's definitely easier for boys in the industry, because they are boys. They're special, even if they're not great dancers. They're special because you know that they're going to get a job someday just because they're a boy. But with girls, it's like you have to be good or else you're not getting anything. So for boys, I think it's a lot easier to win something because they're [boys] and they're more noticeable . . . The girls just kind of blend in together, unless you're like really, really good. So I actually have a lot of boys that go to my studio. And they always tell us, like, "It's not that easy for guys." And [I'm] like, "Well, even if it's not that easy for guys, it's definitely harder for girls."
>
> Female competition dancer, age 14

Unlike most athletic competitions, such as soccer and track and field, boys and girls commonly perform with each other in group, duet, and trio routines and compete against each other in solo categories. When asked if boys and girls are judged by the same technical standards in dance competitions, the majority of survey respondents strongly disagreed or disagreed signifying that boys are judged less stringently. If a boy is a member of group dance routine, nearly two-thirds of survey respondents thought that the boy should wear a different costume than the girls, but at the same time, more than half of survey respondents thought he should also blend in with the rest of the group. Slightly more than half of respondents thought that if there is only one boy in a group number that he should lift and support the girls, and just over one quarter of respondents felt that boys should be featured as soloists in group routines. Few respondents thought it would be proper for boys to wear the same costumes as girls when performing a group routine. The data suggest that there are different expectations for boys and girls in dance competitions and that in some ways boys are considered to be special in dance competition culture.

Interviewees readily articulated what they perceive to be unequal treatment of boys and girls and offered ideas about why this inequality occurs. Several discussed the experience of competing against a boy as a soloist. Marie succinctly portrayed the experience as "kind of scary, because you know if they're good, then the judge is going to like them a lot." Nicole provided more detail explaining "it's difficult because I realize that the boy may place higher than me before I even dance . . . [T]his guy just went in front of [me], and [I] know he'll probably get scored higher than [me] . . . [A]nd [I] still [need to] try to perform to the fullest potential of myself." Because boys are rare in dance competition culture, interviewees posit that there are fewer comparisons that can be made among them, which leads to the use of different criteria when judging boys and girls. Emma explained "girls [are] easier to judge because there's so many of them, and you can compare them to each other. And you can compare what [the judges] feel a good dancer is. And there's not as many boys. So it's kind of hard to say, 'Oh, he's like a good dancer,' or, 'Oh, he's an okay dancer.'" All of the interviewees seemed to agree that boys have a competitive advantage due to their scarcity in dance competition culture.

In competitions that also have conventions, this sense of specialness comes into play in classes. While the interviewees are aware of the advantage that boys may have, they seem to agree that this privilege is situational and stems from the fact that there are so few boys who participate in dance competition culture. Christy described what it is like to take a

Table 5.4. The Specialness of Boys

BOYS AND GIRLS ARE JUDGED BY THE SAME TECHNICAL STANDARDS IN DANCE COMPETITIONS.

	strongly agree	agree	neutral	disagree	strongly disagree
61 respondents	7 (11%)	10 (16%)	6 (10%)	18 (30%)	20 (33%)

IN A LARGE GROUP NUMBER WITH ONLY ONE BOY, THE BOY SHOULD: (*Survey respondents had the option to check all options that applied.*)

	be featured as a soloist	wear a different costume than the girls	lift and support the girls	wear the same costume as the girls	blend in with the rest of the group
60 respondents	17 (28%)	37 (62%)	32 (53%)	4 (7%)	35 (58%)

convention class with over a hundred dancers but fewer than fifteen boys. "It's like, there's so many more girls than boys, it's so hard to be looked at and not just be overlooked. Like especially at like conventions, like, there's a lot less boys than there is girls. And especially like me, I have like just brown hair, pale skin. Like I look like everybody else. So it's so hard to get, like, noticed, I guess. So I think it is easier for boys, but they still have to work hard." In competitions and classes, the data suggest that girls struggle to be seen as individuals because there are so many of them, whereas boys stand out as unique due to the underrepresentation of their gender.

Discussion

The data strongly suggests that adolescent dance competition participants, especially adolescent girls, are aware that there are discernible expectations regulating the expression and performance of gender in competition dance culture. Because dance competition participants are incredibly passionate about dance, they readily embody these expectations as evidenced by their perceptions of what constitutes appropriate appearances, movement, and interactions for each gender while learning and performing competition dance.

In competition dance culture, girls are expected to have bodies that are long and lean but also athletically toned, to pay great attention to their hair and makeup when performing, and to be comfortable wearing costumes that highlight both the movement and the feminine aspects of their bodies. In terms of movement, it is assumed that they will perform in a way that best suits the dancer but is "flowy" and graceful. Choreography should emphasize control and flexibility, although some level of strength is expected. When dancing with boys, girls should hold their own in terms of individual movements but be prepared to be lifted and supported by boys. While they should learn both feminine and masculine dance movement, they should pay slightly more attention to learning feminine aspects of dance. Lastly, when competing against or taking convention classes with boys, girls should be prepared for boys to garner more attention simply because there are so few boys in dance competition culture.

Boys also have a recognizable set of criteria to be aware of in dance competition culture. They are expected to be athletic, maintain a masculine appearance, and wear costumes that support dominant cultural ideas about masculinity. Boys need to be "hard hitting" and strong in their dancing, which tends to emphasize their muscular strength. When dancing with girls, boys have to balance blending in with the group while also being a unique aspect of the choreography, and when performing duets with girls, they are required to lift and support their partner. They need to learn masculine and feminine movement but be prepared to "man-up" so that the movement does not appear too feminine. When participating in competitions and conventions, boys should be ready for the extra attention that their presence will draw and factor that into their experiences of performing, taking classes, and interacting with their peers.

In line with theories about the cultural construction of bodies, dance competition culture reinforces society's attitudes about the binary construction of gender. This is further emphasized through the demands placed on the dancing body in this context. There is a connection between the presumption that girls should perform in a "flowy" and graceful way and bodies that are long and toned, just as there is a connection between the expectation that boys have athletic bodies that move in a hard-hitting way. The movement dynamics and steps that boys and girls train to do shapes their perceptions, bodies, and dancing in very specific ways. This then reinforces ideas about what it means to be feminine and masculine inside of dance competition culture.

Adolescents who participate in dance competition culture are very in tune with Foster's (2013) idea of the industrial body, even if they are unfamiliar with that term. Although adolescent dance competition participants recognize that boys and girls can and should be able to do the same movements, their beliefs about how boys and girls should interact when dancing point to the heterosexual narrative Foster outlines. Girls are expected to yield to their male partners' dominance as they are lifted and supported, and boys are expected to control their female partners as they lift and support them. The expectation of heterosexual desirability is witnessed through dance competition participants' description of girls as "sassy" and boys as "hard hitting"; their preference for costumes that feature girls' arms, legs, and backs, and boys' muscularity; descriptions of what constitutes appropriate hair and makeup styles for girls; and observations of how boys and girls interact when performing together. Data from the interviews confirms that dance competition dancers have their eye on performing in the "industry" as noted by their consistent use of that term in the interviews, so it is not surprising that the rules governing Foster's industrial body are at play in dance competitions.

In dance competition culture, Foster's (2013) assertion of the importance of defining participants' dance experience through an external frontally focused lens is interwoven with the role of the teacher. Dance competition teachers implicitly and explicitly shape their students' ideas about gender and how it is perceived from an external perspective. When interviewees discussed their most memorable dance competition experience, none of them mentioned that their performances felt feminine, yet they gave a great deal of attention to describing the feminizing aspects of their costumes, the amount of flexibility and control it took to perform, and the emotional and sometimes escapist aspects of performing. The messages that dance competition participants receive about gender within choreography, which includes the dance steps, the movement qualities, thematic content, and ways that the genders interact, are largely externally perceived and come from their teachers. These choreographic choices are then normalized when judges award high scores to routines that meet the implicit gender expectations of this culture.

Stinson's (2005) and Risner's (2009a) assertions that traditional approaches to teaching dance breed passivity for girls and create paradoxes for boys directly correlates to survey respondents' and interviewees' experiences with competition dance. This is illustrated most vividly through the example of taking convention classes. Several of the interviewees discussed their frustrations with not being noticed in class because so many of the dancers are girls. In other words, dancing is the normal thing to do, and girls should work hard but should not assert themselves to gain extra attention. They were, however, very sensitive to the complexity of being a boy in dance competition culture. They simultaneously recognized that boys were "prized" due to their scarcity in the culture, but they readily acknowledged the struggles facing boys who dance.

Both in terms of appearance and movement, adolescent dance competition participants internalize and embody messages about gender from a variety of sources. Ideas about gender come from the larger culture; "the industry" they aspire to join; and dance competition culture, which includes judges, teachers, parents, and peers. In relation to Foucault's (1979, 1990) theories connecting power, body, and sexuality, and Loevinger's (1976) assertions about the stages of ego development, adolescent dance competition participants regulate their actions and train their bodies according to what they think constitutes normal gendered behavior. Although the data implies that there is something of a gray area when it comes to delineating gender, it still appears that there are clear criteria for determining what is gender appropriate in terms of appearance, movement, and interaction with the opposite gender in dance competition culture. The data from the survey and the ease with which interviewees discussed ideas about masculinity and femininity indicates that adolescent dance competition participants are well aware of (and keep track of) these gender differences in their own dancing as well as in the dancing of their peers and the dancers they admire.

Conclusion

The October 2014 issue of *Dance Teacher* committed the majority of its content to preparing for competition season, which usually lasts from January to July each year. A remarkable eighty out of 154 pages were dedicated to either advertising dance competitions or providing practical and insider information about how to best prepare for and participate in dance competition season. The amount of page space given to dance competitions in popular publications focused on teaching dance combined with Alexis Weisbrod's (2010) observation that dance competition culture is becoming a significant place for training non-professional dancers speaks to the scope of dance competition culture's reach. As more Americans are exposed to and educated about dance through dance competition culture, it is critical to continue examining this cultural phenomenon through various cultural, political, sociological, and educational lenses.

Working toward a broader perception of gender in dance competition culture is a difficult but not impossible task. Changing the construction and consciousness of gender in dance competition culture is complex because dance studios and dance competitions are businesses (Risner, et al. 2004): both need to make a profit to survive. Therefore, enrollment matters, and winning dance competitions can often help studios recruit new students. To be successful, dance studios and dance competitions may unintentionally promote specific, culturally familiar gender expectations in their choreography, teaching, and business plans. For example, it is not uncommon for dance studios to recruit boys by emphasizing the perceived "masculine" aspects of dance (e.g., developing strength, use of ballet in athletic training) and by offering boys recruitment scholarships, and to distinguish boys, either directly through solos or indirectly by costume choices, in group dance routines. These practices are common in dance competition studios and may go unquestioned.

At the same time, many dance studio teachers wholeheartedly support their gay male students; they also believe in empowering young girls and work diligently to create safe and loving dance studio communities. Taking the time to objectively observe how gender is implicitly and explicitly addressed in the teaching and performing of dance competition dances is an important first step toward creating gender equality in this setting. Pausing to reveal and then reflect on unnoticed assumptions and habits can provide dance teachers greater insight into how their practice relates to (or is perhaps contrary) to their personal values (Risner 2014a).

There are several small changes that dance teachers, judges, and administrators who work in this setting can consider to create gender-neutral approaches to teaching and performing dance. Dance teachers' use of somatic pedagogical approaches, which prioritize the development of an internal, first-person perspective to movement, may lessen the emphasis on the external perception of movement. For adolescent dancers, reducing the importance of their appearance when dancing may reduce their desire to look, dress, and move in certain gender-prescribed ways. Dance teachers, both in studios and conventions, can objectively witness how they observe students and provide feedback in class settings. Bringing awareness to any imbalances between the amount and types of feedback given to male and female students allows teachers to see how their best intentions may contribute to perceived gender inequality. Teachers and competition organizers can reconsider how they market their businesses. Instead of bringing attention to the gendered benefits of studying dance, such as teaching increased poise and grace for girls and strength and power for boys, more emphasis can be brought to the universal benefits of dancing. Increased creativity, physical fitness, coordination, ability to work as part of a team, composure, and confidence are only a few of the recognized benefits of dance. Taking the time to highlight these aspects in advertisements as well as in the teaching, performance, and evaluation of dance in this setting will not only assist students in becoming better dancers but may also broaden gender expectations in dance competition culture.

As demonstrated by quantitative and qualitative components of the research, there are palpable ideas about how gender is constructed and performed in dance competition culture. Understanding the construction and performance of gender in dance competition culture provides a foundation for asking additional questions about the experiences of those who participate in dance competitions. Dance competition culture can certainly help young dancers achieve high levels of technical and artistic proficiency, but it encodes specific expectations about gender into participants' practice of dance.

Note

1. For anonymity purposes, pseudonyms are used throughout the chapter.

6

Boys Only!

Gender-Based Pedagogical Practices
in a Commercial Dance Studio

CAROLYN HEBERT

The State of Boys in Dance

In the April 2009 issue of *Dance Teacher* magazine, an article titled "Separate but Equal?" by Karyn D. Collins highlights the boys-only ballet training program at Eliot Feld's Ballet Tech School in New York City. "One of the biggest trends in ballet during the past 15 years," Collins claims, "has been special programs for boys. . . . many of them offering boys free tuition . . . to address a longtime challenge: how to encourage young American boys to study ballet" (Collins 2009, 36). Accordingly, teachers at Ballet Tech feel that the boys-only classes are "critical to retaining these students" because they "allow for the different learning styles and energy that often differentiate boys from girls" (Collins 2009, 36). In addition, the article features a section of suggested incentives that commercial studio owners and teachers might offer in order to "Get Boys Into Your Studio—and Keep Them There!" (Collins 2009, 38). Ten tips describe various methods, based on stereotypical notions of masculinity, that teachers might employ. Teachers are encouraged to offer hip-hop, breakdancing, and tap classes as they are "very popular male-friendly styles" and because "what boy doesn't love to make noise?" (Collins 2009, 38). Tuition scholarships, lenient dress codes, and leading roles or leadership opportunities are all suggested bonuses studios may provide to "change the perception that dance is feminine" and make male dance students feel comfortable enough to continue studying. The article concludes with a testimonial from an alumnus in praise of the Ballet Tech boys-only program: "It was fun when we got with the girls, but it was a different feeling with the all-boys classes. The boys' classes push you to do your best and see how good you really are" (Collins 2009, 38).

The tips outlined in this *Dance Teacher* magazine article demonstrate the efforts being made by the commercial dance world in North America to reopen the doors of ballet, jazz, and tap dance studios to men. They address the "trouble with the male dancer," which, according to Ramsay Burt (2007), developed in response to mid-nineteenth-century middle-class attitudes toward the male body and social behavior (11). These attitudes plagued the male dancer as "less than masculine" and contributed to the spread of the perception of dance as an inappropriate activity for men in North American culture. But owing partially to a recent surge in the popularity of the male-dominated forms of hip-hop and breakdancing, and the hyper-masculine depiction of male dancers on television shows such as FOX's *So You Think You Can Dance* (Broomfield 2011), few scholars would argue with the claim that the "negative stereotypes about men in [dance] have disappeared in some places today" (Fisher 2009, 35).

Seizing the moment, dance studios seem to be shifting toward implementing gender-based pedagogical techniques that promote dance as a macho activity to encourage male enrollment. Parallels are often drawn between sports and dance, emphasizing competition, jumping, and turning to demonstrate characteristics of hegemonic masculinity (Crawford 1994; Lehikoinen 2006; Fisher 2009; Keefe 2009; Taschuck 2009). Ballet and other genres are marketed to males as "tough as football, a 'real' man's game," reflecting the athletic stamina required to participate (Fisher 2009, 32). Although such efforts may appeal to certain potential male dancers, scholars identify a problematic association between the masculinization of dance and persistent homophobic attitudes toward dance culture (Burt 2007; Risner 2002a, 2002b, 2009a, 2014a; Gard 2001; Lehikoinen 2006).

Furthermore, as discussed by Susan Stinson (2005), the hidden curriculum within single-sex classes potentially reinforces gender stereotypes within the dance classroom and promotes dominant notions of masculinity and femininity. As teachers and scholars, we must critically examine the implications of gender-based pedagogical techniques that potentially assert a singular hegemonic masculinity to counter historical assumptions of the male dancing body being effeminate or homosexual. Conversations with students who experience and participate in a gender-based dance education provide an opportunity to assess these practices and reflect on their value.

Research Methodology

Through an ethnographic case study of a group of male hip-hop dancers who participated in a boys-only jazz technique class between September 2013 and May 2014, this research assesses the effects of gender-based pedagogical practices. According to Soyini Madison, critical ethnographers are committed to participatory fieldwork, so that "empirical methodologies become the foundation for inquiry, and it is here 'on the ground' of Others that the researcher encounters social conditions that become the point of departure for research" (2012, 5). In my role as instructor for the boys-only jazz class, I was "on the ground" with these students, reflecting upon the hidden curriculum of gender embedded in my pedagogical practices, as well as those of other teachers. This research demonstrates the necessity for discussions of gender and dance with nonprofessional dancers so that we may begin to cultivate an understanding of how they observe, encounter, and interpret gender in movement pedagogy. While only a few perspectives are assessed herein, this study contributes to the conversations about the experiences of adolescent male dance students in the context of dance becoming increasingly popular among the male population. Exploring students' interactions with pedagogy allows us to reflect on how commercial dance educators may engage with the male population and ignite in them a love for dance without potentially reinforcing dominant social and cultural norms of masculinity and femininity.

Qualitative research has been used in studies of men in dance education to explore one or a few cases through in-depth interviews or historical material analysis to contribute to valuable pedagogical discourse (King et. al 1994, 4). Much of this research exposes homophobia, bullying, and masculinizing dance practices in professional and recreational dance schools and public education institutions (Risner et al. 2008; Risner 2002a, 2002b, 2009a, 2014a; Pike 2011; Gard 2008; Li 2010; Lehikoinen 2006). While work by Edrie Ferdun focuses on combating gender stereotypes in the studio (1994), some literature geared toward commercial dance teachers (Collins 2009) and physical educators (Taschuk 2009) encourages the employment of gender-based techniques for the engagement of specifically male students.

Participants and Process

Employing qualitative research methods and analysis, this case study focuses on the experiences of nine male dance students as they participated in a competitive hip-hop dance curriculum at a dance studio in a medium-sized city in south-western Ontario. Competitive dance curriculum at this studio required that students participate in a minimum number of hours of dance per week, inclusive of both choreography and technique classes. Students began in September learning and rehearsing choreographed dance pieces in preparation for performance at competitions from March to May of the following year. All nine research participants performed in hip-hop pieces at these competitions, and one of the students performed with a musical theater group as well. Technique classes also were offered in ballet or jazz dance styles, designed to develop technical dancing skills and build strength, endurance, and flexibility. The participants of this research were chosen because they were registered in a boys-only jazz technique class for the 2013–2014 season, taught by the researcher. The student participants were all given pseudonyms, were between the ages of ten and seventeen, appeared Caucasian, and had no more than two years' experience with jazz dancing at the time. Ethics approval for research with human participants was granted through the graduate program in dance at York University.

While there were approximately twenty-five male dance students out of 350 students registered at the studio during this study, only the nine all-boys jazz class students were included in this research. This research excludes the four competitive male dancers who danced in mixed-gender jazz and ballet technique classes; recreational dance students who participated in mixed-gender jazz, ballet, and tap classes; and members of an all-male recreational hip-hop class. Seven of the nine study participants performed in mixed-gender competitive hip-hop routines, but for the purposes of this chapter, data compiled through interviews with the females in these classes were omitted. Input or discussion with the parents or guardians of the students involved was also excluded. Parents were made completely aware of the research process and provided consent for their sons' participation.

Data for this research were compiled through the distribution of three sets of questionnaires between November 2013 and June 2014. The first set of questionnaires was completed by eight of the nine students during one of our classes in November. One student, Brandon, did not complete the first questionnaire. This round of data was collected through handwritten answers to eleven short-answer questions and five opinion statement questions. The second round of questionnaires featured twenty-four short-answer questions and was completed in June 2014, one week after the studio's final recital performance. Five of the eight students completed questionnaires using computers and audio recorders to allow for more in-depth responses. Two of the male students were unable to attend this meeting, so they e-mailed their answers separately. Unfortunately, Peter and Steven could not be reached to complete this second phase. Below are some of the questions used in the male student questionnaires:

- How do you feel when you do jazz dance warmups, exercises, and movements (stretching, split jumps across the floor, arm positions, etc.)? What do you like and dislike about jazz dancing?
- If you had to take jazz dance next year, would you prefer to stay in the all-boys class, or would you like to try dancing with girls who are at the same technique level as you? Why or why not?
- What was it like learning jazz dancing from a female dance teacher? How do you think your experience in jazz dancing would have been different if you had a male dance teacher instead of a female dance teacher?
- If you dance with girls in your other classes, please compare your experience dancing in the all-boys jazz class with your experience dancing alongside girls.
- What, in your opinion, are the advantages and disadvantages to the boys-only environment in jazz class? Do you think all dance classes should be separated for boys and girls? Why or why not?

In November 2013, a third set of questionnaires was distributed to three teachers at the studio who had instructed, or who were at the time instructing these students. The male hip-hop teacher, the female competitive team director, and the female director completed eight short-answer questions along with four opinion statement questions. They were given two weeks to deliver their responses. Throughout this chapter, these three adult participants will be referred to as either "the teachers" or identified by their titles as hip-hop teacher, competition director, and director. Quotations are presented exactly as they were dictated or written, inclusive of spelling and grammar. Below are examples of some of the questions used in the teacher and directors' questionnaires:

- What, in your opinion, draws boys to dance at your school? What, if any, strategies do your school use to increase male enrollment?
- Why are these male hip-hop dancers separated from their female peers in their jazz technique class?
- Do you change your teaching style, exercises, choreography, etc., when working with groups of only boys or only girls? If so, how and why?

Acknowledging the influence of my own position and relationship to the participants throughout the research process was imperative to maintaining as objective a study as possible. As instructor of the student participants, I sought to preserve their complete anonymity and assured them that there would be no effect on our relationship if they chose not to participate. As an independent contractor working alongside and for the teacher participants, it was also important for me to separate the personal and work relationships from the research and analysis. While my roles as both researcher and instructor have undoubtedly influenced the responses and my interpretations, I aimed to diminish the impact of my position on this study.

Theoretical Perspective

As a student of the arts and humanities, I approach this research with an understanding that masculinity and femininity are historically and socially learned performances of the body. This theoretical position reflects the fluidity of gender performance as described by Judith Butler (1990) and the construction of multiple masculinities as is discussed in the work of R. W. Connell (2005). Connell's conviction that masculinity cannot be isolated from the state, the workplace/labor market, and the family, attests that it is not only an aspect produced in interpersonal transaction but also within institutions (2006, 104). As an institution, the dance studio is a place where masculinities and femininities may be (re)produced through student-teacher interaction, pedagogical practices, and choreography.

Outside of scholarly discourse and in the social world within which the subjects of this research mostly interact, sex is considered a biological fact that precedes and reinforces the construction of gender identity (Paechter 1998, 38). Society considers the male chromosomal makeup, "XY," the norm or "neutral," and anything else (e.g., XX, the female) the Other (Paechter 1998, 39). Reflecting this assumption, hierarchical gender roles and expectations of the performance of masculine and feminine traits inevitably pervade aspects of education. Gender roles are normalized, and gendered social relations are reproduced through the hidden curriculum (Stinson 2005). As Jennifer Fisher indicates, the male dancing body is the "marked" category (or the Other) in the female-dominated dance world. Through lack of male genitalia, the female dancer's body becomes the norm (Fisher 2009, 37). Undoubtedly, patriarchal values impact the professional dance world where male directors and choreographers often dominate these positions of power. Despite this, Fisher argues, "Many women and men still [see] ballet as a place where women [rule] and males [take] second place" (2009, 39). Men in Western dance are arguably both a marginalized population and the privileged minority (Risner 2009a).

Results and Discussion

This research demonstrates that irrespective of efforts to cultivate a male-friendly environment at the studio in question, male dancers remain the Other. For example, in their responses, both Peter and Andrew recognized that, as boys, they were treated differently in the dance studio. Andrew noted that the boys' changing room was "a storage room closet. The girls get a actual change room with cabbins when we have a closet." This marginalization of male dancers contradicts the special treatment they received in class and choreography. Teacher participant responses imply an adoption of techniques aimed at encouraging male enrollment similar to those suggested by Collins (2009). Through specific expectations for male movement to be "masculine," and gender segregation in some hip-hop and jazz classes, the dancing body is gendered at this studio.

Beginning with discussions as to why boys decide to dance and continue to do so contributes to an understanding of how they experience their contradictory treatment in the dance studio (Gard 2006; Risner 2009a,b). Andrew and Jesse started dancing three years prior to this study because they had seen how much fun their sisters, who attended classes at the studio, were having. Jesse saw "how much it benefitted them both mentally and physically." Brad took his first class at six years of age because his mom encouraged him to try it. He continues to dance because, "It helps me express who I am, it's fun, good exercise, and I love music." Similarly, Eric began dancing at his mother's insistence, but once he discovered that he was talented, he "continued me [sic] dream." Both Steven and Brian were inspired to take dance classes through their peers. Brian said, "I began dancing because some guy in my fourth grade class could do a flip and all of the other girls in our class loved it and so I asked him where he learned it and he said at a hip hop class so I went home to my mother and said 'hey mom, I need to go do a hip hop class' and . . . ironically I still haven't learned how to do a flip." These examples demonstrate that boys are drawn to dance through a variety of methods and often through the influence of a female figure.

Gendered Role Models

All three teacher participants believed that employing a male instructor drew boys into the dance studio and provided them with a role model. This stance is not unique; Doug Risner (2009a) found a similar correlation between successful programs for male dancers and the presence of a positive male role model. As a fellow dancing male, the male teacher represents an example of an accomplished man in dance who appears accepted within and outside of the dance world. Accordingly, these male students can look to their male teacher to counter narrow societal perceptions of masculinity (Risner 2009a, 71–72). Zihao Li's study of 12 boys (ages 13–16) at a Toronto public school dance program found that the participants felt they could better relate to a male teacher than a female (2010, 156). In contrast, Candace Pike's all-male ballet class participants suggested that they would have been less comfortable with a male teacher than with their female instructor at a Newfoundland dance studio (Pike 2011, 286). The following results demonstrate the pivotal presence of male teachers in this dance studio and the perceived implications of teachers' gender identities in dance education.

The student participants reflected on the importance of male role models within their own dance environments. Four of the students agreed that boys were drawn to dance at this studio because of the male hip-hop teacher. Brad said, "What draws people to dance here is [the male hip-hop teacher] 100% . . . because of [the hip-hop teacher] and his influence in the dance community." Brian agreed, suggesting that the "epic hip hop choreographies" of the male teacher probably drew boys to the studio. He also thought that the female director offered "fantastic ballet for those boys who *do* do ballet," indicating that this class and teacher may be an incentive for boys to join the studio as well. Andrew deduced that because "some people like [a male student] came here because [the hip-hop teacher] came here," the male hip-hop teacher was why boys decided to dance at this studio. Curiously, none of the students specifically mentioned the maleness of the hip-hop teacher as a reason for boys to enroll in his classes. This suggests that it is not necessarily his gender that attracts male students but could be his personality, teaching, or choreography style, as posited by Brian.

Although the presence of a male hip-hop instructor appeared vital to the participation of boys in dance, the students felt that their jazz class would not have been much different with a male instructor. Brian, who stated that he could not "really imagine having a male jazz dance teacher," assumed that "[a male teacher] would either be basically the exact same or it would be a little bit more fitness focused, but maybe that is just me stereotyping." David also said that he could not imagine how a male jazz teacher would be different from a female because he had never had the opportunity to learn from one, but he did propose that a female teacher might have "more feminine dance styles of jazz." Jesse guessed that jazz with a male teacher would not be "too different other than the fact that I feel that with a male teacher they would be easier to relate to." Brad contended that the "only thing probably different over having a female teacher may be the male would have been more assertive and keep the class more on track, but other than that it wouldn't be that much different at all." Though Brad thought that a male jazz teacher would be "more assertive," both Andrew and David felt that the male hip-hop teacher "was more joking" (Andrew) than the jazz teacher: "It's different from [the hip-hop teacher] because [he] more like jokes a lot more" (David). The hip-hop teacher's more relaxed teaching style was also described by Brian: "It's a lot more like sorta here is the basic move, do what you want with it, and learning and watching [the director] teach or learning from [the researcher] . . . they do it very structured, and it's a lot like 'no this move has to be this way or that way' and with [the hip-hop teacher] it is a little bit more free form . . . 'cause [the hip-hop teacher] sorta lets us do our own thing." Students hypothesized that a male jazz teacher would be more masculine, more relatable, and would have more control over the boys-only class than their female teacher. These expectations demonstrate how gender stereotypes influenced the students' perspectives of dance and their teachers.

Hip-Hop, Jazz, and Masculine Movement

Reflections of the societal gender binary within dance exist not only in specific pedagogical practices aimed at engaging male students but also in the actual movement practices. Due to assumptions about the physical differences between male and female dancers and demands for the performance of hegemonic masculinity and femininity, male and female dancers are often expected to execute steps differently or are given separate steps altogether. Judith Lynne Hanna highlights some of these assumptions: "On average, women have a higher proportion of body fat distributed differently, less dense bones, wider pelvises, slightly shorter legs relative to the length of trunk, and less cardiovascular power than men. Men are generally heavier, taller, and more muscular than women, which gives men superior speed and strength" (1988, 157). John R. Crawford argues that while male dancers may prefer certain movement qualities such as higher jumps, larger movements, and quicker shifts of weight, these qualities should be chosen to reflect the interests of *both* male and female dancers, so that all participants may be encouraged to "explore movement outside their usual range" (1994, 42). The "natural" assumptions about the male and female body and their expected performance of gender, however, continue to pervade the dance pedagogies of some commercial dance studios.

The male students involved in this research first encountered formal movement training in hip-hop classes and were later placed in jazz technique classes to supplement their training. Dance education research argues that boys are more likely to continue dancing if they are first exposed to forms of movement that are familiar to them, so that they can have a sense of ownership (Collins 2009; Crawford 1994; Gard 2001; Taschuk 2009). The perception that male dancers prefer hip-hop movement over other forms of dance may stem from hip-hop's early domination by primarily male dancers, and its traditional expression of hyper-masculine qualities (LaBoskey 2001, 112).

Historically, hip-hop dance is rooted in the men's dances that originated in the various cultures of the Hispanic and black populations of New York City (Torp 1986, 29). Although initially female dancers were marginalized by the "male-centered street cultures" that influenced breakdancing and other forms of hip-hop dance, women were always contributing to experimentations with the form (Foster 1998, 16). In a study of the New York City "b-boy" scene, Joseph G. Schloss found that women were "physically accomplishing what men are accomplishing. But they're not setting the standards for everyone. . . . The guys are still the one[s] that are setting the standards" (2009, 65). While hip-hop movement is often perceived as hyper-masculine and heteronormative, Lis Engel contends that men and women are regarded as dynamic bodies who must express "the soft and the hard, the direct and the flexible. . . . a great range between masculine and feminine" (2001, 370–371). Though Engel notes that the hip-hop dance styles avoid "being pretty," the author's discussion of the fluidity of gender performance within Danish hip-hop demonstrates the abilities of male and female hip-hop dancers to transcend normative gender expectations in performance.

In a reflective essay published in *When Men Dance* (Fisher and Shay 2009), Rennie Harris, hip-hop dancer and director of Puremovement Dance Company, discusses the influence of sexuality within hip-hop dance culture: "I think as long as a guy can contract [his hips] back and forth when he's dancing, it's okay. But anytime he moves [them] side to side, it's not okay. It's a sexual thing—it's control, you have to be in control, you're the man. . . . House is probably the one dance that allows you to be feminine and masculine at the same time, and you're not considered anything less than a man because it's such a freestyle dance, a different aesthetic. . . . I think there's still a fear of being too feminine sometimes maybe" (Fisher and Shay 2009, 116). Notions of anxiety regarding appearing effeminate are evident in Harris's reflection, though he asserts that hip-hop dance allows male dancers to play with characteristically masculine and feminine movement. He does not equate the stigma associated with ballet, modern, or jazz dance forms with perceptions of hip-hop dancers, however, noting that "maybe . . . in my community, that was a sign you were gay, but if you were a social dancer, that was okay" (Fisher and Shay 2009, 115). Accordingly, hip-hop dance is seen as a more acceptable movement activity for men than other forms of dance.

Despite convictions of the fluidity between performances of masculine and feminine hip-hop movement as outlined above, all nine male dancers initially perceived jazz dancing as more feminine than hip-hop. Before taking the class, Brad said he "thought dancing jazz was feminine, but after . . . it is no different from taking hip hop, it's just the way you do it personally that makes it look masculine or feminine." Though David claimed that the jazz class helped him learn that "jazz is dancing for boys and girls and it is actually more like hip-hop than any other style," he mentioned feeling "more masculine dancing hip-hop and I do feel more feminine dancing jazz but still it's fine, it's not like I'm embarrassed." Brian felt more masculine in hip-hop: "I mean . . . most hip-hop is either gender-neutral or sorta male type movements, and so in general doing hip-hop it feels a little more masculine and in general doing jazz, I mean there's all the jumps in stuff which originally I am sure was masculine but . . . definitely feel more feminine dancing jazz because of the jumps and splits and stuff like that." On the other hand, though Brandon noted that jazz dancing "looked like more feminine," he later added that "jazz is okay . . . jazz is hip hop in a way." Similarly, Andrew said that he felt "the same dancing jazz as when dancing hip-hop" because "there is not that much difference . . . between the two besides one being jazz and the other hip-hop."

A typical boys-only jazz class began with a cardiovascular warm up, an upper body and leg stretch, and progressions across the floor, including some kicks, leaps, and turns. We also practiced combinations of transitional steps, positions of the arms, and technical aspects of the feet and hips. Though the amount of stretching was modified to account for their minimal flexibility, the structure of the jazz class was no different from those that I teach with female dancers.

The participants found jazz movement to be challenging. Jesse said that he felt "a little awkward because I am still a little bit less comfortable with those positions because my body just isn't as used to [jazz]." Brian also felt less comfortable performing jazz movements than hip-hop. He stated, "I feel . . . when I do jazz dance warm ups, exercises, movements . . . slightly stiff . . . slightly like an old person . . . slightly ridiculous, and that probably has to do with the whole girl/boy stereotype and 'cause we're . . . told to stretch and do the splits and stuff that either hurts or is just plain embarrassing." Though he had low confidence in his abilities, he reasserted that "jazz dancing was ridiculously fun, kinda challenging, especially I am no good at . . . all those jumps, all of them, I am very bad at all the jumps, especially Russians, I just can't get my legs up that far." Four other boys also found that jazz was challenging, and agreed that the stretches and the jumps were the most difficult. Andrew said, "I felt like some of the stretching was a little challenging because I am not as flexible as I would want and [it] helps me to try harder to be better and improve." Brandon noted: "Jazz is ok, kinda challanging, and it's good for you." He found "the spins the kicks the splits and the splats" to be the most difficult part of jazz class. David did not like "the jumps too much . . . the jumps across the floor those I don't really like jumps so I don't really like those." While much of the literature suggests that male dancers prefer large jumps, leaps and turns, the male students in this study found these aspects were the most difficult and least enjoyable. This demonstrates the individuality of each dancer's movement preferences.

Boys-Only Jazz

The main purpose of the *Dance Teacher* magazine article was to demonstrate the success of a program design that included boys-only dance classes (Collins 2009). Li (2010), Pike (2011), and Kai Gunnar Lehikoinen (2006) examine gender-segregating pedagogical methods used to appeal to male students in the public education system, commercial dance studios, and professional training programs. These programs are a common strategy for training male dancers in many parts of the Western world and are usually deemed successful for the resulting increase in male enrollment (Li 2010, 56). Lehikoinen argues, however, that the benefits of coeducational practices outweigh the potential benefits of offering segregated classes (Lehikoinen 2010, 116).

This case-study examines both student and teacher perspectives regarding the boys-only environment. The teacher participants justified the segregation of male students from female students out of concern for their comfort in class. The director and competition director attributed the creation of the boys-only class to feedback received the previous year, when the boys expressed discomfort dancing beside girls who were more advanced than they with jazz technique. The competition director wrote that the boys found "regular jazz tech [with the girls] extremely hard." The teachers assumed that jazz technique was something the boys did not want to do but were forced to do through the program: the hip-hop teacher postulated that the boys "won't be as positive towards jazz [as with hip-hop]" and said that separating them from the girls was ideal because "some boys don't take it serious enough." The director also stated that the boys were more likely to enjoy their own boys-only technique class because they were able to "suffer through it together." Making these assumptions, teachers risk cultivating a culture where male dancers are relegated to hip-hop styles and are only accepted within the jazz studio under special circumstances.

While the competition director argued that "boys have not always been separated from the girls, and they are not all separated now," nine of the thirteen male dancers who took jazz classes did so in a single-gender environment, which indicates a propensity for gender segregation. Young recreational male dancers were also placed in an all-boys hip-hop class. For competitions, there was a boys-only hip-hop group comprising eight of the nine participants and four other male students as well as a girls-only hip-hop group. Despite this (or perhaps to explain this), the hip-hop teacher felt that the "genders should not be separated unless requested."

The statements of both directors suggest not only that the structure of the single-gender class should be altered but also that the movement patterns should be modified to focus on the presumed specific needs of the male dancing body. The competition director wrote that her mixed-gender class "is not geared towards boys so they have to do most of the same exercises as the girls." This suggests that performing the same movements and exercises as the girls places the male students at a disadvantage in jazz technique class. When the director was asked what she would change, she stated the following: "when teaching boys I make their feet and arm positions less feminine. That's about it, I want them to dance and look masculine. . . . My tech class exercises work well for both sexes so they are comfortable. I don't make the boys hold the splits or [center splits] as long as the girls, but they generally try to." Here, the competition director referenced her mixed-gender technique classes in which three of the boys in this study participated the previous year and four other male dancers participated in at the time. Similarly, the director felt that assigning boys to their own class would allow their teacher to focus on "boy steps like more jumps, stronger arms" so they could "hopefully . . . enjoy it more." In comparison to her classes with girls, the director said she would change her boys-only class to focus "more on strength, arms, push-ups . . . not as much on stretch and flexibility. I would jump a lot more. I would make the class more strength than style." These comments promote the reinforcement of singular definitions of masculinity within dance classes and demonstrate how movement pedagogies may gender the dancing body. They signal that certain movement patterns are more acceptable for females than males at this studio.

All of the student respondents preferred participating in jazz technique training in the boys-only class environment. Many of their comments indicate that they felt more confident in the boys-only class because they were all learning the basics together and therefore could not "make fun" of one another. Brian said, "I think it's a good idea if all the boys have to do it together, they can't really make fun of any other boys doing it because they're all doing jazz at the same time . . . I still, even after a year of all-boys jazz, would feel embarrassed joining a girls one." Andrew agreed that the boys felt "safe because all [are] learning the basics . . . and do not judge other people . . . when in the other class we had to start with people that know jazz and already did it when we did not." David also felt more comfortable because "the girls I find are better at jazz so . . . you don't feel like you're the worst in the class," but when asked about dancing with girls in hip-hop, he replied, "I do feel comfortable and safe because I don't care what people think of me that much." Brad blamed a lack of experience in jazz and stated that he would "feel embarrassed" if the class was with girls. Alternatively, in hip-hop he felt more comfortable because "I have more experience and it is not as technical." Like the others, Peter preferred the lack of competition in the all-boys jazz class. He said: "I think it is a very cool and calm environment because if we were with girls I believe we could be compared to them with how are [sic] kicks are and things like that." While most of the literature advocates for the creation of competition within the all-boys class (Pike 2011; Crawford 1994), this group of students preferred the *lack* of competition and enjoyed feeling as though no one was judging them.

Many of the participants felt that the boys-only jazz class was a brotherhood, albeit one that was often distracting. Brandon said "the boys r like bros . . . they don't laugh at u cuz they can't do the same stuff . . . we are more around the same skill level in jazz." Eric's comments also suggested the creation of a community: "Where [sic] in this together. . . . not nervous cuz of girls." In speaking of both the boys-only hip-hop and jazz classes, Jesse said he "noticed that the bond is a lot stronger with the boys and we have a lot more fun goofing around . . . but it did get quite silly sometimes." Brad was similarly concerned with the level of focus in the all-boys class. He remarked, "Girls are a lot more focused and that is 100 percent true . . . that's why I like doing it with girls over guys because we get off track a lot easier . . . boys in jazz class, they didn't want to be there so they just goofed off and they didn't want to pay attention . . . I wish I could have done it with girls because maybe it would have been a . . . better experience for me . . . next year actually . . . I want to be dancing with girls at the same technique level as me so I don't feel like I suck at it and also I can grow with these people and we can grow together." Brad's frustration with the boys and his desire to train with girls the following year suggests that his level of comfort in the boys' class was not necessarily associated with the homogenized gender orientation but with the level of experience of the students.

The participants further contemplated the disadvantages of dancing in classes with and without girls and discussed which option they would choose in the future. One disadvantage was related to discomfort with the female body. Eric said he preferred all-boys classes "cuz I don't want to go to class whit [sic] half naked girls (sports bras and booty shorts)." Brian said that he did feel comfortable in his mixed-gender hip-hop class but that he was "sometimes . . . unsure where to look when girls do a certain part of a choreo that is slightly provocative, I'm never quite sure if I'm allowed to look." Alternatively, David felt that the all-boys class was limiting: "With the girls you can learn more like harder stuff . . . you can learn from them." Brad's comments support this claim as well: "We don't learn how to dance with girls, and we also don't overcome the insecurities." Jesse was concerned with movement styles and argued that "you're not going to get a very diverse dancing environment since girls and guys often dance in different ways . . . maybe the girls want to learn something from the boys and the boys might want to learn something from the girls." Despite their own preferences, all nine participants suggested that there should be two options available—a boys-only class and a mixed-gender class. Brian thought students should be able to "decide for themselves what they're comfortable with" but concluded that, "I would absolutely prefer to stay in the all-boys class because it was ridiculous amounts of fun and I really enjoyed it."

Conclusions

In their final comments, all of the students expressed that their experiences in boys-only jazz were positive. Particularly, Brad's reflection demonstrates how his opinion of jazz dancing changed over time: "Jazz is not what I expected it to be [laughter] it's just, it's actually really fun, it's energetic . . . it was really good for technique wise . . . so I like jazz for the fun factor and the energetic factor . . . overall I believe that hip-hop, jazz and all that stuff, they all work in the same way. You learn a dance, you learn technique, you practice it and perfect it, you go to competition or to the recital and perform it and you feel good after when you're done." Through comparing the experiences of students and teachers at this dance studio with those described in the literature, this chapter demonstrates that while some of the suggested modifications to teaching techniques and class structure successfully encourage student participation, all students respond differently to these practices. The students' experiences in boys-only jazz are indicative of the individuality of each dancer and his body and challenge stereotypical assumptions of male bodies in movement. This research also demonstrates that the dance studio can be a gendered institution, where cultural and social norms of gender roles and identities are often learned and enacted. The boys agreed that male teachers and role-models were a valuable presence in the dance studio. Although they did not disapprove of learning from a female, the students believed that a male would have exercised more control over the all-boys class. Initially the male students perceived that hip-hop dance was more masculine and therefore more "natural" for their bodies than jazz, but once they were exposed to jazz movement, they felt they were able to move with both masculine and feminine qualities. As some dance pedagogies recommend, teachers at this studio adjusted the structure of their classes to accommodate essentialist discourses of the male body. The students in this boys-only jazz class, however, successfully performed the same movements as females with the same amount of experience. Finally, the majority of the students appear to have preferred the all-male dance environment not because they were specifically conscious of their gender identities, but because they appreciated learning alongside students at their technical level.

Overall, although these boys may have experienced some difficulty with the new movement presented by jazz dance, they did not identify this as a challenge to their gender identities, but as a challenge to their bodies. Therefore, perhaps educators should focus their pedagogies on engaging with the abilities of different bodies, instead of those dictated through gender normative discourses. Practices which reinforce assumptions of the gendered body do not necessarily address the varied and multiple "types" of bodies that dance, and therefore may alienate some dancers or inhibit full movement development. While as an institution the dance studio is inevitably a participant in the social construction of bodies, dance teachers may assess their pedagogical techniques to establish methods through which all students are encouraged to explore a wide range of movement possibilities, regardless of their gender identities. Encouraging dancers to move in a variety of styles, forms, and expressions without restrictions based in the "natural" abilities dictated through gender discourses will allow them to explore, discover and transcend.

7

Friendship Formation among Professional Male Dancers

KATHERINE POLASEK AND EMILY ROPER

The purpose of this study is to examine the formation of friendships among professional male ballet and modern dancers. More specifically, qualitative interviews were conducted with professional male ballet and modern dancers regarding the nature and quality of their friendships with men and women in their respective dance companies.

Whereas traditional theories of human development emphasize individualism, autonomy, and separation as key indicators of emotional maturity and psychological health, relational-cultural theory (RCT) suggests that relationships and affiliation are essential to healthy psychological development and well-being (Miller and Stiver 1997, 8). While RCT was initially developed to understand women's psychological experience, it is increasingly being used to gain a better understanding of all human experience, including men's (Bergman 1991, 4).

Although most people tend to believe that men do not connect with other men, research reveals a strong desire for intimacy, empathy, and trust in their close friendships (Bergman 1991, 3). According to Stephen Bergman, most theories devoted to male psychological development focus on a "self" rather than a "self in relation," and as a result, fail to capture men's whole experience in relationships. Bergman suggests that men, like women, strive for connection and that their psychological distress is rooted in disconnection and not forming relationships that are mutually empowering (Bergman 1991, 4).

For the first five years of life, a boy's relational nature is similar to a girl's. It is around age five that boys begin to internalize societal expectations of what it means to be a "real man." The messages disseminated by mainstream culture push boys to disconnect from being in relationships, a disconnection that is intended to encourage their social "growth" into men. "Becoming a man" is associated with aspiring to or portraying hegemonic attitudes and behaviors such as emotional stoicism, physical toughness, strength, individuality, and hyper-heterosexuality. Performing hegemonic behaviors has been associated with a number of negative ramifications for boys (Anderson 2008, 104). As Jane Fonda stated, "It's as though the empathy gene has been plucked from [boys'] hearts and they become emotionally illiterate" (Fonda 2009, 193). Due to disconnection at an early age, boys never really learn to connect with others in the same ways girls do. As a result, boys begin to avoid, devalue, and deny qualities associated with mutually empowering relationships (e.g., empathy, feelings) (Bergman 1991, 4). Rather than being in relationship with others, boys learn to compare themselves to others, which often leads to competition, aggression, and violence (Bergman 1991, 4). Eventually, becoming a self-in-spite-of-relationship leaves less opportunity to practice relationships. While Bergman's work is based on the dominant cultural model for boys in the United States, it is important to recognize that there are many diverse variations of this model that are dependent upon race, ethnicity, religion, sexual orientation, family structure, socioeconomic class, and other cultural identities.

Same-Sex Friendships among Men

Friendship is defined as a type of interpersonal relationship that serves important functions in human experience across the lifespan (Watson 2012, 464). There is extensive research that close friendships are linked to numerous positive outcomes including emotional, social, and physical well-being, as well as academic and career achievement (Way 2013, 201). Researchers note that friendships promoting psychological health and well-being are generally grounded in intimacy, companionship, alliance, affection, and satisfaction (Way 2013, 203).

Friendship differs for males and females, according to research, with females placing greater emphasis on their friendships (Watson 2012, 495). Whereas women's friendships are characterized by intimacy, self-disclosure, and emotional support, men's friendships are more agentic, characterized by less emotional connectedness, and tend to favor instrumental activities (e.g., playing sport) (Felmlee, et al. 2012, 519). Research in developmental psychology has largely reported that males have fewer close friendships and experience lower levels of intimacy within their relationships than females (Chu 2005, 7). Due to the societal pressures placed upon boys to differentiate themselves from anything feminine (e.g., care, empathy, feelings), it has been argued that boys become less interested in developing close and meaningful friendships (Chu 2005, 7). Although research depicts boys as passive recipients of the culture, boys' attitudes and behaviors are not automatically produced by the culture; there are males who resist and challenge societal pressures and expectations by developing close, same-sex friendships (Chu 2005, 15–16).

Judy Chu found that adolescent boys have difficulties forming close friendships with male peers; the findings also indicated a strong desire for genuine relational connections among boys (Chu 2005, 15–16). This desire created a dilemma for the participants and was in direct conflict with pressure they received from their peer group culture that emphasized masculine norms of behavior. As Chu explained, "It seemed socially adaptive, and even advantageous, for these boys to be reserved in their relationships and thereby to protect themselves from the risks of exposure" (Chu 2005, 15–16). There were some boys who overcame the pressures from their peer group and were able to form meaningful close same-sex friendships. These friendships served a protective function for the boys and were an important source of support that helped them overcome pressures experienced within their peer group.

In 2013 Niobe Way called for closer examination of the complexity, emotional nuance, and depth of boys' friendships. Way discussed three factors that influence the development of close same-sex friendships among boys: (a) parent-and-child relationships, (b) social dynamics at school, and (c) ethnic communities (Way 2013, 207–209). If a young boy has at least one emotionally engaged parent that provides a safe space for him to share his feelings, the boy is more likely to develop and maintain male friendships over time. Boys that had greater social power were found to have greater freedom to challenge the "boy code." According to Way, social power was defined as being athletic, physically attractive, having a good sense of humor, and identifying as heterosexual. Race, ethnicity, and social class were also found to influence social power. In Way's study, black, Latino, and working-class boys were considered more "masculine" than white, Asian, and upper-middle-class boys (Way 2013, 208). The ethnic communities that the boys belonged to were also found to influence friendship formation. According to Way, many of the friendships formed early in the boys' lives were not maintained. As Way suggested, boys have two explanations for loss of friendships: (a) having too much to do, girlfriends, changes in schools and neighborhoods; and (b) cultural emphasis and pressure to be "masculine" (Way 2013, 209–210).

Cross-Sex Friendships

While the majority of research has focused on same-sex friendships, there has been some scholarly work dedicated to examining the nature of cross-sex friendships (McDougall and Hymel 2007, 247). According to Diane Felmlee, Elizabeth Sweet, and Colleen Sinclair, "Cultural messages provide scripts for how men and women should interact with each other" (Felmlee, et al. 2012, 519). Children learn from an early age that there are different social worlds for boys and girls; developing a cross-sex friendship may put one at risk of being ridiculed and teased, particularly young boys. Then, as children age, cross-sex friendships begin to increase and are also viewed as normative. However, the mass media romanticizes and sexualizes adult cross-sex friendships, making platonic cross-sex friendships a challenge. In the same way that same-sex friendships enhance people's lives, cross-sex friendships provide a number of emotional and social benefits (Watson 2012, 494–495). In addition to the benefits associated with same-sex friendships (e.g., social support, self-disclosure), research suggests that cross-sex friendships provide a unique "insider perspective" of the other gender (Felmlee, et al. 2012, 520).

For individuals who identify as heterosexual, sexual attraction can present a potential problem for the cross-sex friendship, although it does not always end a friendship (Felmlee, et al. 2012, 520). Heterosexual men have been found to view physical intimacy as more acceptable among cross-sex friends than heterosexual women (Felmlee, et al. 2012, 520–521).

Cross-Category Male Friendships

Research suggests that people seek to connect with those who are similar, commonly referred to as *homophily* (McPherson, et al. 2001, 415).

Friendships also reflect homophily in that people will seek out friends they are similar to on the basis of gender, sexual orientation, race, socioeconomic status and age (McPherson, et al. 2001, 415). Such friendships are important, as they provide a greater likelihood for an equal relationship. For example, Peter Nardi found that gay men are less likely to form friendships with heterosexual men; forming friendships with other gay men provides a more equitable relationship that gay men may not be able to achieve with heterosexual men (Nardi 1999, 14). For heterosexual men, forming friendships with gay men may generate feelings of discomfort due to biases and internalized homophobia (Galupo and Gonzalez 2013, 780). Cross-category friendships among gay and heterosexual men have been characterized as less emotionally connected and supportive (Provence, et al. 2014, 8–9).

Much of the research on cross-category friendships has focused on the inequality and negotiation of difference (e.g., race, sexual orientation) between friends. Despite the unique challenges cross-category friendships may possess, research suggests that cross-category friendships provide the opportunity to acquire greater appreciation for cultural diversity, more critical examination of stereotypes and exposure to different perspectives (Galupo and Gonzalez 2013, 780). Investigations also note that social minorities may be more likely than their majority counterparts to seek out cross-category friendships because they provide an opportunity for acceptance, closeness, and support not found from the dominant culture (Galupo and Gonzalez 2013, 780).

Friendships Formed in the Physical Domain

Despite the fact that sport has always been an acceptable place for males to form and maintain bonds with one another, few studies have examined friendships in the physical domain. As Michael Messner suggested, sport is an arena well suited for the enactment and perpetuation of the male bond (Messner 1987, 193). Messner conducted thirty interviews on male athletes' friendships with former male athletes of a diverse age, race, and socioeconomic status. One of the participants discussed the ways in which sport provided a place where men could enjoy the company of other men—even become close—without having to become intimate in ways that threaten their "firm ego boundaries" (Messner 1992a, 222). Messner argued that while these are often the closest relationships that these men will ever have, athletic battles commonly took place among teammates. One teammate's success might mean another's demotion. Messner conceded that, "Lurking just below the surface of this 'family' rhetoric ... lies intense, often cutthroat competition" (Messner 1992a, 220).

According to Timothy Curry, the men's locker room is known as one of the centers of fraternal bonding (Curry 1991, 119). Curry examined the spoken exchanges within the football locker room culture. More specifically, he explored the jokes and put-downs typically involved in fraternal bonding. Curry found two familiar themes in men's locker room talk: sex and aggression (Curry 1991, 132). He asserted that locker room talk was likely to have a negative cumulative effect on young men because of the ways in which it reinforced the notions of masculine privilege and hegemony.

While mainstream sport culture is considered a site where men confirm and celebrate the physical, social, and psychological attributes associated with hegemonic masculinity, dance is often labeled as a feminine activity. As a field, it is generally more accepting of homosexuality (Risner 2002b, 84). Scant scholarly research has examined the social relations and friendship formation among dancers. Doug Risner examined the ways in which young adult males' experience and make meaning of the social stigmatization associated with men in dance (2002b, 85). Participants consisted of six undergraduate male (three gay/bisexual and three heterosexual) students enrolled in beginning-level dance technique classes. Risner noted that important relationships and social bonds forged in dance class were different for heterosexual and gay/bisexual male dancers (2002b, 86–90). The three heterosexual dancers were especially close with one another, "helping one another with movement combinations, cheering each other on across the floor, partnering with one another on alignment experiences, and working collaboratively on midterm and final practical projects" (Risner 2002b, 88–89). The gay and bisexual participants did not form any bonds with other males, describing a sense of alienation from all males in their classes. Instead, the gay and bisexual participants formed close friendships with the girls and women in their classes.

Risner's investigation provides important insight into an unexamined phenomenon within the dance culture. Context-specific investigations are important. As Chu stated, "Future studies are needed to explore how other populations of boys experience their friendships and how their friendship experiences are shaped by their particular circumstances" (Chu 2005, 19).

The purpose of this study was to examine friendship formation among professional male ballet and modern dancers. More specifically, we examined the nature and quality of professional male dancers' friendships with men and women in their respective dance companies.

Method

Participants

Participants consisted of twelve professional male ballet and modern dancers. All dancers had been dancing for at least five years and had been involved with a major company in ballet or modern dance for a minimum of one year. Professional male ballet and modern dancers were selected because ballet and modern dance are culturally defined as feminine activities in the United States (Risner 2002b, 84) and provide a unique population and context in which to study men's friendship formation.

All of the participants were current professionals when interviewed. Six of the participants (all ballet) were recruited from a ballet company located in a major northeastern city in the United States. The six modern dance participants were recruited through the Internet. These six participants represented three different dance companies in the northeastern United States.

The participants ranged in age from twenty-two to forty-two years of age ($M = 30.3$ years; $SD = 6.4$). Their professional dance experience ranged from three to twenty-seven years ($M = 10.8$ years; $SD = 6.9$). Of the twelve participants, eight self-identified as Caucasian, two as Asian/Pacific Islander, one as African American, and one as Tunisian American. Seven of the participants self-identified as gay while the remaining five participants self-identified as heterosexual.

Interviews

Upon receiving university IRB approval, in-depth semi-structured interviews were conducted with the participants. The six interviews with the ballet participants were conducted in a quiet room at the ballet company. The six interviews with the modern dancers were conducted over the telephone and all interviews (both face-to-face and telephone) were audiotaped. There were no significant differences in the depth or quality of data collected in the face-to-face interviews compared to the telephone interviews. Each participant was given the opportunity to select a pseudonym for confidentiality purposes. A series of probing questions were used in order to promote further clarity and understanding. The interviews ranged in length from sixty to ninety minutes.

Upon completion of the interview, each participant was provided with a final overview of the study and the upcoming timetable for transcription and data analysis. Each participant was informed that he would be e-mailed a copy of the interview transcript and asked to comment on its accuracy and make any additional corrections or additions.

Data Analysis

The first step of the data analysis process was transcribing the interviews verbatim. Each participant was e-mailed a copy of his personal transcript and asked to offer feedback on the interview so as to prevent any misinterpretations or miscommunications. Only three participants provided feedback, and all corrections/additions were minor. All of the participants were invited to contact the researcher at any time throughout the research process to clarify or discuss any information relevant to their experiences.

The transcripts were then studied in order to familiarize the first author with each individual interview. All data were inductively analyzed following the procedures outlined by Juliet Corbin and Anselm Strauss (Corbin and Strauss 2007, 379). Upon reading and rereading the transcripts, an initial set of codes from the collected data was developed. These preliminary codes, or meaning units, were created in order to determine possible categories, themes, or patterns; open and axial coding was used.

The preliminary codes were then sorted into a hierarchical structure for further analysis. The first and second author, both of whom have experience in qualitative research, were involved in the data analysis process. Each individual developed her own coding schemes independently. The authors then met to compare and discuss similarities and differences. As Michael Patton suggests, "Important insights can emerge from the different ways in which two people look at the same set of data, a form of analytical triangulation" (Patton 2001, 464). After several lengthy discussions, consensus was reached, and the data analysis was completed. The findings were then organized and presented in a logical manner. The data that are presented is a rich description of the dancers' experiences.

Results

The purpose of this study was to examine friendship formation among professional male ballet and modern dancers. More specifically, we examined the nature and quality of professional male dancers' friendships with men and women in their respective dance companies. Four themes emerged from the interview data: (a) relational challenges early in life; (b) sexuality and friendship formation; (c) culture of dance; and (d) competition among male dancers.

Relational Challenges with Males Early in Life

Seven of the participants (one heterosexual, six gay) indicated that they had few close friendships with other males while growing up, describing their same-sex youth friendships as "challenging" and "complicated." As Roger[1] stated, "Growing up, in school I think more of my friends were women than men or girls than boys." Several participants discussed being bullied and harassed by peers. Peter described feeling detached from males in the public school system because of being teased and bullied but that involvement in dance provided him an outlet to make friends that accepted him. As he explained, "I think being detached from that whole society . . . I wasn't involved in anything in high school. Any negativity that I got from anybody at school was so much more than offset by the friends that I was making over the summers, and people that I had made friends within dance." Several of the gay participants suggested that the uncertainty surrounding their sexual identity and concerns about being "outed" played a significant role in distancing themselves from males while growing up. As Charles explained, "I wasn't really good at making male friends until not too long ago. Until like maybe ten years ago, I didn't have any male friends and then it started to happen. I just didn't feel comfortable around them. I think I probably didn't feel comfortable with myself being a man, so it was hard to be with another man." When asked what changed within the last ten years, Charles indicated that he had become "much more comfortable with [his] sexuality and gender."

In addition to the challenges associated with forming same-sex friendships, six of the participants (four gay, two heterosexual) described having negative or unaccepting relationships with their fathers and/or brothers while growing up. As Leo stated, "I grew up with my stepdad and he and I weren't ever really close so with the men in my life, I guess I didn't really connect with too much." Marcus noted the tension he felt with his male family members, "I find it sometimes harder to sometimes open up to [men] because I never opened up to my brothers and I never knew my father, I was always with girls." For three of the participants, their fathers held negative attitudes toward their involvement in dance. All three suggested that their father's negative attitudes were related to the stereotypical association of dance with femininity and homosexuality. As Peter explained, "My dance teacher told me years later when I had wanted to really start dancing seriously, he [his father] asked her if dancing would turn me gay."

The low number of male dancers enrolled in dance was another factor that contributed to the lack of same-sex friendships. It was not until the participants became professionals that they began to surround themselves with larger numbers of male dancers. As Jacob indicated, "A lot of times you would be the only one in class by yourself. Coming to a place where you've got 15 other guys doing the same thing, it's great."

Sexuality and Friendship Formation

Sexuality played a significant role in friendship formation for the participants. While all of the participants suggested that the male dancers were generally friendly toward one another, differences across sexuality lines were evident in the interview data. All of the gay participants indicated greater comfort forming friendships with other gay men or females. As Leo stated, "I don't really have many straight guy friends. I have lots of gay friends from living in the city. And I have a lot of female friends." Roger indicated that "60–70% of [his] friends are gay." Gay male dancers were described by three of the heterosexual participants and one gay participant as "cliquey." As Oscar stated, "for a little while it was kind of like the gays and the straights." Charles also suggested a separation between the gay and heterosexual male dancers, "It's of course a little cliquier with the gay guys. We don't get them, and they don't get us."

The heterosexual participants noted having closer friendships with other heterosexual male dancers. As Oscar explained, "My two closest friends in the company are two other straight guys . . . we have a lot more in common. One guy grew up playing hockey, and I grew up playing soccer, so we have some other similar interests. And the other guy plays bass, and I play guitar." While Oscar was closer with the heterosexual male dancers, he indicated that he also had friends in dance that identified as gay. As he stated, "I've got to say that one of the gay guys, I'm really close to him. He and I roomed together in another company for two years." Tony, who self-identified as heterosexual, indicated having several gay friends, but being "standoffish" when he got "vibes that they like me." As Tony suggested, "I have in the past become friends with men who I found out later who were actually attracted to me, and I didn't know it at the time."

There were also differences in how the gay and heterosexual participants described their friendships with female dancers. All of the gay participants discussed having close, intimate relationships with the female dancers. Leo indicated feeling especially close with the female dancers, "I've always gotten along better with women, they didn't make fun of me when I was younger, and we have a good time." Roger described a sense of trust he had with female dancers, "The women have always been very, very nice to me because if they are having trouble with a partner they will come to me and ask me to analyze what they are doing, and I don't know . . . they seem to trust me." Marcus discussed being "one of the girls" in the company: "The relationships I have with women in the company, oh they're great. They think I'm one of the girls (laughing). I mean I sit in their dressing room when they are getting dressed, and they'll get like undressed . . . I have a good time with the girls in the company because we chit chat, we gossip; I can be a big gossip (laughing), and it can be fun." The heterosexual participants also spoke about having close friendships with female dancers. In fact, the dance culture was considered a unique context in which heterosexual men and heterosexual women could form closer friendships due to the nature of their interactions. As Peter indicated, "I think what's interesting is like in this field, because I think I probably have closer relationships with women friends than I think most guys do." Charles spoke to the status heterosexual men receive in the dance culture and how this status influences male and female heterosexual dancers' friendship formation: "A straight male is a little bit like a golden boy. You usually start when you are like two or three men for like 30 women or 30 girls . . . so if you happen to be interested in girls you become like the . . . and also for women, because they assume that the men are gay so if one is straight, if you are a dancer you usually have somehow a good body and you are kind of sensitive and stuff like that so all of a sudden you become this golden boy for all of these women, considering they are straight of course. A lot of gay men or female dancers will tell you that the straight male syndrome in dance is quite funny. Being used to getting everything they want and being adored." Heterosexual male and female dancers dating was considered a common phenomenon and was described by the heterosexual participants as a "perk of the job." Three of the five heterosexual participants were in a committed relationship (one married, one engaged, and one dating) with a female dancer in their respective companies. The other two heterosexual participants had previously dated female dancers but were not presently in a committed relationship. Peter spoke about why he often dated female dancers rather than non-dancers, "I think that they probably see more clearly who I am as a person than I think other women tend to do. I think part of it is that they can understand why, too."

All five of the heterosexual participants indicated that flirting with or inappropriately approaching a female dancer who was in a relationship with another heterosexual male dancer was a common source of conflict among heterosexual dancers. As Tony indicated, "I've not got into confrontations with people but come close to regarding my fiancé. Like they'll be making moves on her or something and I'll have to tell them to back off."

Culture of Dance

All of the participants discussed how being a dancer influenced how they related with other men and women, both in and outside of dance. Eight of the participants suggested that being a dancer provided them a safe environment in which to express themselves artistically and emotionally. Several of the participants suggested that dance helped men to challenge mainstream stereotypical perceptions of masculinity. As Tony stated, "I think in our [mainstream] culture, being able to express yourself or show what you are feeling is considered homosexual or means something gay individually to you. But I don't agree because I'm straight and I feel proud, especially when I express myself [in dance]." Ken stated, "I think being a dancer helps you get in touch with your sensitivity. It helps you learn how to form relationships with other people; it teaches you how to be sensitive." As Peter described, "You have to be very open in dance to (pause) . . . I don't know, maybe be more in touch with certain emotions or just being open to be kind of foolish in situations with costumes and this and that. You can't care so much about your perception of yourself in that way." Several of the participants discussed the uniqueness of their profession, specifically the physical contact and closeness required, fatigue and exhaustion, and psychological stress associated with competing for roles. As Peter stated, "There has to be a mutual respect so nobody gets hurt and so that you can work very intimately with somebody else." Jacob explained, "It's one of those jobs where we have a lot of time to hang out. You are working hard, but you're also kind of just all hanging out in the studio. For the nature of it, the job brings up a lot of joking, goofing-off types of circumstances. Going on tours together, performances . . . you end up spending a lot of time with these people." Due to this uniqueness, several of the participants suggested that dancers formed especially close, almost family-like relationships with one another. As Leo stated, "I think we're just more relaxed around each other because we work together; it really is sort of like a family."

Several of the participants suggested that their involvement in dance fostered a sense of appreciation for and greater understanding of cultural differences. As Peter suggested, "Being around anybody who is different from you can sensitize you to the differences in people. I guess it kind of opens you up to a whole new world and a way of looking at things that I imagine I probably wouldn't have necessarily ever gotten into had it not been for dance." Oscar, a self-identified heterosexual participant, suggested that the stereotypical association of dance with femininity has the potential to influence heterosexual dancers' behaviors and attitudes toward homosexuality. As he stated, "[if not involved in dance] I probably would have been a little less understanding about homosexuality." Oscar recounted a recent experience that he felt served as an example of his acceptance and openness. As he explained, "A guy just left the company last night, and we all threw him a big party and I emceed the whole thing in drag, so there is no problem there. [Sexuality] doesn't really, it doesn't really affect who I make friends with." Peter, who also self-identified as heterosexual, indicated that he would flirt with other male dancers. As he explained, "I'll still flirt with guys to a certain extent, but it's just very different. And it all comes down to tact . . . because I don't really take myself very seriously." Tony, also heterosexual, indicated the following, "Dance is a form of art so as an artist you have to be able to accept different views and opinions. I mean you might be dancing a ballet where you are dancing with other men and you are supposed to be attracted to them and that is what the choreographer wanted—and in that scenario you have to accept that viewpoint." As a result of the uniqueness of their careers, the majority of the participants suggested that few outside the dance world understood the challenges associated. Five of the participants acknowledged that most of their friendships with people outside the dance company were with other artists. As Jonah explained, "They tend to all be artists. That is the type of dialogue that I like to create. Some type of exchange across ... I mean dance is an art form, it's a physical art form, but it is an art that you study and that you train to do. I learn a lot from speaking to playwrights or painters and the men, I guess the male friends that I have tend to be artists, and that is more of a meeting point than the gay-straight position." As Roy stated, "We flock to our comfort zones so I do have a lot of artist friends." As Jacob stated, "I've had a couple of really good friends in dance that have been in the company, which is great. And others are more involved in the arts but not dance at all ... people that kind of understand the arts and who really enjoy it and appreciate it." Three of the participants discussed the arts as an open and accepting atmosphere. As Peter stated, "The arts are absolutely more accepting of everything. Of any type of behavior than a non-artistic organization would be." Similarly, Roger stated, "Theater, dance, and music environments are far more accepting of alternative lifestyles."

Competition among Male Dancers

When discussing their relationships with other dancers, all of the participants acknowledged the competition among male dancers. As Jonah stated, "I do observe the other men in the group do have kind of a competitive streak." Roy stated, "The bottom line here is that we are competing for jobs and roles and better parts and stuff." Leo suggested that many outside the dance culture are surprised by the competition: "I mean it really is such a sport, and it's very competitive and athletic that I think once you get in and sort of experience that world you see how tough it is."

Six of the participants admitted being extremely cautious about the colleagues they got close to within the company due to the competition. As Leo explained, "I'm willing to sort of be more self-deprecating with the women here, and with the men, I'm a little more guarded just because of my position here. And it is a competitive career. You don't want to necessarily open yourself up too much to anybody inside your work space. I think because people, however nice they are, can step on you sometimes, cut you down." As Tony also explained, "Like I said before, the competitive nature of dance . . . so when you're talking to guys in the company, there is more of a standoffishness because of the competition there."

Tony and Roger made a distinction between how competition influences their relationships with male and female dancers. As Tony explained, "With the girls it's just kind of like 'oh well, she's a girl and she'll get her own parts, and you don't have to worry about that." Roger suggested the following: "All of the jealousy tends to fall more toward the roles that people have, and that often manifests in the interactions between the men and the women separately." Four of the participants noted gender differences in competition, with the perception that female dancers experience a higher level of competition. As Jacob explained, "There is so much competition for women. So many girls dream about being ballet dancers, and so few guys dream about being dancers. Guys usually get scholarships to all kinds of places—not everywhere but most places. And you don't have to be as good to get accepted in the schools. You can't be horrible but whereas women, they are taking the best of the women, and a lot of girls are getting left behind. And if you are taking the best of the men and only fifteen men show up, well that's pretty much everybody. So you get a lot of breaks in that way." Several of the participants discussed the ways in which they attempted to cope with the competition. Brendan and Jonah made a distinction between their personal and professional lives as a way in which to cope with the intense competition. As Jonah stated, "I do tend to keep a healthy distance from all the people that I work with because the job is so intense . . . I like to have just a little bit of distance in my own life." Ken's method of coping was to focus on himself, "For some people there is a lot of competition, but for me I never try and compete with other males. I just try and do my job. It's a better concept." Charles indicated that his age and years of experience taught him to distance himself from the competition: "It's not competitive, so that's a good thing. It also of course has to do with where you are in your life. I mean it was more competitive at times . . . I'm not so competitive anymore because I'm just so happy with where I am at career wise, and I have other things going on in my personal life; it just doesn't matter that much."

Discussion

The purpose of this study was to examine friendship formation among professional male ballet and modern dancers. More specifically, we examined the nature and quality of professional male dancers' friendships with men and women in their respective dance companies.

Seven of the participants described challenges making friends with other males while growing up. Several of the participants noted being teased or bullied by peers. Researchers have found that boys who are interested in non-traditional activities or forms of movement that are counter to the bodily practices of contact sports, such as dance (Gard 2008, 185), often face bullying, ridicule, and teasing and may be ostracized from their peer group. Furthermore, for boys who identify as gay or who may be questioning or exploring their sexuality, mainstream boy culture can be especially hostile and intimidating. The fear of being labeled "gay" keeps boys from getting involved or remaining involved in certain activities; it also forces those individuals who may be struggling with their sexual identity into a deeper state of denial. Researchers have also found that adolescent males who identify as gay or are questioning their sexuality may not only distance themselves from feminized spaces but also purposefully avoid males they perceive may be unaccepting or who may tease or harass them (Galupo and Gonzalez 2013, 787–788). For the young male dancer who faces rejection from the mainstream culture, the dance community can become a safe and welcoming environment. Risner shared his personal experiences as a gay student and dancer. Like several of the participants in the present study, Risner found dance to be an escape from the bullying and abuse he experienced while growing up (2002a, 67). Furthermore, Risner found that male dancers received most of their support and care from their best friends in dance and school.

One of the most significant relationships people have in their lives is with their families. The relationship between a father and his children has been found to have a major impact on a child's development, especially on a male child's development. Six of the participants in the present study detailed negative or unaccepting relationships with their fathers and/or brothers while growing up. Fathers and brothers, and male family members in general, play an especially important role in boy's physical development and involvement in physical activities (Messner 1992b, 26). The physical domain, and sport in particular, is often considered to be one realm where fathers and sons connect. Research indicates that fathers tend to hold more rigid standards with regard to gender-appropriate behavior and roles compared to mothers (Messner 2002, 19). Consistent with the participants in the present study, researchers have reported that fathers, compared to mothers, tend to harbor more negative and stereotypical attitudes toward male involvement in dance due to its association with femininity and homosexuality (Polasek and Roper 2011, 180). Risner found that only 28 percent of male dancers indicated their fathers were "supportive" or "helpful." Male dancers were also more likely than females to report social support dissatisfaction (2009a, 112). Katherine Polasek and Emily Roper indicated that three (25 percent) of the twelve professional male dancers' fathers in their study held negative attitudes toward their son's involvement in dance (Polasek and Roper 2011, 180).

Sexuality played an important role in friendship formation for the participants in the present study. Consistent with research (Risner 2002b, 89), the heterosexual participants in the present study formed their closest friendships with other heterosexual male dancers, citing similar interests and activities. In contrast to Risner, who found that the gay dancers in his study felt a sense of alienation from all other males in dance, the gay participants in the present study indicated forming close friendships with other gay dancers (Risner 2009a, 89). Research indicates that friendship is a central element in gay men's lives and that gay men are more likely to form friendships with other gay men than heterosexual men. Gay men's friendships are likely to be more equitable than friendship with a heterosexual man.

Consistent with Risner (2002b, 89), the gay participants in the present study also noted having especially close friendships with female dancers. A growing amount of research has examined the "straight female-gay male" friendship; however, the majority of this research has focused on the value and benefits for heterosexual women. Some research reports that gay men place a high value on their friendships with heterosexual women (Grigoriou 2004, 14). Tina Grigoriou found that gay men view their heterosexual female friends to be trustworthy sources of information regarding their romantic lives, describing their friendships with women to be "meaningful" and "deep" (2004, 14).

All five of the heterosexual participants reported dating female dancers throughout their careers. Like most workplaces, "office romances" and dating are not uncommon. The potential to date female dancers was described by some of the heterosexual participants as a "perk of the job." Research examining heterosexual males involved in cheerleading, another feminized domain, reports that one of the most common narratives used to explain a heterosexual male's transgression into feminized space is related to the access to "beautiful women" (Anderson 2005, 345). As a heterosexual male cheerleader interviewed by Anderson indicated, "Yeah, there are a lot of hot chicks in cheerleading. That is why I came out for the team" (Anderson 2005, 345). Referred to as defensive heterosexuality, Eric Anderson suggests that such reasoning is used to justify or defend involvement in an activity associated with femininity and homosexuality.

Male dancers have been found to receive preferential or special treatment (e.g., access to schools, scholarships) within the dance culture (Polasek and Roper 2011, 185). The participants in the present study spoke about the "golden boy" status of heterosexual male dancers. As dance is primarily viewed as a feminine art form and a culture that is perceived to have a large number of dancers who identify as gay, the heterosexual male dancer represents a distinctive and rare being.

Due to the association of dance with femininity, it is often perceived that dancers are more likely to challenge the physical, social, and psychological attributes associated with hegemonic masculinity. All of the participants in the present study indicated that their involvement in dance provided them a space to express themselves artistically and emotionally. According to Risner, dance may be an important vehicle for boys to examine dominant notions of masculinity, gender, sexual orientation and the body (2007c, 144).

Several of the participants suggested that being a professional dancer fostered a sense of appreciation for and greater understanding of cultural differences, particularly with regard to attitudes toward homosexuality. According to contact theory (Allport 1954, 6), interpersonal contact is one of the most effective ways to reduce prejudice between majority and minority group members. By interacting and communicating with others, a person is more likely to understand and appreciate different points of view. Research suggests that heterosexuals who know someone who identifies as lesbian, gay, bisexual, or transgender are more likely to hold positive attitudes toward gay men and lesbians (Herek and Capitano 1996, 418). Anderson found that heterosexual male cheerleaders' relationships with gay men and women helped them reconstruct their views on homosexuality and femininity (Anderson 2005, 345).

All of the participants acknowledged that there was competition between the male dancers. Competition among men is a well-documented phenomenon across a variety of settings (e.g., sport, work, relationships). Interpersonal competition is defined as "a dynamic, ongoing process between two people that is initiated by social comparison and motivated by self-evaluation as the individuals vie to out-do one another on various tasks, abilities and status dimensions" (Singleton and Vacca 2007, 618). Researchers have addressed the competitive element in male friendships (Singleton and Vacca, 2007, 618). Lillian Rubin found that male friends, compared to female friends, were more likely to report competition as a common theme in their same-sex friendships (Rubin 1985, 23). Royce Singleton Jr. and Jessica Vacca surveyed U.S. college students and found male friendship dyads to have significantly more competition than female friendship dyads. Such competition has the potential to negatively affect the quality of friendships. While competition does not automatically end a friendship, as Rubin suggested, it undermines the emotional support and closeness that friendship requires (Rubin 1985, 23). As the findings from the present study suggest, competition forced several of the participants to be cautious of whom they got close to within their respective companies. Such concerns regarding competition restricted the formation of same-sex friendships as well as the participants' friendship quality.

Conclusion

Socially defined as a feminine context, dance provides a unique setting in which to study men's friendship formation.

The purpose of this study was to qualitatively examine friendship formation among professional male ballet and modern dancers. While no noteworthy differences were found across the ballet and modern dancers in the present study, it is important to acknowledge the mixed group of dancers studied. The findings provide insight into the ways in which male ballet and modern dancers connect (and disconnect) with both male and female dancers and how gender and sexuality influence their social interactions and relationships.

For some of the participants, their early experiences of bullying by peers hindered their desire and opportunity to form friendships with their peer group while growing up. During data collection, however, all of the participants indicated satisfaction with their friendships both in and outside the dance setting. For most, involvement in dance was especially helpful in allowing them to be themselves, providing them a safe place in which to express themselves emotionally and artistically.

The dance culture also influenced the ways in which the participants related with other men and women, reaffirming and challenging stereotypical norms surrounding same-sex, cross-sex, and cross-category friendships. Sexuality played a significant role in friendship formation for the participants, with the gay participants forming stronger friendships with other gay dancers and female dancers and heterosexual male dancers aligning more with other heterosexual male dancers. For the heterosexual participants, friendships with female dancers were also common but not without complications associated with physical attraction. While such division across sexuality has been found in dance and other social settings, the participants in the present study suggested that such division was not exclusionary or discriminatory. In fact, many of the participants stressed the unique nature of their work and the emotional and physical connection needed among dancers. Furthermore, the heterosexual participants in particular noted that their experiences in dance and working in an environment that was less traditionally "masculine," fostered a greater appreciation for cultural differences and challenged their personal definitions of masculinity. Based upon the findings from the present study, it appears that the dance culture buffers and reduces some of the stereotypical norms and attitudes toward same-sex, across-sex, and cross-category friendship formation.

Note

1. All of the participants selected a pseudonym for confidentiality purposes.

8

"Boys are Morons" ...
"Girls are Gross"

Let's Dance!

KAREN E. BOND

This chapter focuses on student meanings of gender as found in an evolving dance studio course titled "Embodying Pluralism." Since 2008 the course has fulfilled Temple University's general education requirement in race and diversity.[1] From the current syllabus: "We will explore theories and practices of race, ethnicity, gender, and other social constructions that form the fabric of American society. Embodying Pluralism combines dance and movement experiences with viewing of videos and performances, theoretical inquiry and lively discussion.... No dance experience necessary!" An earlier study of collaborative learning across four sections of the course (2011–2012) identified a strong interest in gender (Bond and Gerdes 2012). The present research elaborates on this finding, drawing on 348 students' Blackboard gender discussions in seventeen sections of the course from 2008 to 2014.

Topography of the Study

"Embodying Pluralism" (EP) attracts a diverse demographic. Students span racial-ethnic categories similar to the university profile as a whole.[2] Classes support a cross-section of university years, majors, abilities, and religious and spiritual orientations. As typical for a public university, most students come from urban, suburban, and rural locations in Pennsylvania and nearby states. In this study, forty-nine out of seventy-two males (68 percent) and 151 out of 276 females (53 percent) entered the course with dance knowledge—practical and/or theoretical; of these, fourteen males (29 percent) and 106 females (70 percent) had experiential dance background. Students' self-described dance backgrounds ranged from "none" to "all my life."

The only social variable skewed in all seventeen sections was gender. In classes numbering twenty-five to thirty (fewer in summer sessions), individuals identifying as male ranged from one to six, composing 21 percent of total enrollments over the six years. A low ratio of males to females is common in most dance education settings, with the exception of K-12 schools that include dance in core curriculum,[3] and the rare males-only settings.

Methodology

The study aligns philosophically with feminist phenomenology, "by definition a critical phenomenology" (Simms and Stawarska 2013, 11) concerned with lived experience, gender, ethics, and the illumination of human possibility. The research privileges students' experiences and meanings of gender and dance, so no review of background literature is provided to orient the reader to a particular theoretical framework (Bond and Stinson 2001). Sources include 348 student Blackboard entries totaling 106,000 words. The study has been approved as an ethical research design by Temple's Institutional Review Board.

Student writings are from one Blackboard assignment that involves a reading and then a 300-word response to this (or a similar) question: "What messages about gender did you receive as a child . . . ?" This prompt encourages description and memoir. The reading, "How 'Wild Things' Tamed Gender Distinctions" ("Wild Things"), reports on action research in a multicultural K-3 dance class in an Australian inner suburban primary school (Bond 1994). Dancing in large, self-decorated cardboard box body masks inspired by the sexless creatures in Maurice Sendak's (1963) *Where the Wild Things Are*, eight boys and six girls (ages five to eight) overcame gender inhibitions and role playing to become a cohesive performing group.

Analytic procedures were adapted from Max van Manen's (2014) three coding methods for isolating themes: detailed (line by line), selective (highlighting lived experience anecdotes as meaning units), and holistic (meaning statement for each text as a whole), also drawing on conventional qualitative content analysis procedures (Saldana 2009). In addition to their lived experiences of gender, I was interested in students' theories (beliefs, assumptions, critical perspectives) and hopes for the future of gender in dance and life. The first cycle of coding and clustering of codes generated nine broad gender categories: female associated, male associated, gender neutral/crossing, agency/resistance, stereotypes, sexuality, outside influences, judgment, and developmental perspectives (changes with maturation).[4] I performed multiple further cycles, developing a layered part-whole analysis of EP students' conversational writings.

Research findings are presented thematically, followed by theoretical discussion and reflection. Each theme is illustrated abundantly with individual excerpts (coded by sex and year written, e.g., F2008), distillations of whole entries, and/or research poems created from students' language (Bond and Stinson 2001; Prendergast, et al. 2009).[5] I edited individual verbatim excerpts for extraneous words, seeking to accentuate thematic focus without compromising the writer's meaning. Criteria for selection of excerpts were to present the maximum range of gender meanings and an equitable representation of female and male writers. Since females comprise 79 percent of the study population, presentation of themes may read like "herstory" (Ashby and Ohrn 1995), although male voices, like any minority, have substance, individually and collectively.

Male writings as a whole suggest some shared characteristics of those who were willing to take a general education dance studio course. As a group, they appear to diverge from stereotypical maleness in a number of ways. While most, including some self-identified gay males, described themselves as masculine and competitive, they do not self-describe as an athletic group. Males wrote proportionately less about sports and cars than females did and proportionately more about peer pressure as an influence on gender performance.[6] Male writers connected more with memories of high school than elementary and in general cited "school" less than female writers (67–92 percent). Majors from other art forms, particularly music and theater, were well represented but were not a majority.

This research provides a cross-cultural retro-validation of Bond's 1994 "Wild Things" study (Bond 1994). In its year of publication, most EP writers were around the same ages as children in the Australian primary school where the project took place. To my knowledge, the study has not been replicated formally, which is a weakness of dance education research. While some may associate replication with quantitative research or legal process, the word has qualitative meanings as well, including *echo*, *reverberate*, and *reply* (Dictionary.com 2015).

The Gender Binary (TGB): A Meta-Narrative

Also writing around the time EP students were young children, feminist scholar Judith Lorber (1994) noted, "Everyone 'does gender' without thinking about it" (13). Some referred to this unconscious aspect of gender socialization: "My parents installed gender roles in me without my knowledge" (F2011). Here is an elaborated perspective: "The restrictions society places on gender make it impossible to let one's true self shine through, and after many years we are tricked into believing that we developed as masculine or feminine by our own accord" (M2009). A large number of studies, however, show that from a young age children accept gender stereotypes as fact, whether or not parents consciously enforce them (Cook and Cook 2009, Fine 2010, Jacobson 2011). Cordelia Fine (2010) observes, "It's hardly surprising that children take on the unofficial occupation of gender detective. They are born into a world in which gender is continually emphasized." (147)

Based on keywords analysis,[7] a majority of study participants continued the status quo. Perhaps the shared reading led students down the proverbial garden path to the meta-narrative of TGB that pervades the writings. Alternatively, the similarity of male and female word use might be related to the Blackboard social writing environment. Nevertheless, the striking alignment of males' and females' descriptions of gender qualities observed in childhood is not something one would necessarily expect from groups of "opposites." I will return to this paradox in concluding reflections. On balance, the rich meanings that emerged through rigorous micro-analytic and inductive coding methods give me no reason to doubt that students were engaged in genuine memoir and reflection.

Simone de Beauvoir's ([1949] 2010) assertion in *The Second Sex*, "One is not born, but rather becomes, woman" (330), has been a mantra for feminist scholars devoted to theorizing gender as social process. However, while some students noted that biological facts are misused, for example, to "spin stereotypes" (M2009), many conflated sex and gender, as in this firm online retort (female to male): "You stated gender does not have a biological basis. I disagree. I was born with the female gender" (F2009). The following excerpts connect biological difference with roles in dance.

> Certain steps compliment the female body and others the male. We naturally consider bigger to be stronger and since males are built larger, they seem more powerful. Females look small and fragile, and the choreography they get matches their body type. (F2008)

> Body types are passed on. You don't picture a large man leaping around a stage or gracefully turning like you can see a female doing. (F2008)

In different ways, the above students accept gender stereotypes of females as fragile and graceful and those of males as "naturally" powerful and big.

Students detailed outside influences on TGB in memories of school (especially peers, teachers, recess, gym class, and "sports"), private dance studios, and media, including TV, toys, and other "things" of popular culture that children embody through personal attraction and social contagion. "School" (P-12) was noted as a major zone of gender differentiation (imposed and by choice) and peer pressure, but few students referenced dance in school. Moving on from the meta-theme of TGB, the next section highlights people and places of first influence.

Dance in/and the Family

Students recalled gender experiences in close and extended families, females writing proportionately more about mothers and brothers, and males highlighting sisters. Fathers received relatively equal mention. About twice as many authors described having parents who reinforced gender differences than those who supported similarity or malleability. The following excerpts illustrate family as a place where specific gender roles may be encouraged, imposed, imitated, negotiated, debunked, or absent altogether.

> My sister and I did recitals at home. My older brother thought our dances were stupid, yet when asked to participate he took it seriously, even choreographed. He always played a monster attacking us or included dramatic movements like falling. My sister and I wore tutus; he stayed in sweatpants and T-shirt. (F2009)

> I was athletic, but my mother dressed me girly. In seventh grade I quit sports and started cheering and dancing. I don't think dancing made me more feminine. My parents supported whatever activities I wanted to participate in. (F2009)
>
> I dressed my little brother like the Sugar Plum Fairy. (F2010)
>
> I never hesitated to dance. There was no male figure to tell me what is or isn't masculine. (M2010)
>
> My mother wanted me to carry pocketbooks, but I liked wrestling with my brother and cousins. It's weird though . . . now I'm a dancer and love bags . . . lol! (F2012)
>
> I wanted to imitate mom. Dad got me to play soccer but I didn't like getting dirty. I danced in the goals. After my mother put me in dance classes and pageants, I couldn't be bothered with anything remotely masculine. (F2012)
>
> My father was enthusiastic about dance. This broadened my view of what a man was. A man could do most anything—especially dance. (M2013)

Students wrote about mirroring siblings' dance qualities, both same and "opposite" sex.

> My older sister danced like Lisa Left Eye and Sporty Spice, so I learned to move like them. (F2011)
>
> My brothers were praised for quickness, balance, etc. I became a quick, energetic dancer rather than a typical ballerina. (F2011)

A number of self-described tomboys recalled being enrolled in dance to bring out femininity.

> My mother put me in dance when I was five hoping I would become more of a lady. I am so thankful! I wouldn't be a dance major if it wasn't for her. (F2009)
>
> My mother found my boyish qualities disturbing. She enrolled me in dance where I became more feminine. My cousins then teased me for becoming a "sissy girl." (F2011)

Maternal feminization strategies don't necessarily work: "My mom enrolled me in dance to put some 'girly' in me, but it was not for me!" (F2011)

No males described being "put into" dance classes by a parent. Even when families support male involvement, boys may eventually experience pressure not to dance: "As we got older, gender stereotypes affected my brother and he quit dance" (F2011). Males who entered EP with dance background seldom wrote about parental influence. The following illustrates an extreme of nonsupport, providing a segue to the next theme: "'Dancing is for girls!' 'If you dance you are gay.' Males in my life never appreciated my love for dance. I received strict messages about the difference between males and females" (M2012).

Dancing Is for Girls!

> "Ballet at Two"
> Pink leotard, pink tights, pink shoes
> All girls!
> Graceful and delicate
> Quiet, gentle, and reserved
> I wanted to be a prima ballerina.
> Beautiful, sparkly
> The tutus!
> Dance was a place to dress up, move, and be beautiful.
> Pristine and proud
> Like a Disney princess in the ballroom
> Freedom to feel feminine

I created the above research poem from female students' language to acknowledge the many who remember the early lure of ballet with its opportunities to "dress up, move, and be beautiful." No males wrote about beauty, although attraction to dressing up is a cross-gender phenomenon in students' writings (including males in tutus and females in action hero costumes). Some females' descriptions are more socially aware than the above "pure fem" poem.

> I was taught to use feminine movements, never the harsh, violent or joking movements associated with boys. (F2008)

Dance had a lot to do with going to my studio and learning to dance with girls. (F2010)

I had all girl birthday parties. NO BOYS ALLOWED. These were DANCE parties, not something boys would be interested in. (F2011)

While some recalled seeing boys at regional dance competitions, many females had never or rarely experienced dance class with a male: "There were no boys at my dance school. Boys are grossly underrepresented in dance" (F2011).

"Is that a Boy?"
I was shocked!
We retreated to the barre giggling and blushing.
The teacher had to force us to interact with him.
He was always trying to be the loudest tapper.
He wanted to use each prop as a weapon.
He never wanted to do ballet movements . . .
It was weird.
He was only interested in stomping around and falling.
I never understood boys . . .
Actions, movement, thought process—completely different.
I thought it was silly . . .
My brothers were playing sports, not pliéing in ballet class.

Relatively few females wrote positive memories of dancing with a boy in class. Here are two exceptions:

He was better than most of the girls . . . I always admired him. (F2010)

The few I danced with were strong yet gentle enough to make some girls jealous. (F2011)

An Irish dancer recalled mixed feelings: "I was distracted. The boy became a lot more fascinating to concentrate on than my teacher" (F2011). Some students wrote about dancing in mixed sex contexts such as pre-school, daycare, camp, ethnic dance classes outside of ballet, community performances, and school dances. The following excerpts depicting group dance show gender affiliations and movement preferences reminiscent of the parallel play of two-year-olds (Cook and Cook 2009). I remember dance in daycare. I felt flowing and graceful while the boys were throwing their hands around and rolling on the ground like cavemen. (F2009)

At our middle-school dance guys made jokes with their moves. Girls moved with the music, swaying bodies side to side. (F2009)

Not until I found out I would get to dress up like a soldier with a rifle did I get excited! I got in trouble for playing war with the other boys, but we were willing to dance. (M2009)

We girls performed as in the article—graceful and timid, while the boys ran and jumped as high as they could, not thinking about the actual move. (F2011)

During rehearsal the boys romped around battling invisible monsters, while the girls rolled their eyes and chainéed across the stage. (F2011)

Shall We *Not* Dance?

Most students confirmed that by elementary school, gender separation and often aversion were the norm, maintained by school, personal choice, and "peer policing" (M2012). EP students narrated a culture of disaffection between the sexes: "I thought boys were morons" (F2011); "I thought girls were gross" (M2011). Descriptions of gender aversion alluded to complex circumstances, behaviors and affects.[8]

Girls were not allowed to lead! No wonder I hate square dancing. (F2008)

The boys made fun of the girls! Society trains males to hate anything prissy. (F2009)

I hated the idea of dance—it made me feel sissy. (M2009)

Guys in our recitals were ridiculed. It was okay if they were gay, but not if they were straight. (F2009)

The girls scolded him as someone who would ruin the flow of the dance because he didn't fit in. (F2010)

> I felt embarrassed dancing with the boys watching. They were not caring. (F2011)
>
> My class performed for St. Patrick's Day. Dancing with the opposite sex was a nightmare. I survived, but the humiliation burns as if it were yesterday. (F2011)
>
> I pretended to like boyish things. I was afraid of being made fun of. It was not normal to like to dance. (M2011)
>
> I teach beginners and once in a while there is a boy among the tutus. At first you see everyone's shyness and the boy realizing where he is. His attention span is usually that of a fly with gracefulness near zero. He will be the one to act up and show anger learning a new move. (F2011)
>
> In dance I would do gymnastics moves to impress the girls. When I got to middle school the boys called me gay and asked me if I did ballet. I started to question if what I was doing was "girly." (M2011)

Students of both sexes wrote about difficulties fitting into gender norms.

> When I first signed up for this class my peers gave me funny looks; like, why do you have a dance class? (M2008)
>
> Being told to dance in a feminine way has been a problem. I feel my dance should be an expression of me... not movements copied from an instructor. (F2009)
>
> I was either trying to convince everyone that dance is a sport or I was flaunting my femininity, flitting around in costumes. I wanted to defend and defy my gender at the same time, and it's the same today. (F2011)
>
> I hated the way tights felt under my leotard and being told to stand up straight. I had to smile, do the positions and perform for audiences. I started gymnastics at six and learned more about good posture. I had to keep my hair tight, point my toes, and pretend I was holding an egg with my fingers. They stretched me to where my muscles tore. (F2012)

Writers recalled performing outside of stereotypes, exercising choice of gender roles or at least acknowledging the potential. Apart from the explicit tomboy and fem-boy narratives, students wrote about observing or performing gender agency "under the right conditions" (F2010). These unique individual experiences "troubled gender" (Butler 1990).

Outside the Box

> I got a buzz cut and started ballet. I wore mismatching baggy clothing to class, yet my friends were jealous of my long muscular legs. (F2008)

> I wanted to break dance like my best friend's brother. Once I performed for my class. The boys loved it, but the girls called me "boyish" for three years, until I started belly dance and ballet. (F2010)

> As the tall girl I sometimes had to switch roles. I enjoyed this! I was a tomboy in real life. I wanted to be better than the boys. (F2011)

> A boy in the three to fours loved to wear tutus. The mom's sister-in-law told her she's letting her son turn gay, but the mom said it's wrong to label a child. Why should a boy not get to dress up for dance class? (F2011)

> I fell in love with dance in high school junior year. A few people said stuff but I didn't care. (M2011)

> In early dance experiences I was competitive and boisterous. In high school I began to find the balance with my feminine side. (M2011)

> I put my all into dance. I was not afraid to explore outside the box. (M2011)

> I expanded from my ballerina identity, chasing boys and kicking butts in soccer. Girls and teachers ostracized me. (F2012)

> I always felt more "boy" and it's still there in my dance—no light and airy delicacy. I clump my legs around, crash, and slide. But there is still a beauty that only a female dancer can produce. (F2012)

> I danced a partner dance on stage... to endless teases and jokes. But I never backed out. I earned respect. (M2012)

> In fifth grade I tried out for the cheer competition team. All the girls accepted me, but I got hell in school. I was called "princess" and "flower boy." (M2014)

Some students suggested it's easier for females to be "different."

> It's OK for girls to be tomboys, but boys are looked down on for showing female interests. (F2009)

> Girls could act aggressive in performances and not surprise people, but if a boy acted feminine he was considered uncool and questioned. (M2010)

I identified gender agency in students' writings about overcoming bias. These young women described changed attitudes towards males in dance.

> Today I'm more open to male dancers and find them as beautiful as females. (F2011)

> Dance can be a level ground to explore roles and break boundaries that once seemed set in stone. (F2011)

> At competitions, my friends and I were baffled. Some of the male dancers were phenomenal! We put them into a category—gay. Now I know that anyone can love dancing, sexuality no matter. (F2012)

Males also showed reflexivity about gender aversion.

> Thankfully much has changed—my pretentious, arrogant ways are past. (M2010)

> I let peers pressure me to play sports, hang out with all guys, and act like a clown. I can honestly say I didn't like a lot of things I did when I was young but did them anyway to fit in. (M2013)

Reflecting on children's behavioral transformation in "Wild Things," students recalled their own experiences of releasing or observing the release of gender stereotypes in dance. Many noted that commitment to group goals and practice can moderate individual temperament and social-cultural difference for the sake of community.

Communities of Practice

> The more I practiced the dance with my class, the more I felt a communal understanding. We were sharing and did not focus on our different genders. (F2009)

> He refused to do a move because it was too girly. I told him just because you're a boy doesn't mean you can't enjoy this. After that he did everything and had a great time. (F2009)

> Working with the "Wild Things" age group in summer camp, I created some partner choreography. At first both girls and boys seemed iffy, but as the weeks went on they put their differences aside. (F2011)

> The guys didn't flinch at the makeup. They were immersed in the roles, overcome by the dances. (F2013)

More than two-thirds of student writers referred to the power of mask and costume to liberate dance expression. Males in particular highlighted this aspect of "Wild Things" pedagogy, some recalling similar experiences: "We had to move showing our personalities. Even though we were fourteen, we behaved like the kids in the article. The boys moved percussively with a lot of running; the girls were flowing and legato. The next week we were given blank masks to make up characters with. Just like the wild things, I let my inhibitions go and shifted away from stereotypical movements" (M2009). Masks need not hide or erase the dancer's subjectivity (Fraleigh 2004, Manning 2006). Masking can be part of micro-culture in the making, in the moment, through the marking of local knowledge and lived experience—individual, inter-individual, and collective (Bond 1999). Some students noted this paradox of masking: "While hiding their faces they were able to reveal their true identities" (F2009).

Fast-Forward

Although the Blackboard assignment is oriented to childhood memories, students wrote about the present also, describing gendered behavior of younger siblings and cousins and in work and study settings (studios, camps, daycare, and schools).

> Last night my little cousins had a talent show. The girls did girl moves and my cousin did his karate moves.

> The toddler mirrored the girls; because they were girls she did their moves. (F2009)

> As a dancer and teacher, I find this article accurate. Boys and girls develop different styles and any variation makes them subject to ridicule. (F2011)

> I student-teach dance classes and the little girls act just like those in the study, using mostly dainty movements that differ from child to child based on their personalities. (F2012)

Some referred to gender behaviors described in "Wild Things" as "normal."

> I loved to dress up and go to ballet class. Even without societal influences I would be very feminine. We have no control over acting feminine if female or masculine if male. Why do people have such a hard time accepting this? Does it matter if genders move differently? (F2008)

> When boys and girls dance together they become excited and distracted. This is normal when we put them in the same room. (F2011)

> We have known since we were little that most boys are rowdy and competitive, and most girls are delicate and like to act like ballerinas . . . this is common knowledge. (F2011)

> The attitude that girls are quieter or more timid than boys and that this makes them less interesting dancers is something I observe in all ages. (F2012)

Finally, students wrote about gender stereotyping in themselves and contemporaries:

> Boys are embarrassed to acknowledge themselves as dancers—they see dance as female. I feel bad for males who truly want to dance but get ridiculed for it. (F2012)

> Dance is classified as feminine. Instilled early, this still holds true in our age group. For example, the makeup of our class—six boys compared to about twenty girls. (M2012)

> I notice that female dancers are expected to be both beautiful and able. (M2012)

> Even in our class I find it difficult to move freely for fear I will do something too feminine. I don't want to embarrass myself. Gender stereotypes continue to control me. (M2012)

Transition

Through exhaustive qualitative analysis grounded in phenomenological procedures, themes were identified in 348 general education students' memories of gender experiences in dance and beyond. To an extent, the study supports textbook explanations of typical childhood gender development as the embodiment of stereotypes within a matrix of bio-phenomenological, social, and cultural influences. At the same time, students' stories exceed stereotypes, offering nuanced portrayals of gender agency.

Presentation of findings began with a section on the meta-narrative of the study, "The Gender Binary (TGB)" followed by sections on "Dance in/ and the Family," "Dancing is for Girls!" "Shall we *not* Dance," "Out of the Box," and "Communities of Practice." "Fast-Forward" offered a longitudinal perspective, depicting the persistence of gender movement stereotypes in the present. To illuminate maximum variation of gender meanings, each section was liberally illustrated with text excerpts, research poems, and other distillations based on close analysis of students' conversational writings in "Embodying Pluralism." The chapter turns now to discussion of findings in relation to salient literature. The meta-narrative of TGB led me to sources in evolutionary biology, neuroscience, and social and cognitive psychology, extending my feminist phenomenological perspective.

Zooming Out

As analysis unfolded, it became evident that in spite of a disciplined intention to mine students' writings for gender phenomena in dance, it was impossible to ignore the big picture. Without a specific prompt, students across sections theorized sex and gender as a global problem, with dance a small part of the story.

> Many of us are dancers and realize the gender differences that come with that, but polarization of the sexes goes much further . . . from the sports we play, to what we watch on TV, to how we spend free time. This topic is universal. (F2009)

> Dance is not the only principle defined to us as "feminine" or "masculine" at a young age. How one should act, socialize, be active, etc. are thrust upon us by society, culture, and families. (M2012)

Further, student writings suggest that boys who are averse to dance and girls who are averse to dancing with boys might be understood better if situated in the macro-culture (or cultures) of childhood gender segregation.

> Boys and girls really do separate themselves at a young age. They learn to recognize gender and form flocks, boys with boys and girls with girls. (M2011)

> I rejected anything of the slightest feminine quality. I hated the color pink... and I *certainly* rejected anything "pretty." "Speed, explosiveness... competition"—that pretty much sums up my experience of how a young boy thinks it's appropriate to act. (M2012)

> I believe I was searching for myself within others who have common characteristics. (M2012)

While EP writings overall suggest that males tend to generalize about dance, specific descriptions relate mostly to the princess dance offered in the segregated pink ghetto sphere of American private dance instruction and other "strictly girly" spaces (see Orenstein 2011). "Gender roles have been part of my entire life. I have seen how strong they are in dance. When watching almost any type of dance, you see such girly things as makeup, glitter, and rhinestones. It is almost impossible to picture any masculine qualities in the art" (F2011). The development of gender segregation is well researched. Joan and Greg Cook (2009) claim, "gender segregation exists. In fact, it is nearly universal, occurring in every cultural setting in which researchers have observed children selecting playmates" (423). Fine (2010) cites homophilia, as in "birds of a feather flock together," as a deterrent to cross-gender rapport and equality throughout life. Why would the socio-culturally feminized behaviors and spaces of dance be exempt? Encouraged by nostalgic mothers, princess media (fairy tales, romantic ballets, Disney movies) and other influences, American girls are entering "pre-ballet" as young as two years. Boys at eighteen months are joining pre-football. Myriad websites advertise these twenty-first-century toddler-training industries.

Turning to biological discourse on gender difference, David Barash and Judith Lipton (2002) assert that, "Genetically primed male-to-male competition underpins the gender gap" (xi), suggesting also that male-female differences in brain function influence "tendencies to violence, parenting inclinations, [and] behavior of infant boys and girls . . ." Further, these "robust phenomena" appear across "widely separated populations" (ix). The authors state, "Females really are the gentler sex" (31), a premise on which most student writers of both sexes seemed to concur (see endnote seven).[9] Few students (mostly the self-identified "tomboys") wrote about female same-sex social aggression or, in popular terms, the "mean girl" meme unleashed in the blockbuster film of that name (*Mean Girls*, 2004) and narrated since in film sequels and a substantial body of popular literature.

Research on the subject is contradictory, indicating variously that the "mean girl" may be biologically potentiated, a cultural stereotype, or perhaps a liminal stage in the development of female agency (Horn 2004). In any case, both scholarly and popular sources suggest that females do not have a monopoly on same-sex social aggression (Dowd 2005, Underwood 2003). What does a "mean girl" look like in dance? Might the controversial Abby Lee Miller of the hugely popular *Dance Moms* (2011) "reality" TV show be dance education's mediated adult "mean girl"?

Clearly, it is difficult to sort out biological influences from those of culture. I want to think like Fine that "as conscious, thinking creatures we are able to say no to our biological tendencies. . . . Evolution gives the 'is' not the 'ought'" (Fine 2010, 201). A student wrote, "Why is it 'normal' for girls to be pleasant and shy?" (F2009). To my "beginner's mind" (one capable of logic but not possessing expert knowledge to offer the biology/culture debate), it seems probable that humans are both primed by biology and shaped by culture.

As far as I can discern, few general texts on gender development consider dance; however, Fine's (2010) *Delusions of Gender* is notable for its incidental attention to dance in two studies of parental attitudes. First, a mother discusses her preference for having a female child: "A girl, I wanted that more . . . to dress her up and to buy the dolls and the dance classes . . . do all the things that you like to do, more than you could a boy" (135). The second comes from a study of parents committed to gender-neutral childrearing. A father states, "If [my] son really wanted to dance, I'd let him . . . but at the same time I'd be doing other things to compensate . . ." (141). As introduced in "Dance in/and the Family," about twice as many Embodying Pluralism students reported having parents who emphasized gender difference than those who modeled similarity and equality.

Based on current knowledge, emphasis on difference seems counterintuitive, given the brain's capacity to support behavioral plasticity (Fine 2010). Some students wrote about the harmfulness of socially enforced movement differences, given that both sexes are born with similar expressive potential and range, graceful to rough. I argue that once the gender binary is fully embodied, both sexes are developmentally delayed or, as Saul Keyworth (2001) put it, each is "half of a crippled whole" (123).

Fine (2010) discusses "the half-changed mind" (142), as exemplified by the father quoted above who would permit his son to dance, but would "compensate" with other (read "masculine") activities. Students' writings portray complexity of parental attitudes to gender, although none as extreme as this father: "If my son wanted to dance, I would kill myself" (Kirby 2013). Butler asserts a variation on the theme: "We are talking about an extremely deep panic or fear . . . Someone says: you must comply with the norm of masculinity otherwise you will die. Or I kill you now because you do not comply" (*Judith Butler* 2006). Parents may think "gender norms be damned" but continue to "craft their children's 'gender performances,' especially for boys" (Fine 2010, 142). Again citing Judith Lorber and a number of EP writers, this may happen unconsciously or "without thinking" (Lorber 1994, 24).

Current studies in cognitive and social psychology suggest that "without thinking" is actually a form of thinking. Fine (2010) explains that even those who don't subscribe to stereotypes can find themselves enacting them "rapidly, automatically and unintentionally" (21) through "implicit associations" picked up from the environment, for example, childhood family patterns and cultural patterns, including attitudes to dance. An EP student illustrates the phenomenon, as others have in the chapter: "I think gender acts are done almost naturally. For example, I worked at a summer dance camp with a group of 7–8 year olds and I would constantly refer to the girls as 'sweetie' and the boys as 'dude'" (F2013). Efforts to identify a neural basis for implicit association are showing promise (Stanley, et al. 2008).

Dance's feminization, a historical-social-political construction, has been examined extensively, including its impact on boys and men (Ferdun 1994, Gard 2008, Keyworth 2001, Risner 2009a, 2014b).[10] In EP writings, dance's femininity reads as a taken for granted fact of childhood, both implicitly embodied and explicitly trained. This study lends empirical support for Susan Stinson's (2005) theoretical analysis of the "hidden curriculum" of gender difference in dance education. Dance historian Ann Daly (2002) challenges that dance will never be common ground for males and females as long as the "myth of masculine-feminine difference" is perpetuated, since "it is due to this polarity that dance was dubbed 'effeminate' in the first place" (292).

While many EP students wrote about gender as a global problem, some expressed a dance-focused view: "We can notice in the dance circle that gender is even a bigger issue than it is in real life!" (F2008). One may smile at the writer's innocent dance centrism, but she was not the only one to distinguish between dance and "real life," suggesting an implicit association between dance and play. Some studies suggest that the earliest child-initiated gender segregation may be based on play compatibility. Cook and Cook (2009) observe, "The most active and disruptive boys differentiate from the most socially sensitive girls" (423), the latter perhaps being the ones who are able to comply with the social discipline of pre-ballet.

Yet boys and girls are capable of sharing stereotypically gendered activities: "My sister and I played Battleship and ballet and were just as happy" (M2011). A student wrote that parents at her studio requested a boys-only class to "allow the boys to roughhouse more than if they were mixed in a class with mostly girls" (F2011). Maxine Sheets-Johnstone (2009) suggests that rough-and-tumble play is an evolutionary marker of dance. My question is whether in the rarified milieu of girls' dance culture there is enough roughhousing to enable female dancers to exercise their potential for free and full movement in space (see Young 2005).

Theorists have long situated dance in play (Ellis 1923, Huizinga 1955, Kealiinohomoku 1976). In *Homo Ludens,* Johan Huizinga's ([1949] 1955) germinal treatise on play, he asserts: "The connections between playing and dancing are so close that they hardly need illustrating. It is not that dancing has something of play in it or about it, rather that it is an integral part of play: the relationship is one of direct participation, almost of essential identity. Dancing is a . . . particularly perfect form of playing" (163–164). Further, Huizinga cites freedom as a requisite of play: play "is in fact, freedom" (8). Previous research has found that many young people, including EP students, connect dance with experiences of freedom (Bond 2013; Bond and Stinson 2001; Frichtel 2012). If, as bell hooks (1994) has long advocated, education becomes defined as a "practice of freedom," will more boys choose to dance in school?

Student Reflections

EP writers reflected on the past, present, and future of gender. Although some said, "I never really thought about it" (meaning pre-EP), the collective body had experienced TGB as "real life" with a long history. As for its entrapment in dance, students took this seriously as well, with some noting that progress is being made: "It's awesome today how a woman can run for president and a male ballet dancer can feel masculine while looking graceful" (F2008). A large majority of EP students advocated for change, offering visions, ethical commentary, and concrete suggestions for "undoing gender" (Butler 2004).

> A dance class like "Wild Things" should be implemented in all grade schools so boys and girls can become free with individuality and not fear what others think. (M2008)

> If boys are allowed to become more graceful, dance will be looked down upon less. It is important for children to become well rounded. (F2009)

> Hopefully we can erase the feminine connotation of the word "dance." The male dancer's masculinity should not be questioned. (F2010)

> I would love to see the same experiment at high school level. (M2011)

> Movement shouldn't have a gender. People should be free to move however they want. Gender-specific movements are shields. (M2011)

> Reinforcing stereotypes is not healthy for children. My philosophy is congruent with the article. Treat children as individuals. Don't divide them and treat each group differently. (M2012)

I don't believe in gender. (F2012)

We need to teach from a young age that there is no "male" or "female" dance or action. There is only "dance," only "action." (M2012)

Growing up was hard. Being more "feminine" than other boys, I searched to define myself and found I didn't have to apologize. Education like "Wild Things" is the future of humanity: appeal to the senses and challenge people in a gentle way. (M2013)

Educators need to do more to close the gender gap. (F2014)

Many EP writers argued for inclusion of dance education in public schools, an important finding. Relatively few children are able to benefit from dance's holistic content, affective power, and socializing rhythms with any enduring curricular coherence (see endnote 3). A student disclosed, "When I was the ages of children in the article, only kids of parents with financial means got to do dance, which I would have loved to be part of" (F2011).

Conclusion

Asia Friedman (2013) argues that neither sex nor gender is fixed, countering the "neurosexism" (Fine 2010) of recent popular science literature attributing gender behavioral differences to biological sex differences in the brain (see Sax 2006). She notes, "Binaries invite oppositional logic, rigid thinking, and disproportionate attention to differences (and therefore disproportionate inattention to similarities)" (3). Given that the genetic difference between the sexes is much less than between individuals of the same sex (Gowaty 1997; Friedman 2013), let's be clear: there is no logical or just reason for the perpetuation of socially enforced gender binaries. Friedman notes that the term "opposite sex" implies "difference to the greatest degree possible," when "genetically, males and females are in fact 98 per cent identical . . . only by social measures are we more different than similar" (4). Shouldn't children then be learning to actively search across difference for elements of common humanity? Both "Wild Things" and the present study show that genders are capable of creating shared worlds, including dance worlds, for example, in spaces that allow "parallel play" where difference is accommodated.

Art historian Barbara Stafford (2001), an advocate for détente between humanities and neurosciences, argues for recuperation of analogy in order to "construct a more nuanced picture of resemblance and connectedness" (9). She observes, "We possess no language for talking about resemblance, only an exaggerated awareness of difference" (10), challenging, "Both the intellectual and the practical emphasis on extreme otherness . . . have resulted in an aesthetic, philosophical, ethical, and social calamity. We seem to be obsessed with identity, not recognition. . . . The search for . . . reconciliation never seemed more urgent than today" (180). Fine (2010) notes, "It is remarkable how similar the two sexes become, psychologically, when gender fades into the background," aligning with Michael Kimmel's declaration in *The Gendered Society:* "Love, tenderness, nurturance; competence, ambition, assertion—these are human qualities, and all human beings—both women and men—should have equal access to them" (Kimmel quoted in Fine 2010, 161). One of my practices as a feminist phenomenologist is to offer final words from or about those who may not be published otherwise. The following complete EP Blackboard entry captures some of the rich ambiguity of gender meanings found in the writings of 348 general education dance students in "Embodying Pluralism": "Boys and girls dance different. Boys are wild and girls are tame. I cannot say boys and girls dance different, they just dance. In my opinion boys dance horrible and girls dance good. When boys and girls dance together they dance better. I do not know if they dance different because I never paid attention."[11]

Notes

1. Initiated by Edrie Ferdun, this course in dance pluralism for the general undergraduate population has been offered at Temple University since the early 1990s.

2. See http://www.collegefactual.com/colleges/temple-university/student-life/diversity/.

3. The National Dance Education Organization (NDEO) estimates that 6 percent of 99,000 schools nationwide offer dance as core curriculum. http://www.ndeo.org/content.aspx?page_id=22&club_id=893257&module_id=55774

4. I thank Ellen Gerdes and Elisa Davis for assistance with preliminary content analysis.

5. Research poems were created from students' descriptions and metaphors, selected and structured for thematic impact.

6. All references in the chapter to proportional relationships serve qualitative interpretation—meta-analytic rather than precisely mathematical.

7. A word-count tool was employed to carry out keyword analyses. Words most used to describe gender behavior in childhood were the same for male and female writers across sections: female qualities—girly, light, graceful, delicate, gentle, quiet, soft. Male qualities were strong, rough, aggressive, masculine, competitive, loud.

8. Content analysis identified ninety-nine negative effects, descriptors, and behaviors that students recalled feeling, seeing, hearing, or expressing in childhood gender relations ("opposite" and same sex when the latter acted outside of gender norms).

9. As with race, genetic differences between the sexes are quite small (Cook and Cook 2009). While female reproductive biology may prime for gentleness, it is also learned behavior of which both sexes are capable.

10. The feminization trope is also best viewed in a larger framework; for example, the feminization of poverty and farming are global phenomena in 2015.

11. In 2012 "Embodying Pluralism" was selected by Temple's Academy of Adult Learning to accommodate students with intellectual disabilities. The concluding text is an academy student's response to the assigned article.

9

Leadership and Gender in Postsecondary Dance

An Exploratory Survey of Dance Administrators
in the United States

DOUG RISNER AND PAMELA S. MUSIL

The place dance holds as an academic area of study in colleges and universities in the United States today can be directly traced to the work of Margaret H'Doubler at the University of Wisconsin–Madison and other visionary women of the early twentieth century. Their pioneering leadership forged uncharted territory to establish dance as an independent discipline in academe (Ross 2002). The primary tenets, influence, and momentum of their leadership led to the mid-century expansion of dance departments in the 1950s, increasing numbers of dance faculty (primarily women), and the resultant postsecondary dance "boom" of the late 1970s through the early 1990s—buttressing the academic presence and relevance of dance (Hagood 2000).

From this wider acceptance of dance as a valid and viable area of study in higher education, as well as gender shifts in the professional dance world, male faculty hires began to increase in the 1990s. As Jan Van Dyke (1996) noted at the time, "Once clearly the domain of women, now many college dance faculties are striving for gender equity regardless of the numerical dominance of women as dance students" (537). According to Higher Education Arts Data Services (HEADS 1994), 37 percent of postsecondary dance faculty were male in 1994; however, women continued to lead the vast majority (80 percent) of dance departments and programs as chairs, directors, heads, and coordinators (Stern 1994 cited in Van Dyke 1996). Yet, gender questions remained: Will more gender diverse dance faculties satisfy the large population of female students' needs? Or will young women "come to regard academic dance programs as just one more place where men are given special consideration? Will male dance student enrollment rise with the increase in male faculty?"(Van Dyke 1996, 538).

Two decades later, female students still account for the wide majority population—86 percent of all postsecondary dance majors (HEADS 2013)—while males comprise 34 percent of dance faculties (down 3 percent from 1994). However, according to data from the National Association of Schools of Dance, men now lead over 42 percent of dance departments and programs (HEADS 2014), an increase of 5 percent in just the last two years alone (HEADS 2011, 2014). This chapter presents an exploratory yet comprehensive status report of administrative leadership in postsecondary dance today through critical analyses of gender representation, equity, workplace issues, professional motivations, and career choices—the first empirical study of its kind conducted in the United States.

Research Design and Methodology

The present study was drawn from a larger mixed-method empirical study (n=75) that investigated the professional lives of administrative leaders in postsecondary dance departments and programs in the United States. For the purposes of this research, administrative leaders were defined as chairs, directors, and heads who lead schools and departments of dance, as well as coordinators, area heads, and directors who lead dance programs within larger organizational structures (colleges, schools, and departments). The purpose of the investigation was to develop a comprehensive status report, comprising quantitative data and qualitative narratives, of administrative leadership in postsecondary dance today with particular attention to gender. The present study focuses on quantitative and qualitative survey data and findings.

A three-part methodology was employed for this research: (1) review of literatures in postsecondary dance leadership, administration, and historical perspectives; (2) analysis of data assembled annually by Higher Education Arts Data Services (HEADS) in conjunction with the National Association of Schools of Dance (NASD) from 1994 to 2014; and (3) findings from the authors' mixed-method study of dance administrators (n=75) leading postsecondary dance departments and programs, described later in this section.

Research Design

Interpretive research designs allow researchers to render a better understanding of a particular phenomenon in the world and to bring forth meaning and understanding rather than proving or disproving facts (Denzin and Lincoln 2011). Participant meanings are revealed in diverse ways and necessitate that researchers engage conceptual frameworks and employ methodologies that account for multiple perspectives, contexts, and complexities. The lives and experiences of participants are considered multiple, socially constructed, and contextual (Creswell 2014).

Beyond HEADS annual reports of data from NASD-accredited postsecondary institutions, the dearth of published empirical research on dance administration and leadership in higher education required gathering significant quantifiable data. Thus, collecting quantitative survey data on a relatively large scale was necessary.

Concurrently, and from an interpretive research perspective, the processes and methods of qualitative research and data generation allow researchers to draw out concepts, develop grounded theories, and pursue emergent patterns through interpretation and contextual analyses (Denzin and Lincoln 2011). Further, when teamed with a critical approach, "Qualitative dominant mixed methods research is the type of mixed research in which one relies on a qualitative, constructivist-poststructuralist-critical view of the research process, while concurrently recognizing that the addition of quantitative data and approaches are likely to benefit most research projects" (Johnson, Onwuegbuzie, and Turner 2007, 124).

By articulating the kind of primary question a researcher asks, Frederick Erickson (2005) summarizes interpretive design from a critical perspective: "The interpretive qualitative researcher would say that the question 'what is happening?' is always accompanied by another question: 'and what do those happenings mean to those who are engaged in them?' And a critical qualitative researcher would add a third question, 'and are these happenings just and in the best interests of people generally?'" (7).

Methodology

Procedures for the larger study included: an extensive online survey generating quantitative and qualitative data from seventy-five participants from across the United States and in-depth interviews with nine participants of geographic diversity. The online survey required twenty-five to forty minutes to complete. Each of the nine participants selected was interviewed once; interviews were forty-five to seventy-five minutes long. Due to space limitations, interview data are not included in the present study.

Human subject investigation approval was obtained from Wayne State University. Comprising seven sections, the online survey generated the following participant data: (1) demographic and institutional information; (2) workload, responsibilities, and salary; (3) support satisfaction and work satisfaction; (4) meaning/purpose, strengths, and challenges; (5) influential experiences and people; (6) quality of professional lives and work-life balance; and (7) qualitative comments organized by open-ended questions. Risner conducted and aggregated the online survey. When appropriate, gender asymmetries and divergences will be discussed.

Background and Literature Review

A review of published literature presents a hopeful yet troubling portrait of how much (and how little) has changed in roughly the past century since dance made its debut in academe in 1917 (Ross 2002). The matriarchy within postsecondary dance leadership is well represented, documenting the important roles figures such as Blanche Trilling, Margaret H'Doubler, Gertrude Colby, Mary Shelly, Martha Hill, and Bessie Shönberg, among others, played in dance's debut and legitimization within higher education (Hagood 2000; Ross 2002). These sources among many others also raise dialogue about equity within a decidedly female discipline in a male institution, offering sentient commentary on historic and evolving societal attitudes concerning gendered bodies. Critical, multicultural, and feminist commentary and burgeoning bodies of literature have infused and transformed pedagogies, curricula, research agendas, and attitudes within the discipline. Data gathering regarding gender, social issues, equity, and leadership in higher education have provided critical information about where the discipline currently stands and where it may need to go (Garber, et al. 2007; McGreevy-Nichols, et al. 2014; Risner 2007a, 2009a, 2010a,b; Van Dyke 1996). So, while it is clear that substantive progress has been made in some arenas, questions that have been part of the discipline's discourse throughout several decades—particularly those related to gender and equity—remain unanswered; and importantly, in surprising ways dance parallels other disciplines in academe, particularly the arts and humanities (Garber, et al. 2007; Wolf-Wendel and Ward 2014; Zwirn 2006).

In the quest to keep dance at the center of focus while fulfilling the accelerating demands of the increasingly corporate-driven world of academia, effective leadership becomes progressively more important (Fichter 2002), particularly as the shifting of dance administrators into executive ranks has become more commonplace in recent decades (Kahlich 2011). Literature regarding dance leadership and administration is sparse, though what has emerged raises important issues for further inquiry. The Dance 2050 initiative (McGreevy-Nichols, et al. 2014) and other voices (Musil 2010; Risner 2004, 2007a, 2010a) have set in motion opportunities for current leadership to consider the direction dance is headed in academe and to respond with strategic and visionary planning.

Presentation of Survey Data

Participant and Institutional Data

For the purposes of this study, administrative leadership positions held by participants (f=72 percent; m=28 percent) were identified in three categories: (1) department chair (head or director), (2) associate/assistant department chair (head or director), and (3) dance program coordinator (area head or director). As table 9.1 indicates, the majority of participants' positions were equally split between department chairs (48 percent) and dance program coordinators (47 percent). Depending upon the leadership position, size of the dance unit, and particular institution, differences in workload, responsibilities, authority, and salary vary considerably. For example, smaller institutions and programs may be administrated by a program coordinator who functions as the sole full-time dance faculty, oversees two or three adjuncts, and reports to the department chair, head or director while larger programs are led by a department chair who oversees two associate chairs, four area heads, fifteen full-time faculty, and

Table 9.1. Position Title by Gender

	Female (n = 54)		Male (n = 21)		Total [%]
	n	%	n	%	
Department Chair, Head or Director	23	43	13	62	36 [48]
Associate/Assistant Department Chair, Head or Director	3	5	1	5	4 [5]
Dance Program Coordinator, Area Head or Director	28	52	7	33	35 [47]
Total	54	100	21	100	75 [100]

scores of adjuncts. Clearly, such differences in program size impact the scope and nature of workloads, responsibilities, and level of authority, both within the unit and across campus.

Most males (62 percent) held department chair positions, while females (52 percent) were more likely to hold dance program coordinator positions. On average, female participants had served as dance administrators for ten years, while males on average had served six years. Sixty-nine percent of participants worked on nine- to ten-month academic year contracts, while eleven- to twelve-month academic contracts were held by 35 percent of participants; there were no significant gender differences found between contract subgroups.

The average age of the participant population was 53.4 years (females 53.4, males 53.5); females comprised the vast majority of participants (72 percent female, 28 percent male). Most participants held tenured positions (68 percent) and the plurality of participants were full professors (see table 9.2). Males held full and associate professor ranks (86 percent) more frequently than females (72 percent). Females were twice as likely as males to hold non-tenure eligible lecturer/instructor and assistant professor ranks. In terms of highest degree earned, 24 percent of participants reported doctorate (30 percent female, 10 percent male), 41 percent reported MFA (34 percent female, 57 percent male), 26 percent held initial master's degrees (34 percent female, 5 percent male), and 7 percent held bachelor's degrees (2 percent female, 18 percent male). Ten percent of male participants reported no academic degree. Participants self-reported ethnicity as follows: 87 percent white or Caucasian (94 percent female, 67 percent male); 5 percent Hispanic or Latino (4 percent female, 10 percent male); 4 percent black or African American (2 percent female, 10 percent

Table 9.2. Rank and Tenure Status by Gender

	Female (n = 54)		Male (n = 21)		Total [%]
	n	%	n	%	
Professor	23	42	10	48	33 [44]
Associate Professor	16	30	8	38	24 [32]
Assistant Professor	9	17	2	9	11 [15]
Lecturer/Instructor	6	11	1	5	7 [9]
Tenured	36	68	14	67	50 [68]
Tenure Track	5	9	1	5	6 [8]
Non-tenure Track	12	23	6	28	18 [24]

male); 3 percent other ethnicity (0 percent female, 10 percent male); and 1 percent Asian (0 percent female, 5 percent male). Sixty-five percent of participants administered dance programs in public institutions (35 percent in private institutions), which is commensurate with current data reported by HEADS (2014). With regard to NASD accreditation, 71 percent of male participants administered NASD-accredited programs as compared to only 35 percent of females.

Participants reported the following administrative structure in which the dance department or program is housed at their institution: department or school of theater and dance (41 percent); department or school of dance (37 percent); department or school of performing arts (8 percent); department or school of music and dance (7 percent); and any other configuration (7 percent). Males were more likely than females to serve as dance administrators in departments of theater and dance.

The survey data establish clear evidence of a continued dearth of ethnic and racial diversity in female leadership and raise questions of gender equity as well. While males outnumbered females as department chairs by nearly 20 percent, males had served in administrative positions for six years versus ten for women. Males outnumbered females by 14 percent in associate and full professor ranks while females were twice as likely as males to hold lecturer and assistant professor ranks (even though the number of females holding doctoral degrees was triple that of males).

These statistics indicate that men advance more quickly through professorial rank and administrative leadership despite having far fewer academic credentials than women. It is important to identify what choices women and men in leadership may have made regarding child rearing and whether these choices impacted their career advancement.

The disparity among genders relating to degree obtained also warrants further scrutiny. Nearly 30 percent of male participants' highest degree earned was either a bachelor's degree or no academic degree at all. Beyond the merits of academic credentials, extended time spent learning and teaching in postsecondary settings is vital to understanding academic culture and administrative leadership. The data suggest that female participants are better prepared in this respect than their male counterparts.

Workload, Responsibilities, and Salary Data

With regard to participants' overall workload, females indicated more time spent on teaching than males, who reported slightly more time on administration than females (see table 9.3). No significant gender differences were found for time expended on research, creative activity, and service. When asked to report "actual number of hours on average spent each week in order to accomplish the work required of your current position," the plurality of females indicated fifty-six to sixty hours, while the plurality of males reported sixty-one to sixty-five hours.

The survey also asked participants to rate their level of involvement in the following administrative responsibilities: faculty affairs, student affairs, and alumni and community outreach. Each area of responsibility was delineated more specifically within the survey questions. All participants indicated high levels of involvement in faculty recruitment, searches, mentoring, and professional development; however, male participants reported significantly higher involvement in faculty review (annual evaluation, tenure and promotion review) than females. Participants' responsibilities for student affairs were equitable across genders with the exception of student advising, for which females reported a higher level of involvement than males.

Table 9.3. Workload as Percent Time by Gender

	% Female	% Male	% All
Administration	40	44	42
Teaching	35	28	31
Research/Creative Activity	11	13	12
Service	10	11	10
Fund-raising/Development	4	4	4

Table 9.4. Average Salary by Rank, Annual Appointment, and Gender

	Female	Male	Overall
11–12 Month Appointment			
Professor	$103,600	$102,500	$103,500
Associate Professor	$75,600	$75,000	$75,500
Assistant Professor	$75,000	nr	$70,800
9–10 Month Appointment			
Professor	$88,200	$82,500	$86,300
Associate Professor	$66,500	$63,300	$65,300
Assistant Professor	$50,400	nr	$50,400

As a preface to discussing participant salaries as dance administrators, we turn to dance faculty salary data from the Higher Education Arts Data Survey (HEADS) of postsecondary dance institutions accredited by NASD. This preface is important because dance administrators' salaries are often tied directly to their faculty salary base. In terms of tenured and tenure track dance faculty, HEADS (2014) salary data for public and private institutions accredited by NASD report that average salaries of females are higher at the rank of full professor ($86,664) than males ($83,042). However, average male salaries are higher at both associate professor ($69,271) and assistant professor ($55,017) ranks than female faculty (respectively, $65,493 and $54,809).

In the present study, average salary data by participants' rank, academic year contract length, and gender are presented in table 9.4. Although reported male salaries of participants are lower than females, it is important to remember that on average female participants had served as dance administrators for ten years, while males on average had served six years. Because an administrator's salary is frequently tethered to the faculty member's base salary, these differences may make sense. Additionally, closer inspection of the data may explain the anatomy of these seeming disparities: overall, female faculty receive the lowest individual salary at each rank (HEADS 2014). These data provide strong indicators of starting salaries for assistant professor hires, as well as initial salary increases when faculty are promoted to associate professor and full professor. In short, female faculty start well behind their male colleagues' salaries for the same job and the same work. The fact that women's salaries tend to catch up to (and then exceed) men's by the time they hold full professorships could be explained by higher level of merit pay increases for women over time, in conjunction with female longevity as full professors. The idea that gender equity in salary remains elusive until promotion to full professor, when in fact females comprise the significant majority of postsecondary dance faculty (66 percent), raises wage parity concerns for the field and its future administrative leadership.

Work Support Satisfaction and Influential Experiences

The survey employed an adapted version of Williams Social Support Scale (Williams 2003) to gather participants' insights about important persons, groups of people, institutions, and organizations that provide support for their work as dance administrators. The majority of participants identified the following as very helpful or supportive: department chair, head or director (45 percent female, 67 percent male); department secretarial and clerical staff (54 percent female, 78 percent male); and department professional staff (38 percent female, 69 percent male). Male data clearly indicate significantly higher levels of perceived support satisfaction from these individuals and groups. Participants' overall support satisfaction showed similar gender differences (see table 9.5): the majority of males (47 percent) reported highly satisfied and satisfied, while only 36 percent of females reported the same combination. Females (43 percent) also indicated somewhat satisfied at nearly twice the rate of males (23 percent).

Statistically, the fact that females expressed considerably lower levels of support satisfaction brings up important questions about the environments in which women administrators work and lead dance programs, as well as others' perceptions and attitudes about female leadership in the academic workplace.

When participants were asked to identify "the most influential experiences or persons in the development of their effectiveness as a dance

Table 9.5. Support Satisfaction by Gender

	% Female	% Male	% All
Highly satisfied	6	6	6
Satisfied	30	41	33
Somewhat satisfied	43	23	38
Dissatisfied	17	18	17
Highly dissatisfied	4	12	6

Table 9.6. Most Influential Experiences and Persons by Gender

	% female	% male	% all
Learning on the job	74	78	75
Teaching and academic experience	71	50	66
Mentors and role models	64	61	63
Trial and error	47	72	54
Formal education, training, and leadership in arts	61	76	51
Learning from other administrators	38	61	44

administrator" (see table 9.6), the majority of all participants reported the following: learning on the job, mentors and role models, and formal education, training, and leadership in the arts. However, some gender divergences were found: the majority of female participants also reported "teaching and academic experience" as highly influential to their work as dance administrators, while the majority of males identified the influence of "trial and error" and "learning from other administrators."

Highlights and Questions

The gender disparities within this data set are significant. Most apparent are female leaders' perceptions of lack of support, which suggest deficiencies within existing support structures for females that may not be as prevalent for males. Questions arise regarding differences in male-female approaches and methods of working that might contribute to such consistent disparity in satisfaction levels. For example, are female administrators less likely to have support structures in place than males, and/or are males better able to negotiate and justify the need for support structures? Or do differences in working, interacting, and leadership styles lead to differing satisfaction levels among male and female administrators working within similar support environments? Identifying whether males statistically receive more assistance and attention than females from support staff and other stakeholders may help further explain the perceptual disparities that seem to exist.

Motivation, Strengths, and Challenges

When asked to describe their motivations for entering the field of dance administration, participants completed the survey's selected response statement, "I became a dance administrator because . . ." most frequently with the following:

- I enjoy supporting students and faculty. (72 percent females, 50 percent males)
- It was a logical progression in my career. (51 percent females, 56 percent males)
- I felt the need to guide the program. (53 percent females, 44 percent males)
- At my core, I'm a leader. (49 percent females, 56 percent males)

Females (43 percent) reported being "specifically hired for the position" more frequently than males (27 percent). Whereas male administrators were three times more likely than females to report "I wanted to increase my income," and "My previous experiences in leadership were positive." The most divergent gender response was "I had a strong mentor/role model," which men selected at five times the rate of women.

It is important to note that male participants reported both their primary strengths and challenges as a dance administrator at a higher frequency than females. The majority of all participants selected the following strengths:

- Creating a learning culture of respect, curiosity, and equity. (87 percent females, 83 percent males)
- Problem solving and proactive approaches to challenges. (77 percent females, 83 percent males)
- Advocating for the department/program. (75 percent females, 72 percent males)
- Insuring the program's rigor and integrity. (72 percent females, 83 percent males)

A number of gender divergences were found in participants' perceived strengths as administrators. Wide majorities of male responses included:

- Providing strong administrative leadership. (83 percent males, 57 percent females)
- Guiding the unit's artistic direction and production values. (78 percent males, 53 percent females)
- Forward thinking and developing a collective vision. (72 percent males, 57 percent females)

- Managing the unit's business, budget, and fiscal health. (67 percent males, 41 percent females)

Although less pronounced, divergent perceived strengths of female participants included: "leading faculty in collaborative and productive ways" (70 percent females, 55 percent males); and "supporting junior faculty and faculty development" (59 percent females, 44 percent males).

When asked to complete the survey's selected response statement, "As a dance executive, I believe my primary challenges are in" the plurality of participants reported administrative bureaucracy, and budget and fiscal management (see table 9.7). On the whole, male participants reported challenges at a significantly higher frequency than females. Gender divergences were shown in which males reported greater challenges in facilities (males 50 percent, females 29 percent), conflict resolution (39 percent males, 19 percent females) and policy and procedures (33 percent males, 13 percent females), while females indicated significantly greater challenges in personnel and staff issues (females 48 percent, males 22 percent).

Highlights and Questions

The data in this segment reflect significant gender differences in how male and female administrators perceive themselves in the leadership role. Whereas male administrators' perceived strengths aligned with the abilities of providing, guiding, forward thinking, and managing, female administrators' perceived strengths aligned more with the ability to lead through collaboration and support of students and faculty.

The challenges identified by administrators in this section also parallel previous data where males were more likely to be satisfied with existing support structures while females were less satisfied with support overall. Whereas females were more than twice as likely to report problems with

Table 9.7. Primary Challenges by Gender

	% female	% male	% all
Administrative bureaucracy	48	50	49
Budget and fiscal management	44	39	43
Personnel/staff issues	48	22	41
Recruitment	38	39	39
Fund-raising and development	35	44	37
Facilities	29	50	34

personnel and staff issues, males were five times more likely to identify a strong mentor/role model. Though these two data bytes may seem disparate, when aggregated with support data they reinforce male-female differences in seeking and obtaining support. Could the disparity with personnel and staff issues be connected to male administrators being perceived as more authoritative than females, or are there other factors at play? Are male faculty and students more likely to be mentored than female faculty and students, or are they more likely to seek out mentors than their female counterparts?

Quality of Professional Lives, Work-life Balance, and Satisfaction

The survey posed a series of Likert scale questions about participants' professional lives and work life. When asked to respond to the statement, "As dance administrator, I have been able to maintain an active research/creative activity profile," participants reported strongly agree (10 percent), agree (48 percent), disagree (36 percent), and strongly disagree (6 percent). There were no significant gender differences. In response to the statement, "As dance administrator, I have been able to maintain my teaching effectiveness and pedagogical expertise," participants' answers varied widely by gender (see table 9.8). Females were nearly twice as likely to agree as males. Additionally, combined responses for disagree and strongly disagree diverged considerably by gender (males 44 percent, females 10 percent).

When asked to respond to the statement, "As dance administrator, I have been able to maintain a healthy work–life balance," participants reported strongly agree (3 percent), agree (31 percent), disagree (42 percent), and strongly disagree (24 percent). There were no significant gender differences, though males (50 percent) reported disagree more frequently

Table 9.8. Participant Responses by Gender, Ability to Maintain Teaching
"As a dance administrator, I have been able to maintain my teaching effectiveness and pedagogical expertise."

	% Female	% Male	% All
Strongly agree	24	22	24
Agree	66	34	58
Disagree	8	33	14
Strongly disagree	2	11	4

Table 9.9. Participant Responses by Gender, Perception of Others

"As a dance administrator, I am confident that my gender does not affect the way my work, approach, leadership, or decision making is perceived by others."

	% Female	% Male	% All
Strongly agree	11	24	14
Agree	34	41	36
Disagree	49	35	46
Strongly disagree	6	0	4

than females (40 percent). The final survey item of this series asked participants to respond to the statement, "As dance administrator, I am confident that my gender does not affect the way my work, approach, leadership, or decision making is perceived by others" (see table 9.9). Significant gender asymmetries were found: male participants were more than twice as likely as females to strongly agree, while the majority of females (55 percent) reported disagree or strongly disagree compared to males (35 percent) for the same combination.

Finally, in terms of overall satisfaction with their work as dance administrators, participants reported highly satisfied (16 percent), satisfied (41 percent), somewhat satisfied (32 percent), dissatisfied (11 percent), and highly dissatisfied (0 percent). Gender differences were found for participants who were somewhat satisfied (males 39 percent, females 30 percent) and dissatisfied (females 13 percent, males 5 percent).

Highlights and Questions

Gender differences among male and female respondents regarding teaching effectiveness and pedagogical expertise warrant discussion with particular attention to why dance administrators feel their pedagogy either remains strong or suffers. Given that males in the study were more likely to be department chairs while females were more likely to be area heads or coordinators, the disparity is likely related to the position: department chairs normally teach fewer classes and have less time to hone and sharpen their pedagogical skills. This assumption correlates with section 3.2, where males reported spending slightly more time on administrative duties while females spent more time teaching.

Work-life balance also raises questions, with 66 percent of respondents reporting the inability to maintain work-life balance. What specific mechanisms or structures contribute to the imbalance? Do singles, couples, and parents feel equally accountable to maintain balance? How do family and child-rearing responsibilities influence perceptions of work-life balance?

Finally, the considerable gap between male-female responses, with 55 percent of females indicating that their gender impacts how their work is perceived by others, warrants further inquiry. In what specific settings does gender seem to play most prominently?

Open-Ended Responses: Most Meaningful, Least Gratifying Work

The survey concluded with open-ended questions that asked participants to share their responses to the following questions: (1) What is most meaningful to you about your work as dance administrator? (2) What is least gratifying to you in your work as dance administrator? For the purposes of this study, we present this open-ended qualitative data by gender.

Female participants found meaning in their work as administrators primarily in the value and worth of dance itself, followed closely by meaningful experiences with dance faculty and students, especially their development. Female administrators also discussed the overarching importance of their dance programs, highlighting enjoyment, learning, and future directions. Like their female counterparts, male participants located meaningfulness in faculty and student opportunities, development, and achievement. However, males also cited the creative aspects of dance, the importance of education and its value, and creating positive and supportive environments.

With regard to the least gratifying aspects of participants' work as dance administrators, males focused on difficulties with upper administration, management, and bureaucracy—especially the lack of understanding of the arts in higher education. Mediating faculty conflicts was also a source of frustration. Females described the least gratifying aspects of their work primarily in administration—"endless" reporting, justifying, and defending the dance program. Lack of support for the dance unit at all levels (secretarial/clerical, professional, production) was also reported as a source of frustration. Somewhat similar to males, negotiating faculty management and evaluation (disharmony, negative evaluations, and professionalism) figured prominently for female administrators.

While the most meaningful and least gratifying aspects of dance administrators' work contain many similarities among male and female respondents, the most pervasive gender difference in open-ended responses mirrors data in previous sections: females' perceived lack of support at all levels contrasts starkly with their male counterparts. This disparity, whether perceived or real, demands further study and unpacking: why do female dance administrators perceive or receive less support than their male counterparts?

Open-Ended Responses: Increasing Male Leadership

The final open-ended survey question asked participants to respond to recent gender data from NASD-accredited institutions, which indicate a significant gender shift occurring in postsecondary dance executive positions, with males increasingly assuming leadership roles. Since 2011 male leadership has increased over 10 percent, and now men comprise over 42 percent of dance executive positions. At the same time, the dominant population of female students in postsecondary dance maintains its stable majority at 86 percent of all dance students. The survey prompt asked participants, "As a current dance executive and from your experience, what are your thoughts on this shift?"

Male Reponses

A number of men addressed the shift by indicating they don't see a dance administrator's gender as important, as a male dance department director asserted, "I think genderless. The right person should do the job." A chair of a department of theater and dance suggested, "It seems to me that effective leadership is effective leadership. Also, often those of us in this position are the only ones willing to do the job." Similarly, a department chair of dance noted, "Oddly enough, I currently have a faculty that is much heavier in male teachers than in female teachers. Perhaps because this is a ballet program and historically it has been a discipline dominated by men. This is not a subject that ever comes to mind. I just don't think about gender at all."

Some male responses attempted to explain the gender shift in dance administration, as the following narratives illustrate:

> There may be a default setting internalized by men that success means advancing along a path or ladder. In turn, there may be a default setting/prejudice, still in society that men are better suited

to leadership. In any case there is something here about roles that society bestows out of long-held habit based on long held perceptions and prejudices. I have the perception that higher-education dance programs exist primarily because of women who started them, persevered against administrative prejudices and prevailed even though not part of the "old boys' network."

Associate Chair, Department of Theater and Dance

Everything to do with gender in dance is unfair, and I say that as a male. I feel it is [due to] the greater support and opportunity afforded a larger percentage of men in the dance field at large. Those opportunities often lead to opportunities in administration and elsewhere. For some faculty searches, depending on area of specialization, we have seen a slightly larger pool of qualified men than women, (qualified mainly meaning that they have had greater life/professional opportunity). I have actually tried to hire women over men [because] of the disproportionate representation of the sexes between the faculty and student body, and been met with opposition by the female faculty.

Chair, Department of Dance

A few males saw the shift as a positive direction for dance leadership, as a dance area head in a department of theater and dance expressed, "I hope that more men continue to take up such positions in dance education. It is important for future male dancers to see that there is a continued path for their careers in dance. It also serves as an example that dance is not a feminine profession and art form." Some male participants tethered their responses to the need for increasing the number of male dancers:

> More research should be encouraged for including positive male role models to students in PreK–12 settings so that majoring in dance is a more viable option.
>
> Dance Area Head, Department of Communication and Theater Arts

> Boys need to be encouraged to dance—or rather, not discouraged from dancing. Redefine masculinity. Certainly we are up against the influence of materialism and money-accumulation with living a meaningful life. And conformity. Girls dance, boys don't.
>
> Associate Chair, Department of Theater and Dance

A few male participants responded more anecdotally, offering insights into their own experience, as a school of dance chair indicated: "I have found that a higher percentage of men are willing to accept leadership roles in dance higher education." Another dance chair participant stated, "I have always preferred to work for women in this field (though I am male)" and a dance program coordinator clarified "As a male in this position, I am here because duty called, not as a reflection of any trends."

Highlights and Questions

These responses raise and reinforce a familiar dichotomy within the dance discipline: the simultaneous need and desire for more male students in the discipline along with male role models to serve them—and the prevalence of female students who deserve successful female role models. Male respondents seem to recognize overwhelmingly the dichotomy, though not all indicate the imbalance within the male to female ratio as problematic. Though prevailing societal attitudes about gender are acknowledged as possible reasons for the gender disparity in dance higher education leadership, responses also offer evidence that gender is not an issue that males often think about. Why might gender be invisible to these participants?

Female Responses

Many female participants found the gender shift in dance administration to be problematic on a number of levels, as one program director in a department of performing arts asserted, "I find this disturbing. There is a lack of leadership of women in academia in general. Dance should be the leader in promoting women since we are the majority of the field." Another female department chair noted, "It is unfortunate. I think it is important for the overwhelming number of female students in these programs to have female role models." Others focused on leadership competence and effectiveness, and male dominance:

> I believe it is best to maintain strong leadership of competent and well equipped women in postsecondary dance executive dance positions.
>
> Head, Department of Dance

> In my experience, males are least able to be effective administrators. My strongest role models have always been women.
>
> Head, Department of Music and Dance

It is echoed in my program. Unfortunately, this exists within the larger department of theater and dance that is extremely male-dominated; only one play in the last twenty seasons has been directed by a woman. Male faculty members dominate the programs, though the female faculty are the ones doing the more difficult work in curriculum planning and assessment. As a new female faculty member, the larger landscape does not look encouraging.

Dance Area Head, Department of Theater and Dance

I find the trend uncomfortable. If it were balanced by a greater percentage of men in the student ranks, I would not be so dismayed. This trend may also reflect an even more entrenched cultural ideology that places the female on display and well-paid man in power.

Chair, Department of Dance

Some female participants linked gender inequity with race disparities in the field, as an associate chair in a department of dance stated, "This is disturbing. I have also read about a decline in diversity. It echoes the field, where the majority of dance presenters are white men, and the majority of artistic directors of companies that are presented are also white men. I have heard presenters say that men make more interesting work." Another female participant, a school of dance director, noted "Problematic—moving from a matriarchal-based history to one that is patriarchal—from college and university presidents to dance program heads. White males dominate, as they do in larger society. There is also an imbalance of white female students when compared to black and brown students, and dance faculty for that matter."

A number of female participants responded with explanations for the gender shift in dance administration, as a dance program director suggested, "Women probably want to have children and decide to spend time with their families. Because this job requires so much time women are not finding the time justifies giving up on a family and/or possible health concerns due to stress?" Others focused on male experiences in postsecondary education, as one dance area head stated, "I feel like men are respected more by the upper administration in the institution and that may be part of the reason for the shift." Looking at the field more broadly, a department of dance director posited: "I think this trend is reflective of the role of males in the field of dance overall. As more men have joined the field as performers, choreographers, and artistic directors, it seems a natural shift that many of them would move into academia at some point in their careers as well. As many have come into academia with experience from directing their own organizations, similar to many women dance artists, it is logical these males would assume leadership roles in academia as well. My only concern is payment equity—we continue to see huge disparities in academia between female and male salaries." Other women addressed the shift cautiously. "I think it depends a great deal on the individual, more than gender," suggested a dance department chair, "However, I would hate to see this shift undermine the power of women in higher education dance." An assistant chair responded, "Does not make sense to me. My student population is overwhelmingly female," while a dance area head felt "uncertain—perhaps it's a natural shift as more men have worked their way up through the field?"

Unlike male participants, many females cited gender bias as the two following responses summarize:

> We need to look above the dance leader to leadership in the upper administration as men are automatically members of the 'good old boy' club, and women have to fight tooth and nail to stand up for the department and the needs of the students. The glass ceiling exists because men understand men and not women, so it's important to have equality from the top down.
>
> Head, Department of Dance

> The gender divide is alive and well. Studies need to be initiated that look at why we still hire on this basis. Usually opinion factors into the equation and professionals are reticent to fight for what they believe in. There is also the myth of men having a more rational basis for making decisions. They are just very competitive and do not like it when the door is not as open to them.
>
> Dance Program Director, Department of Dance

Some female participants viewed increasing numbers of male administrators as a positive direction for postsecondary dance. A department chair of theater and dance believed, "It is heresy, but I think it's good. Men prefer to work with men and I think this is good for dance. It's not good for women, but in an age where the business model runs and informs every attitude it can be good for dance. We are headed into a bad time, but this is what I see." A dance area head from a theater and dance department suggested, "We need more men in dance. I'm fine with men increasing leadership in dance." Another dance department chair suggested, "I think that it is good to have more male faculty and executives on faculty because often there are too many women. It offers a balance that is sometimes needed," but she was unsure of the overall impact, noting, "In terms of them dealing with the female student body, I am not sure how it will have an effect long term. Most of the men, frankly, are atypical men (how do I say this and not sound non-PC?) They might be more empathetic perhaps or be more sensitive to a woman's perspective."

Though far less frequently than male participants, a few females indicated that a dance administrator's gender was inconsequential, as one dance program director put it, "It doesn't matter to me who leads as long as they are effective." A department chair of theater and dance noted, "I have not been aware of this shift, as all of the dance executive positions in my geographic area are female. I am the head of a department of mostly male faculty, and it has not been a problem for me personally."

Highlights and Questions

Differences between female respondents and their male counterparts are strikingly evident in their attitudes about the gender shift in higher education dance leadership. Whereas males overwhelmingly welcomed the shift as a means to attract more male dancers to the discipline, many female respondents found the data troubling. Simultaneously acknowledging the need for more male role models within the discipline, female respondents also recognize the dichotomy that may necessarily exist within a discipline that is predominately populated by females. Possibly the most striking difference between male and female responses was an overwhelming female perception of gender bias in academe, whereas males were less likely to perceive gender bias as an issue. How does the invisibility of gender for males produce misperceptions of gender bias?

Further Thoughts

The purpose of this exploratory study was to develop a comprehensive status report of administrative leadership in postsecondary dance today with particular focus on gender and its role within leadership structures and practices. The study data reveal both expected and unpredicted outcomes regarding gender representation, equity, workplace issues, professional motivations, and career choices among leaders currently or recently serving within postsecondary dance education programs. The first empirical study of its kind conducted within the United States, this exploratory study uncovers and confirms the existence of long-standing issues within postsecondary dance and raises some new ones. At the same time, it would be imprudent to make sweeping generalizations or firm conclusions at this time. Instead, we revisit some primary themes and pose a number of questions for readers' contemplation—ones that we hope will inspire future research in this area.

Van Dyke (this volume), in her chapter "Dance in America: Gender and Success" offers a number of insights on gender differences in the professional dance realm. Some are applicable to postsecondary dance leadership: (1) girls in dance are socialized for obedience, perfection, and being heard but not seen, which often results in adult females who avoid risk taking and making mistakes (Stinson 1998a); (2) males overestimate their abilities and performances, "while women underestimate both, although performances do not differ in quality" (Van Dyke 1996, 538); and (3) females who realize that their success depends largely on male-dominated structures and practices may elect to take a different career path or direction.

This study's findings revealed additional gender differences and disparities among male and female participants. Carol Gilligan's (1982) contradiction of male-centric psychologies is useful in exploring the troubling chasm that separates male and female perceptions of support systems. Gilligan asserts that women's moral compasses and views of what is important in life lead them to prioritize care, relationships, and responsibility over justice, fairness, and rights, which put them consistently at odds with psychological developmental theories founded on male-centric behaviors. Given that women in higher education leadership continue to function within a male-centric administrative structure where they may sometimes feel shut out or lack a strong support system, Gilligan provides a potential model for better understanding gender differences in which she contrasts a feminine ethic of care with a masculine ethic of justice based on individual images of self. Em Griffin (1991) explains that Gilligan "realizes there are women who view moral questions in terms of justice, duty, and rights. There are also men who make moral decisions based on whether their actions help or harm the people involved. She merely sees two separate but noncompeting ways of thinking about moral problems. One is associated with men; the other is typical of women" (81). However, the stark contrast between male and female participants' perceptions regarding the influence of gender on how others perceive their work reinforces struggles that women encounter within male-centric environments, especially when males are not as inclined to think about gender. How might this gender blind spot develop for some male dance administrators?

Peggy McIntosh (2008), in addressing male privilege, notes men's unwillingness to acknowledge privilege "even though they may grant that women are disadvantaged." Further, she asserts that this behavior protects "male privilege from being fully recognized, acknowledged, lessened, or ended" (1988, 1). Defining privilege as "an invisible weightless knapsack of special provisions, assurances, tools, maps, guides, codebooks, passports, visas, clothes, compass, emergency gear, and blank checks," McIntosh believes that while "whites are carefully taught not to recognize white privilege, males are taught not to recognize male privilege"(1988, 1).

From the time they begin dance study, adolescent boys and young males confront a double bind situation of simultaneous privilege in the dance studio and marginalization in their larger social world. Boys in dance, unlike their male peers in athletics and team sports, are participating in an activity that already sheds social suspicion on their masculinity and heterosexuality (Risner 2009a). At the same time, dance teachers frequently emphasize the need to make boys and young men in dance "feel more comfortable" by inviting them to take leadership roles and to contribute ideas for movement, music, costumes, and choreographic theme. Doug Risner (2009a) asserts, "Over time this bias creates a paradox wherein men in dance are at once devalued by the culture, yet prized by the field" (27). This complexity requires close attention to the marginalization of male student dancers in a culturally feminized field, tempered with a full understanding of the privilege, benefit, and authority of being male in a patriarchal society and the dance world. Therefore, challenging the social status quo also involves a struggle to not make postsecondary dance merely another area in which males are privileged simply because their participation is rare. More to the point, how can we address young males' marginalization as dancers without reproducing traditional male privilege and its invisibility to many men?

At the same time and based on Risner's findings, Van Dyke (this volume) posits that, "Because of the challenges they face, perhaps most boys who make the decision to train for the dance profession are determined to make a success of it from the beginning. Or perhaps they are made resilient by the social stigma that usually accompanies such a decision. On the other hand, often they start training later than girls and it might be argued, do not absorb as much of what Risner calls the 'hidden curriculum' in traditional dance classes, teaching passivity and taking direction along with building strength and grace" (p. 34). Van Dyke's assertions may explain "trial and error" as the majority of male participants' (72 percent) most influential experiences in the development of their effectiveness as dance administrators, compared to 47 percent of females. Trial and error approaches promote taking risks and making mistakes, which females often avoid when socialized in dance for obedience and perfection (Stinson 1998a). In terms of postsecondary career progression, Kate Bahn (2014) notes, "Studies have shown that women generally apply only to those jobs for which they're totally qualified, whereas men tend to have no compunction about applying if they meet some, but not all, of a job's requirements. Women are less likely to tout [and cite] their own research and more likely to be saddled with excessive service commitments than men are, too" (14).

In closing, one gender assumption widely held by both female and male participants deserves further attention: postsecondary dance needs more male students. This hegemonic supposition—broadly accepted and rarely questioned—has fueled popular and scholarly discourses since the academic dance boom of the 1970s. Based largely on heterocentrism and influenced heavily by the professional dance world, the obsession for attracting and retaining male students, often at the expense of highly skilled females, may ultimately contribute significantly to the gender inequities and bias elaborated in this study. Even if we truly believe more male students would importantly benefit our academic dance programs, we must at some point ask, "How many is 'enough'?" And "what and who are we willing to sacrifice to achieve this goal?"

While the percentage of male faculty in postsecondary dance has remained relatively unchanged over the past two decades (37 percent in 1994; 34 percent in 2014), the number of male dance majors has steadily increased from 8 percent in 1994 to 14 percent in 2014—a 75 percent gain (HEADS 1994; HEADS 2014). Although research indicates that young males (age twelve to twenty-two) believe having more male faculty role models in dance is essential (Risner 2009a), it appears that the current 34 percent may be sufficient.

This exploratory study presents multiple opportunities for future research regarding lack of support structures among female administrators; how male and female administrator's strengths reflect what they value in leadership traits; and issues surrounding male privilege including disparities relating to academic credentials, salaries, and career advancement. Matters impacting both genders include the role of child rearing and family structures in tenure, advancement, and work-life balance, as well as the impact of increasing male leadership on both male and female students. Further inquiry on these and similar topics will help transport the discipline toward establishing a more informed—if not always level or balanced—playing field.

References

Aalten, A. 2005. In the presence of the body: Theorizing training, injuries and pain in ballet. *Dance Research Journal* 37(2): 55–72.

Acosta, N. Kickstarter website, "I shot Denzel" project funded Jan. 2014. https://www.kickstarter.com/projects/nivacosta/niv-acostas-world-premiere-of-i-shot-denzel.

Adair, C. 1992. *Women and dance: Sylphs and sirens.* New York: New York University Press.

Alksnis, C., S. Desmarais, and J. Curtis. 2008. Workforce segregation and the gender wage gap: Is women's work valued as highly as men's? *Journal of Applied Social Psychology* 38(6): 1416–1441.

Allegranti, B. 2011. *Embodied performances: Sexuality, gender, bodies.* New York: Palgrave Macmillan.

Allen, G. 2005. Is the art market rational or biased? *New York Times*, May 1.

Allport, G. 1954. *The Nature of Prejudice.* Massachusetts: Addison-Wesley.

Alterowitz, G. 2014. Embodying a queer worldview: The contemporary ballets of Katy Pyle and Deborah Lohse. *Dance Chronicle* 37(3): 335–366.

Alvin Ailey American Dance Theater website. Alvin Ailey American Dance Theater. Accessed December 7, 2014. http://www.alvinailey.org/about/company/alvin-ailey-american-dance-theater.

American Association of University Women. 2015. Economic justice report: The simple truth about the gender pay gap. http://www.aauw.org/research/the-simple-truth-about-the-gender-pay-gap/

American Dance Festival. 2012–2014. Festival season programs. *ADF Archive.* www.americandancefestival.org.

American Dance Festival website. Six Week school. Accessed December 11, 2014. http://www.americandancefestival.org/education/school/2015-school-summer-home-draft/2015-school-6ws-main-draft/2015-school-6ws-faculty-and-musicians-draft/.

Anderson, E. 2005. Orthodox and inclusive masculinity: Competing masculinities among heterosexual men in a feminized terrain. *Sociological Perspectives* 48(3): 337–355.

———. 2008. Being masculine is not about who you sleep with . . . : Heterosexual athletes contesting masculinity and the one-time rule of homosexuality. *Sex Roles* 58: 104–115.

Anderson, J. 1987. *The American Dance Festival.* Durham, NC: Duke University Press.

———. 1997. *Art without boundaries: The world of modern dance.* Iowa City: University of Iowa Press.

Angus, K. 2010. Dancing caricatures: Race and gender in ballroom dancing. MA thesis, York University, Canada. Abstract in ProQuest, UMI Dissertations Publishing, publ. nr. MR68285, 2010.

Arkin, L. 1994. Dancing the body: Women and dance performance. *Journal of Physical Education, Recreation and Dance* 65(2): 36–43.

Ashby, R., and D. Ohrn, eds. 1995. *Herstory: Women who changed the world*. New York: Viking Press.

Atencio, M. 2008. "Freaky is just how I get down": Investigating the fluidity of minority ethnic feminine subjectivities in dance. *Leisure Studies* 27(3): 311–327.

Atencio, M., and J. Wright. 2009. Ballet it's too whitey: discursive hierarchies of high school dance spaces and the constitution of embodied feminine subjectivities. *Gender and Education* 21(1): 31–46.

Atkins, J. 2008. Setting the stage: Dance and gender in old-line New Orleans carnival balls, 1870–1920. PhD diss., Florida State University. Abstract in ProQuest, UMI Dissertations Publishing, publ. nr. 3321453.

Bahn, K. 2014. Faking it: Women, academia, and impostor syndrome. *The Chronicle of Higher Education*, December 12.

Bailey, M. 2013. *Butch queens up in pumps: Gender, performance, and ballroom culture in Detroit*. Ann Arbor: University of Michigan Press.

Banes, S. 1998. *Dancing women: Female bodies on stage*. London: Routledge.

Barash, J., and J. Lipton. 2002. *Gender gap: The biology of male-female differences*. Piscataway, NJ: Transaction Publishers.

Barr, S., and D. Risner. 2014. Weaving social foundations through dance pedagogy: A pedagogy of uncovering. *Journal of Dance Education* 14(4): 136–145.

Bauerlein, M., and E. Grantham, eds. 2009. *National Endowment for the Arts: A history 1965–2008*. Washington, D.C.: NEA.

Beauvoir, S. de. [1949] 2010. *The second sex*. Translated by C. Borde and S. Malovaney-Chevallier. New York: Alfred A. Knopf.

Bentham, J. [1787] 1995. *The panopticon writings*. Introduced and edited by M. Bozovic. New York: Verso.

Berger, A. 2003. Dance and masculinity: Shifting social constructions of gender. MA thesis, Boston College. Abstract in ProQuest, UMI Dissertations Publishing, publ. nr. 1419014, 2003.

Bergman, S. J. 1991. Men's psychological development: A relational perspective. Wellesley, MA: Stone Center, Wellesley College 1–14.

Bindler, N. 2014. Ugly numbers part I: Just the facts. *Thinking Dance,* September 3. http://thinkingdance.net/articles/2014/09/03/Ugly-Numbers-Part-I-Just-the-Facts.

Blume, L. B. 2003. Embodied [by] dance: Adolescent de/constructions of body, sex and gender in physical education. *Sex Education* 3(2): 95–103.

Boccadoro, P. 2006. The best and worst of Maurice Bejart. http://www.culturekiosque.com/dance/reviews/maurice_bejart.html.

Bond, K. 1994. How "wild things" tamed gender distinctions. *Journal of Physical Education, Recreation and Dance* 65(2): 28–33.

———. 1999. Perspectives on dance therapy: The lived experience of children. In *Dance therapy collections II*, edited by J. Guthrie, E. Loughlin, and D. Albiston, 1–7. Melbourne: Dance Therapy Association of Australia.

———. 2013. Recurrence and renewal: Enduring themes in children's dance. In *Revisiting Impulse: A contemporary look at writings on dance, 1950–1970*, edited by T. Hagood and L. Kahlich, 61–91. Youngstown, NY: Cambria Press.

Bond, K., and E. Gerdes. 2012. Student performance in a dance-based humanities course at "Diversity U." In *Dance, young people and change: Proceedings of the World Dance Alliance/Dance and the Child International Conference*, edited by S. W. Stinson, S-Y. Liu, and C. S. Nielsen. http://www.worlddancealliance.net/Publications.html.

Bond, K., and S. Stinson. 2001. "I feel like I'm going to take off!": Young people's experiences of the superordinary in dance. *Dance Research Journal* 32(2): 52–87.

Bordo, S. 1993. *Unbearable weight: Feminism, western culture, and the body*. Berkeley: University of California Press.

Bradford, G., M. Gary, and G. Wallach, eds. 2000. *The politics of culture*. New York: The New Press.

Brooklyn Academy of Music. www.brooklynacademyofmusic.org.

Brooklyn Academy of Music. 2012–2014. Season Programs. *BAM Archive*.

Broomfield, M. A. 2011. Policing masculinity and dance reality television: What gender nonconformity can teach us in the classroom. *Journal of Dance Education* 11(4): 124–128.

Brustein, R. 2000. Coercive philanthropy. In *The politics of culture*, edited by G. Bradford, M. Gary, and G. Wallace, 218–225. New York: New Press.

Bryant, R. 2003. Shaking big shoulders: Music and dance culture in Chicago, 1910–1925. PhD diss., Univ. of Illinois at Urbana-Champaign. Abstract in ProQuest, UMI Dissertations Publishing, publ. nr. 3086023, 2003.

Burt, R. [1995] 2007. *The male dancer: Bodies, spectacle, sexualities*. London: Routledge.

———. 2001. The trouble with the male dancer. In *Moving history/dance cultures: A dance history reader*, edited by A. Dils and A. C. Albright, 44–55. Middletown, CT: Wesleyan University Press.

Butler, J. [1990] 1999. *Gender trouble: Feminism and the subversion of identity*. New York: Routledge.

———. 2004. *Undoing gender*. New York: Routledge.

Butler, S., R. Mocarski, B. Emmons, and R. Smallwood. 2014. Leaving it on the pitch: Hope Solo's negotiation of conflicting gender roles on *Dancing with the Stars*. *Journal of Gender Studies* 23(4): 362–375.

Campbell, M. S. 2000. A new mission for the NEA. In *The politics of culture*, edited by G. Bradford, M. Gary, and G. Wallach, 141–146. New York: New Press.

Capezio Dance Foundation website. Brief history, aims, and objectives. Accessed December 6, 2014. http://www.capezio.com/spotlight/the-capezio-dance-foundation/.

Carter, R. 2004. When will we dance in French? Jazz, gender, and dancing French identity in the "Annees Folles." PhD diss., Purdue University. Abstract in ProQuest, UMI Dissertations Publishing, publ. nr. 3166601, 2004.

Casey, C. 2009. Ballet's feminisms: Genealogy and gender in twentieth-century American ballet history. PhD diss., University of California, Berkeley. Abstract in ProQuest, UMI Dissertations Publishing, publ. nr. 3411215, 2009.

Casey, K. 2010. Cross-dressers and race-crossers: Intersections of gender and race in American Vaudeville, 1990–1930. PhD diss., University of Rochester. Abstract in ProQuest, UMI Dissertations Publishing, publ. nr. 3430979, 2010.

Cash, T. 2012. *Encyclopedia of body image and human appearance.* Philadelphia: Elsevier Science.

Chambliss, D. F. 2012. *Making sense of the social world: Methods of investigation.* Thousand Oaks, CA: Sage.

Chatterjea, A. 2004. *Butting out: Reading resistive choreographies through works by Jawole Willa Jo Zollar and Chandralekha.* Middletown, CT: Wesleyan University Press.

Christ, S. 2010. Matchines dancers in the Midwest: Religion, gender and Mexican-American identity. MA thesis, University of Central Missouri. Abstract in ProQuest, UMI Dissertations Publishing, publ. nr. 1486565, 2010.

Chu, J. Y. 2005. Adolescent boys' friendships and peer group culture. *New Directions for Child and Adolescent Development* 107:7–22.

Clark, D. 1994. Voices of women dance educators: Considering issues of hegemony and the education/performer identity. *Impulse* 2(2): 122–130.

Cohen, S. J., et al., eds. 2005. *The international encyclopedia of dance.* Pas de deux. http://www.oxfordreference.com/view/10.1093/acref/9780195173697.001.0001/acref-9780195173697.

Collins, K. D. 2009. Separate but equal? *Dance Teacher* 31(4): 36–40.

Connell, R. W. 2002. *Gender.* Cambridge, UK: Polity Press.

———. 2005. *Masculinities.* Berkeley and Los Angeles: University of California Press.

———. 2006. The big picture: Masculinities in recent world history. In *The Routledge-Falmer reader in gender and education,* edited by M. Arnot and M. Mac an Ghaill, 101–114. New York: Routledge.

Cook, J., and G. Cook. 2009. *Child development principles and perspectives.* Boston: Allyn & Bacon.

Copeland, R. 1993. Dance, feminism and the critique of the visual. In *Dance, gender and culture,* edited by Helen Thomas, 139–150. London: Macmillan.

Corbin, J., and A. Strauss. 2007. *Basics of qualitative research: Techniques and procedures for developing grounded theory.* 3rd ed. Thousand Oaks, CA: Sage.

Craig, M. L. 2014. *Sorry I don't dance: Why men refuse to move.* Oxford and New York: Oxford University Press.

Crawford, J. R. 1994. Encouraging male participation in dance. *Journal of Physical Education, Recreation and Dance* 65(2): 40–43.

Creswell, J. W. 2009, 2014. *Research design: Qualitative, quantitative, and mixed method approaches.* Thousand Oaks, CA: Sage.

———. 2013. *Qualitative inquiry and research design: Choosing among five approaches.* Thousand Oaks, CA: Sage.

Croft, C. 2014. Feminist dance criticism and ballet. *Dance Chronicle* 37(2): 195–217.

Curry, T. J. 1991. Fraternal bonding in the locker room: A profeminist analysis of talk about competition and women. *Sociology of Sport Journal* 8: 119–35.
Daly, A. 1987a. At issue: Gender in dance. *The Drama Review: TDR*, Summer, 22–26.
———. 1987b. Classical ballet: A discourse of difference. *Women and Performance—A Journal of Feminist Theory* 3(2): 57–66. doi: 10.1080/07407708708571104.
———. 1991. Unlimited partnership: Dance and feminist analysis. *Dance Research Journal* 23(1): 2–3.
———. 1994. Gender issues in dance history pedagogy. *Journal of Physical Education, Recreation and Dance* 65(2): 34–35, 39.
———. 2002. Classical ballet: A discourse of difference. *Critical gestures: Writings on dance and culture*. Middletown, CT: Wesleyan University Press, 288–292.
Dalzell, J. 2014. At a crossroads. *Dance Magazine*, February, 56.
Dance Magazine website. *Dance Magazine* Awards. Accessed February 12, 2015. http://dancemagazine.com/dance-magazine-awards.
Dance Moms. 2011. Produced by Collins Avenue Productions. Distributed by Lifetime Television.
Dempster, E. 2010. Women writing the body: Let's watch a little how she dances. In *Moving history/dance cultures: A dance history reader*, edited by A. Dils and A. C. Albright, 229–235. Middletown, CT: Wesleyan University Press.
Denzin, N., and Y. Lincoln. 2011. Discipline and practice of qualitative research. In *The Sage handbook of qualitative research*, edited by N. Denzin and Y. Lincoln, 1–19. Thousand Oaks, CA: Sage.
Desmond, J. 2001. *Dancing desires: Choreographing sexualities on and off stage*. Madison: University of Wisconsin Press.
Dictionary.com. 2015. Replication. *Dictionary.com Unabridged*. Random House.
Dorsey, S. Sean Dorsey Dance Company website. http://www.seandorseydance.com/
Dowd, M. 2005. *Are men necessary? When sexes collide*. New York: G. P. Putnam's Sons.
Downey, D. J., J. J. Reel, S. Soohoo, and S. Zerbib. 2010. Body image in belly dance: Integrating alternative norms into collective identity. *Journal of Gender* 19(4): 377–393.
Drummond, Kent G. 2003. The queering of Swan Lake: A new male gaze for the performance of sexual desire. *Journal of Homosexuality* 45(2–4): 235–255.
Duerden, R., and B. Rowell. 2013. Mark Morris' Dido and Aneas (1989): A critical postmodern sensibility. *Dance Chronicle* 36(2): 143–171.
Dunning, J. Dance notes: Modern field out of balance. *New York Times*, September 3, 2001.
———. Has dance evolved into a man's world? *New York Times*, June 25, 2004.
Edmonds, W. A., and T. D. Kennedy. 2013. *An applied reference guide to research designs: Quantitative, qualitative, and mixed methods*. Thousand Oaks, CA: Sage.
Ellis, H. 1923. *The dance of life*. Boston: Houghton Mifflin.
Engel, L. 2001. Body poetics of hip hop dance styles in Copenhagen. *Dance Chronicle* 24(3): 351–372.
Erickson, F. 2005. Arts, humanities, and sciences in educational research and social engineering in federal education policy. *Teachers College Record* 107(1):4–9.

Etnyre, B., and E. Lee. 1988. Chronic and acute flexibility of men and women using three different stretching techniques. *Research Quarterly for Exercise and Sport* 59(3): 222–228.

Felmlee, D., E. Sweet, and H. C. Sinclair. 2012. Gender rules: Same and cross-gender friendship norms. *Sex Roles* 66: 518–29.

Ferdun, E. 1994. Facing gender issues across the curriculum. *Journal of Physical Education, Recreation and Dance* 65(2):46–47.

Feuer, J. 2001. A mistress never a master? In *Dancing desires: Choreographing sexualities on and off stage*, edited by J. Desmond, 385–390. Madison: University of Wisconsin Press,

Fichter, S. N. 2002. The quest for center: Creating a culture for learning in a corporate world. *Arts Education Policy Review* 103(5):3–7.

Fine, C. 2010. *Delusions of gender: How our minds, society and neurosexism created difference*. New York: W. W. Norton.

Fisher, J. 2007. Tulle as tool: Embracing the conflict of the ballerinas as powerhouse. *Dance Research Journal* 39(1): 3–24.

———. 2009. Maverick men in ballet: Rethinking the making it macho strategy. In *When men dance: Choreographing masculinities across borders*, edited by J. Fisher and A. Shay, 31–54. Oxford: Oxford University Press.

Fisher, J., and A. Shay, eds. 2009. *When men dance: Choreographing masculinities across borders*. New York: Oxford University Press.

Fonda, J. Gender and destiny. *Studies in Gender and Sexuality* 10:190–194.

Foster, S. L. 1997. Dancing bodies. In *Meaning in motion: New cultural studies of dance*, edited by J. Desmond, 235–258. Durham, NC: Duke University Press.

———. 2013. Performing authenticity and the gendered labor of dance. In *Choreographie, medien, gender*, edited by Y. Hardt, L. Angerer, and A. Weber, 125–138. Zurich: Diaphanes.

———. 1998. Choreographies of gender. *Signs* 24(1): 1–33.

Foucault, M. 1979. *Discipline and punish: The birth of the prison*. New York: Vintage.

———. 1990. *The history of sexuality*. New York: Vintage.

Fraleigh, S. 2004. *Dancing identity: Metaphysics in motion*. Pittsburgh, PA: University of Pittsburgh Press.

Frichtel, J. 2012. Freedom, transformation, and community: Student meanings of engagement in a dance-based general education course. PhD diss., Temple University.

Friedler, S. E., and S. B. Glazer. 1997. *Dancing female: Lives and issues of women in contemporary dance*. Amsterdam, The Netherlands: Harwood Academic Publishers.

Friedman, A. 2013. *Blind to sameness: Sexpectations and the social construction of male and female bodies*. Chicago: University of Chicago Press.

Galupo, M. P., and K. A. Gonzalez. 2012. Friendship values and cross-category friendships: Understanding adult friendship patterns across gender, sexual orientation and race. *Sex Roles* 68: 779–90.

Gaquin, D. 2008. *Artists in the workforce, 1990–2005*. Washington, DC: National Endowment for the Arts. PDF e-book.

Garber, E., R. Sandell, M. Stankiewicz, and D. Risner. 2007. Gender equity in the visual arts and dance education. In *Handbook for achieving gender equity through education,* edited by S. Klein, 359–380. Mahwah, NJ: Lawrence Erlbaum Associates.

Gard, M. 2001. Dancing around the problem of boys who dance. *Discourse: Studies in the Cultural Politics of Education* 22(2): 213–225.

———. 2003a. Being someone else: Using dance in anti-oppressive teaching. *Educational Review* 55(2): 211–223.

———. 2003b. Moving and belonging: Dance, sport and sexuality. *Sex Education* 3(2): 105–118.

———. 2006. *Men who dance: Aesthetics, athletics and the art of masculinity.* New York: Peter Lang.

———. 2008. When a boy's gotta dance: New masculinities, old pleasures. *Sport, Education and Society* 13(2): 181–193.

Gilligan, C. 1982. *In a different voice: Psychological theory and women's development.* Cambridge, MA: Harvard University Press.

Golden, K. 1994. What do girls see? *Ms. Magazine,* April 1994, 52–61.

Gowaty, P., ed. 1997. *Feminism and evolutionary biology.* New York: Chapman & Hall.

Green, J. 1999. Somatic authority and the myth of the ideal body in dance education. *Dance Research Journal* 31(2): 80–100.

———. 2000. Emancipatory pedagogy? Women's bodies and the creative process in dance. *Frontiers* 21(3): 124–140.

———. 2001. Socially constructed bodies in American dance classrooms. *Research in Dance Education* 2(2): 155–173.

———. 2002–2003. Foucault and the training of docile bodies in dance education. *Arts and Learning* 19(1): 99–126.

———. 2004. The politics and ethics of health in dance education in the United States. In *Ethics and politics embodied in dance,* edited by E. Anttila, S. Hamalainen, and L. Rouhianen, 65–76. Helsinki, Finland: Theatre Academy of Finland.

Griffin, E. 1991. A different voice of Carol Gilligan. In *A first look at communication theory,* edited by E. Griffin, 81–91. New York: McGraw-Hill.

Grigoriou, T. 2004. Friendship between gay men and heterosexual women: An interpretative phenomenological analysis. MSc diss., London South Bank University.

Guarino, L. 2014. Jazz dance training via private studios, competitions, and conventions. In *Jazz dance: A history of the roots and branches,* edited by L. Guarino and W. Oliver, 197–206. Gainesville: University Press of Florida.

Guggenheim (John Simon) Memorial Foundation website. About the fellowship. Accessed December 7, 2014. http://www.gf.org/about-the-foundation/the-fellowship/.

Guo, J. 2014. Establishing male choreographers' artistic identity in early modern dance. MFA thesis, Mills College. Abstract in ProQuest, UMI Dissertations Publishing, publ. nr. 1557476, 2014.

Hagood, T. 2000. *History of Dance in American higher education.* Lewiston, NY: Edwin Mellen Press.

Hanna, J. L. 1987. Patterns of dominance: Men, women, and homosexuality in dance. *The Drama Review: TDR* 31(1): 22–47.

———. 1988. *Dance, sex, and gender: Signs of identity, dominance, defiance, and desire.* Chicago: University of Chicago Press.

Harris, A. 2012. Gendered discourses in American ballet at mid-century: Ruth Page on the periphery. *Dance Chronicle* 35(1): 30–53.

Hart, A. 2014. Queering choreographic conventions: Concert dance as a site for engaging in gender and sexual identity politics. MFA thesis, California State University, Long Beach. Abstract in ProQuest, UMI Dissertations Publishing, publ. nr. 1527949, 2014.

Haseman, B., and D. Mafe. Acquiring know-how: Research training for practice-led researchers. In *Practice-led research, research-led practice in the creative arts*, edited by R. T. Dean and H. Smith, 211–228. Edinburgh: Edinburgh University Press. http://qut.eblib.com.au.ezp01.library.qut.edu.au/patron/FullRecord.aspx?p=475756. Accessed 12 May 2013.

Heiland, T., D. Murray, and P. Edley. 2008. Body image of dancers in LA: The cult of slenderness and media influence among dance students. *Research in Dance Education* 9(3): 257–275.

Heilbrun, J., and C. M. Gray, eds. 2001. *The Economics of art and culture.* 2nd ed. Cambridge, UK: Cambridge University Press.

Higher Education Arts Data Services. 1994. *Dance data summaries 1993–1994.* Reston, VA: Author.

———. 2004. *Dance data summaries 2003–2004.* Reston, VA: Author.

———. 2011. *Dance data summaries 2010–2011.* Reston, VA: Author.

———. 2014. *Dance data summaries 2013–2014.* Reston, VA: Author.

Hildebrand, K., ed. 2014. *Dance Teacher.* October.

Hochman, D. 2014. A vote of confidence for her stance. *New York Times*, September 21. http://www.nytimes.com/2014/09/21/fashion/amy-cuddy-takes-a-stand-TED-talk.html?_r=0.

Holdsworth, N. 2013. Boys don't do dance, do they? *Research in Drama Education: Journal of Applied Theatre and Performance* 18(2): 168–178.

hooks, b. 1994. *Teaching to transgress: Education as the practice of freedom.* New York: Routledge.

Horn, S. 2004. Mean girls or cultural stereotypes? *Human Development* 47(5): 314–320.

Horwitz, C. 1995. Challenging dominant gender ideology through dance: Contact improvisation. PhD diss., University of Iowa. *Dissertation Abstracts International* 56(6), 2023.

Hubbard Street Dance Chicago website. Meet the dancers. Accessed December 10, 2014. http://www.hubbardstreetdance.com/dancers.

Huizinga, J. [1949] 1955. *Homo ludens: A study of the play-element in culture.* Boston: Beacon Press.

Ireland, R. 2009. Choreographing theory: An analysis of Edouard Lock's *Amelia* (2002) questioning the limits of feminist and poststructuralist perspectives. *Research in Dance Education* 10(1): 49–61.

Jacobson, T., ed. 2011. *Perspectives on gender in early childhood.* St. Paul, MN: Redleaf Press.

Jacob's Pillow Dance. 2012–2014. Festival season programs. *Jacob's Pillow Archive.* www.jacobspillow.org.

Jennings, L. 2013. Sexism in dance: Where are all the female choreographers? *Guardian*, April 28, 2013. http://www.theguardian.com/stage/2013/apr/28/women-choreographers-glass-ceiling.
———. 2014. Put two and two together for raw, sexual curiosity: 4D. *Observer*, June 29, 34.
Jensen, I., S. Heymsfield, Z. Wang, and R. Ross. 2000. Skeletal muscle mass and distribution in 468 men and women aged 18–88 years. *Journal of Applied Physiology* 89(1):81–88.
JoAnna Mendl Shaw: The Gender Project. 2004. *New York Foundation for the Arts Quarterly*, Summer, http://www.nyfa.org/level4.asp?id=320&fid=1&sid=5&tid=172.
Johnson, C. 2014. *Physical manifestation of ascent*. YouTube video, posted Jun 12, 2014. Accessed February 15, 2015. https://www.youtube.com/watch?v=bqIuCYccjhg.
Johnson, R., A. Onwuegbuzie, and L. Turner. 2007. Toward a definition of mixed methods research. *Journal of Mixed Methods Research* 1(2):112–133.
Jordan, S., and H. Thomas 2010. Dance and gender: Formalism and semiotics reconsidered. In *Routledge dance studies reader*, edited by A. Carter and J. O'Shea, 149–157. 2nd ed. London: Routledge
Jowitt, D. 2010. Dancing masculinity: Defining the male image onstage in twentieth-C America and beyond. *Southwest Review* 95:228–242.
Judith Butler: Philosophical encounters of the third kind. Directed by P. Zjadermann. 2006. Brooklyn, NY: First Run/Icarus Films.
Kahlich, L. 2001. Gender and dance education. *Journal of Dance Education* 1(2): 45–47.
———. 2011. Dancing deans: Dance educators move into the executive ranks. *Journal of Dance Education* 11(3):90–99.
Karthas, I. 2006. Nation, modernism, gender and the cultural politics of ballet. PhD diss., Brown University. Abstract in ProQuest, UMI Dissertations Publishing, publ. nr. 3227861, 2006.
Kay, K., and C. Shipman. 2014. The confidence gap. *The Atlantic*, May. Accessed January 6, 2015. http://www.theatlantic.com/features/archive/2014/04/the-confidence-gap/359815/.
Kealiinohomoku, J. 1976. Theories and methods for an anthropological study of dance. PhD diss., University of Indiana.
———. 1983. An anthropologist looks at ballet as a form of ethnic dance. In *What is dance?*, edited by R. Copeland and M. Cohen, 533–549. Oxford: Oxford University Press.
Keefe, M. 2009. Is dance a man's sport too? The performance of athletic-coded masculinity on the concert dance stage. In *When men dance: Choreographing masculinities across borders*, edited by J. Fisher and A. Shay, 91–115. Oxford: Oxford University Press.
Keersmaeker, A. T. de. 1984. *Elena's aria*. Performed Vienna, Volkstheatre: Rosas. Performance: Dance (viewed 22 & 23 July, 2011).
Kelly, J., J. Laurito, and L. Byargeon. 2012. Dance workforce census: Earnings among individuals 21–35. *Dance/NYC Junior Committee*.

Kemmis, S., and M. Wilkinson. 1998. Participatory action research and the study of practice. In *Action research in practice: Partnerships for social justice in education*, edited by B. Atweh, S. Kemmis, and P. Weeks, 21–35. London and New York: Routledge.

Kennedy Center website. Kennedy honors history. Accessed May 4, 2015. http://www.kennedy-center.org/programs/specialevents/honors/history.cfm.

Kerr-Berry, J. 1994. Using the power of Western African dance to combat gender issues. *Journal of Physical Education, Recreation and Dance* 65(2): 44–45, 48.

Keyworth, S. A. 2001. Critical autobiography: "Straightening" out dance education. *Research in Dance Education*. 2(2): 117–137.

Killerman, S. 2013. *A guide to gender*. Austin, TX: Impetus.

Kinetz, E. 2005. Budding dancers compete, seriously. *New York Times* July 7. Accessed February 18, 2014. http://www.nytimes.com/2005/07/07/arts/dance/07danc.html?pagewanted=all&_r=1&.

King, A. 2008. In vivo coding. In *The SAGE encyclopedia of qualitative research methods*, edited by L. M. Given, 473–474. Thousand Oaks, CA: Sage. doi: 10.4135/9781412963909.n240

King, G., R. O. Keohane, and S. Verba. 1994. *Designing social inquiry: Scientific inference in qualitative research*. Princeton, NJ: Princeton University Press.

Kirby, J. 2013. If my son wanted to dance, I would kill myself. *Chicago Now,* August 1, 2013. http://www.chicagonow.com/cheaper-than-therapy/2013/08/

Koresh Dance Company website. Koresh Dance Company-Dancers. Accessed December 7, 2014. http://www.koreshdance.org/dancers.php.

Koritz, A. 1995. *Gendering bodies/performing art: Dance and literature in early twentieth-century British culture*. Ann Arbor: University of Michigan Press.

Kylian, J. 1981. *Jiri Kylian—Nomaden/Nomad*. YouTube video, posted May 4, 2013. Accessed February 24, 2015. https://www.youtube.com/watch?v=1dwIydJS3JE.

LaBoskey, S. 2001. Getting off: Portrayals of masculinity in hip hop dance in film. *Dance Research Journal* 33(2): 112–120.

Lang, J. Interview with Rachel Strauss. 2012. PillowTalk: Jessica Lang on creating a company. *Jacob's Pillow Archive*. July 27.

Lanier, C., and L. Byargeon. 2011. State of NYC dance: Who, what, where, how, and how much? *Dance NYC*.

Lansdale, J., ed. 2008. *Decentering dance texts: The challenge of interpreting dances*. Hampshire and New York: Palgrave Macmillan.

LaPointe-Crump, J. 2007. Competition and dance education. *Journal of Physical Education, Recreation, and Dance* 78(7): 4–5, 9.

LaRocco, C. 2012. Dance competitions for youngsters: Tap-tap-tapping into a national obsession. *New York Times* September 2. http://www.nytimes.com/2012/09/03/arts/dance/dance-competitions-for-youngsters.html.

Lee, A. 2014. The poetics of dance in nineteenth-century France: Transcribing movement, gender, and culture. PhD diss., Washington University. Abstract in ProQuest, UMI Dissertations Publishing, publ. nr. 3670321, 2014.

Lee, F. 2011. New report cites strong start-up culture of dance in the city. *New York Times,* November 15.

Lehikoinen, K. G. 2006. *Stepping queerly? Discourses in dance education for boys in late 20th century Finland*. Bern, Switzerland: Peter Lang.

Lehmert, A., and J. Killian. 2014. So you think you can hold political office? Join the club. *News and Record*, October 20, 2.

Letts, W., and C. Nobles. 2003. Embodied [by] curriculum: A critical pedagogy of embodiment. *Sex Education* 3(2): 91–94.

Li, Z. 2010. Adolescent male dancers' embodied realities. PhD diss., University of Toronto.

Lodge, M. J. 2001. Dancing up the broken ladder: The rise of the female director/choreographer in the American mU.S.ical theatre. PhD diss., Bowling Green State University. *Dissertation Abstracts International* 63(1), 29.

Looseleaf, Victoria. 2012. "Modern vs. Contemporary." *Dance Magazine* 86(12): 53-60. http://gateway.library.qut.edu.au/login?url=http://search.ebscohost.com/login.aspx?direct=true&db=afh&AN=83631869&site=ehost-live.

Lorber, J. 1994. *Paradoxes of gender*. New Haven, CT: Yale University Press.

MacArthur Foundation website. MacArthur fellows, dance and choreography. Accessed May 4, 2015.http://www.macfound.org/fellows/search/?area=dance.

Macaulay, A. 2010. For ballet, plots thicken, or just stick? *New York Times*, Aug 8, AR.4.

———. 2013a. Ballet choreographer's duets of disconnection. *International Herald Tribune*, June 5, 10.

———. 2013b. Changing dance in leaps and bounds: A new generation of American ballerinas sheds traditional image. *International Herald Tribune*, July 5, 10.

MacBeth, P., July 5, 1994. Personal communication.

Madison, S. D. 2012. *Critical ethnography: Method, ethics and performance, second edition*. Chapel Hill, NC: Sage.

Maggie Allesee National Center for Choreography website. Florida State University. Welcome to MANCC. Accessed December 11, 2014. http://mancc.org/.

Manning, S. 2006. *Ecstasy and the demon: The dances of Mary Wigman*. Minneapolis: University of Minnesota Press.

Marcotte, A. 2014. Best way for professors to get good student evaluations? Be male. *DoubleX* (blog), *Slate*. December 9. http://www.slate.com/blogs/xx_factor/2014/12/09/gender_bias_in_student_evaluations_professors_of_online_courses_who_present.html.

Marques, I. 1998. Dance education in/and the postmodern. In *Dance, power, and difference: Critical and feminist perspectives on dance education*, edited by S. Shapiro, 171–185. Champaign, IL: Human Kinetics.

Martha Graham Dance Company website. Company bios. Accessed December 7, 2014. http://marthagraham.org/the-martha-graham-dance-company/company-bios/#Brdnik.

McDougall, P., and S. Hymel. 2007. Same-gender versus cross-gender friendship conceptions: Similar or different? *Merrill-Palmer Quarterly* 53: 347–80.

McGreevy-Nichols, S., K. Ferris Lester, and M. Pfohl Smith. 2014. DANCE 2050: The future of dance in higher education. *Journal of Dance Education* 14(1): 41–42.

McGuire, L. 1999. The year of the angry young men: Performing gender at championship tap dance events. Master's thesis, York University. *Dissertation Abstracts International,* 38(3), 498.

McIntosh, P. 2008. White privilege: Unpacking the invisible knapsack. In *White privilege: Essential readings on the other side of racism,* edited by P. Rothenberg, 123–127. New York: Worth.

McKernan, M. 2002. Persistence and change in gender role-reversal phenomena in American social dancing. PhD diss., Boston University. Abstract in ProQuest, UMI Dissertations Publishing, publ. nr. 3037377, 2002.

McLean, A. 2008. *Dying swans and madmen: Ballet, the body, and narrative cinema.* New Brunswick, NJ: Rutgers University Press.

McMahon, T. 1999. Is reflective practice synonymous with actions research? *Educational Action Research* 7(1): 163–169.

McMains, J. 2003. Glamour lessons: Race, class, and gender in the American dancesport industry. PhD diss., University of California, Riverside.

McPherson, M., L. Smith-Lovin, and J. M. Cook. 2001. Birds of a feather: Homophily in social networks. *Annual Review of Sociology* 27: 415–44.

Mean Girls. 2004. Directed by Mark Waters. Produced by SNL Studios.

Meglin, J., and L. M. Brooks. 2012. Where are all the women choreographers in ballet? *Dance Chronicle* 35(1): 1–7.

Messner, M. 1987. The meaning of success: The athletic experience and the development of male identity. In *The making of masculinities: The new men's studies,* edited by H. Brod, 193–209. Boston: Allen & Unwin.

———. 1992a. Like family: Power, intimacy, and sexuality in male athletes' friendships. In *Men's friendships,* edited by P. M. Nardi, 215–237. Thousand Oaks, CA: Sage.

———. 1992b. *Power at play: Sports and the problem of masculinity.* Boston: Beacon Press.

———. 2002. *Taking the field: Men and women in sports.* Minnesota: University of Minnesota Press.

Midgelow, V. 2007. *Re-working the ballet: Counter narratives and alternative bodies.* London: Routledge.

Miller, J. B., and I. P. Stiver. 1997. *The healing connection: How women form relationships in therapy and life.* Boston: Beacon Press.

Moss, I., C. Blake, L. Harwell, and L. Byargeon. 2012. State of NYC dance: Discovering fiscally sponsored NYC dancemakers. *Dance/NYC.*

Mozingo, K. 2008. Crossing the borders of German and American modernism: Exile and transnationalism in the dance works of Valeska Gert, Lotte Goslar, and Pola Nirenska. PhD diss., The Ohio State University. Abstract in ProQuest, UMI Dissertations Publishing, publ. nr. 3375422, 2008.

Mulvey, L. 1975. Visual pleasure and narrative cinema. *Screen* 16(3): 6–18.

Munger, J. 2007. A census of New York City dancemakers. *Dance/NYC.*

Munson, L. 2000. *Exhibitionism.* Chicago: Ivan R. Dee.

Musil, P. 2010. Perspectives on an expansive postsecondary dance. *Journal of Dance Education* 10(4): 111–121.

Nardi, P. M. 1999. *Gay men's friendships: Invincible communities.* Chicago: University of Chicago Press.

National Assembly of State Arts Agencies. 2014. State arts agency legislative appropriations preview: Fiscal year 2015. *National Assembly of State Arts Agencies.* July 14. http://www.nasaa-arts.org/Research/Funding/NASAAFY2015SAALegAppropPreview.pdf.

National Endowment for the Arts. 2004. 2002 survey of public participation in the arts. Research Division Report, 45.

National Endowment for the Arts website, various articles below: 1987–2013 Annual Reports. *National Endowment for the Arts.* Accessed December 5, 2014. http://arts.gov/about/annual-reports.

———. About the NEA. Accessed December 14, 2014. http://arts.gov/about/national-council-arts.

———. National medal of arts. *National Endowment for the Arts and National Council on the Arts.* Accessed December 5, 2014. http://permanent.access.gpo.gov/lps76264/NEA_MOA_eBook.pdf.

———. Panelists. Accessed December 5, 2014. http://arts.gov/grants/recent/panelists.

———. Recent grant search. Accessed December 5, 2014. http://arts.gov/grants/recent-grants.

National Women's Law Center. Equal pay and the wage gap. Accessed January 6, 2015. http://www.nwlc.org/our-issues/employment/equal-pay-and-the-wage-gap.

Netzer, D., and E. Parker. 1993. *Dancemakers.* Washington, DC: National Endowment for the Arts.

Newstadt, K. 2007. Swinging the pendulum: Dance, gender, Reform Judaism, public artmaking. MPAS thesis, University of Southern California. Abstract in ProQuest, UMI Dissertations Publishing, publ. nr. 1443863, 2007.

New York City Ballet website. Dancers by rank. Accessed December 7, 2014. http://www.nycballet.com/Dancers/Dancers-by-Rank.aspx.

New York Live Arts 2011. Lobby talks: Transgender in dance. Podcast posted Oct. 19, 2011. http://www.newyorklivearts.org/blog/?p=302.

Novack, C. 1990. *Sharing the dance: Contact improvisation and American culture.* Madison: University of Wisconsin Press.

———. 1993. Ballet, gender and cultural power. In *Dance, gender and culture,* edited by H. Thomas, 34–48. London: Macmillan.

O'Flynn, G., Z. Pryor, and T. Gray. 2013. Embodied subjectivities: Nine young women talking dance. *Journal of Dance Education* 13(4): 130–138.

Oliver, W. 1994. Are we feminists? How our own antifeminist bias permeates dance academe. *Impulse* 2(3): 157–164.

———. 2005. Reading the ballerina's body: Susan Bordo sheds light on Anastasia Volochkova and Heidi Guenther. *Dance Research Journal* 37(2): 38–54.

———. 2008. Body image in the dance studio. *Journal of Physical Education, Recreation, and Dance* 79(5): 18–25.

Orenstein, P. 2011. *Cinderella ate my daughter.* New York: Harper & Row.

Osweiler, L. 2011. Dancing in the fringe: Connections forming "An evening of experimental Middle Eastern dance." PhD diss., University of California, Riverside. Abstract in ProQuest, UMI Dissertations Publishing, publ. nr. 3465362, 2011.

Ovalle, P. 2006. Shake your assets: Dance and the performance of Latina sexuality in Hollywood film. PhD diss., University of Southern California. Abstract in ProQuest, UMI Dissertations Publishing, publ. nr. 3257767, 2006.

Paechter, C. F. 1998. *Educating the other: Gender, power, and schooling.* London: Falmer.

Patton, M. Q. 2001. *Qualitative research and evaluation methods*, 3rd ed. Thousand Oaks, CA: Sage.

Paul Taylor Dance Company website. Dancers. Accessed December 7, 2014. http://www.ptamd.org/artists-dances/ptdc/dancers/.

Perron, W. 2008. Curtain up. *Dance Magazine*, April, 10.

———. 2014. What exactly is contemporary ballet? *Dance Magazine* 88(9): 34–36.

Peterson, G. T. 2011. Clubbing and masculinities: Gender shifts in gay men's dance floor choreographies. *Journal of Homosexuality* 58(5): 608–25.

Pew Research Center. 2008. "Men or women: Who's the better leader?" Pew Research Center, Social and Demographic Trends. August 25, 2008. http://www.pewsocialtrends.org/2008/08/25/men-or-women-whos-the-better-leader/.

Philadanco website. Philadanco dancers. Accessed December 7, 2014. http://www.philadanco.org/about/dancers.php.

Picart, C. 2006. *From ballroom to DanceSport: Aesthetics, athletics, and body culture.* Albany: SUNY Press.

Pickard, A. 2013. Ballet body belief: Perceptions of an ideal ballet body from young ballet dancers. *Research in Dance Education* 14(1): 3–19.

———. 2015. *Ballet body narratives: Pain, pleasure and perfections in embodied identity.* Oxford: Peter Lang.

Pike, C. 2011. Black tights and dance belts: Constructing a masculine identity in a world of pink tutus in Corner Brook, Newfoundland. In *Fields in motion: Ethnography in the worlds of dance*, edited by D. Davida, 277–303. Waterloo, ON: Wilfred Laurier University Press.

Polasek, K. M., and E. A. Roper. 2011. Negotiating the gay male stereotype in ballet and modern dance. *Research in Dance Education* 12(2): 173–193.

Polhemus, T. 1993. Dance, gender and culture. In *Dance, gender and culture*, edited by H. Thomas, 3–15. London: Macmillan.

Prendergast, M., C. Leggo, and P. Sameshima, eds. 2009. *Poetic inquiry: Vibrant voices in the social sciences.* Rotterdam, The Netherlands: Senses Publishers.

Provence, M. M., A. B. Rochlen, M. R. Chester, and E. R. Smith. 2014. Just one of the guys: A qualitative study of gay men's experiences in mixed sexual orientation men's groups. *Psychology of Men and Masculinity* 15(4): 427–436.

Reed, S. 1998. The politics and poetics of dance. *Annual Review of Anthropology* 27: 503–532.

Richard, B. 2009. "Daddy, root me in": Tethering young sons in the context of male, inter-generational, child-centered dance education. PhD diss., Temple University. Abstract in UMI Dissertations Publishing, publ. nr. 3359701, 2009.

Richmond, P. 2003. Gender and the forms of modernism: Dancers and painters. PhD diss., Case Western Reserve University. Abstract in ProQuest, UMI Dissertations Publishing, publ. nr. 3097358, 2003.

Risner, D. 2002a. Rehearsing heterosexuality: Unspoken truths in dance education. *Dance Research Journal* 34(2): 63–78.

———. 2002b. Sexual orientation and male participation in dance education: Revisiting the open secret. *Journal of Dance Education* 2(3): 84–92.

———. 2004. Dance, sexuality, and education today: Observations for dance educators. *Journal of Dance Education* 4(1): 6–10.

———. 2005. Dance & sexuality: Opportunities for teaching and learning in dance education. *Journal of Dance Education* 5(2): 41–42.

———. 2006. Equity in dance education: Where are we now? *Journal of Dance Education* 6(4): 105–108.

———. 2007a. Current challenges for K-12 dance education and development: Perspectives from higher education. *Arts Education Policy Review* 108(4): 17–24.

———. 2007b. Dance education in social and cultural perspective. In *Dance: Current Selected Research*, edited by L. Overby and B. Lepczyk, 153–189. Brooklyn, NY: AMS Press.

———. 2007c. Rehearsing masculinity: Challenging the "Boy Code" in dance education. *Research in Dance Education* 8(2): 139–153.

———. 2008. The politics of gender in dance pedagogy. *Journal of Dance Education* 8(3): 94–97.

———. 2009a. *Stigma and perseverance in the lives of boys who dance: An empirical study of male identities in Western theatrical dance training*. Lewiston, NY: Edwin Mellen.

———. 2009b. What we know about boys who dance. In *When men dance: Choreographing masculinities across borders*, edited by J. Fisher and A. Shay, 57–90. Oxford: Oxford University Press.

———. 2010a. Dance education matters: Rebuilding Post-secondary dance education for twenty-first century relevance and resonance. *Arts Education Policy Review* 111(4): 123–135.

———. 2010b. The rise and fall of postsecondary dance education: Charting an expansive recovery. *Journal of Dance Education* 10(4): 93–94.

———. 2014a. Bullying victimization and social support of adolescent male dance students: an analysis of findings. *Research in Dance Education* 15(2): 179–201.

———. 2014b. Gender problems in Western theatrical dance: Little girls, big sissies & the "Baryshnikov Complex." *International Journal of Education & the Arts* 15(10): 1–22. http://www.ijea.org/v15n10/2.

Risner, D., and S. Barr. 2015. Troubling methods-centric "teacher production": Social foundations in dance education teacher preparation. *Arts Education Policy Review* 116(2): 78–91.

Risner, D., H. Godfrey, and L. C. Simmons. 2004. The impact of sexuality in contemporary culture: An interpretive study of perceptions and choices in private sector dance education. *Journal of Dance Education* 4(1): 23–32.

Risner, D., and D. Prioleau. 2004. Leadership and administration in dance in higher education: Challenges and responsibilities of the department chair. In *Conference Proceedings of the National Dance Education Organization: Merging Worlds: Dance, Education, Society and Politics*, edited by D. Risner and J. Anderson, 343–351. East Lansing, MI: National Dance Education Organization.

Risner, D., and S. W. Stinson, 2010. Moving social justice: Challenges, fears and possibilities in dance education. *International Journal of Education and the Arts* 11(6). Retrieved [November 11, 2015] from http://www.ijea.org/v11n6/.

Risner, D., and S. Thompson. 2005. HIV/AIDS in dance education: A pilot study in higher education. *Journal of Dance Education* 5(2): 70–76.

Ritenburg, H. 2010. Frozen landscapes: A Foucauldian genealogy of the ideal ballet dancer's body. *Research in Dance Education* 11(1): 71–85.

Ronen, S. 2010. Grinding on the floor: Gendered scripts and sexualized dancing at college parties. *Gender and Society* 24(3): 355–377.

Ross, J. 2002. Institutional forces and the shaping of dance in the American university. *Dance Chronicle* 25(1): 115–124.

Rossen, R. 2006. Dancing Jewish: Jewish identity in American modern and postmodern dance. PhD diss., Northwestern University. Abstract in ProQuest, UMI Dissertations Publishing, publ. nr. 3213017, 2006.

Rubin, L. 1985. *Just friends: The role of friendship in our lives*. New York: Harper and Row.

Saldana, J. 2009. *The coding manual for qualitative researchers*. Thousand Oaks, CA: Sage.

———. 2011. *Fundamentals of qualitative research*. New York: Oxford University Press.

Samuels, S. 2001. Study exposes dance gender gap. *Dance Magazine*, March, 35–37.

Sanderson, P. 2001. Age and gender issues in adolescent attitudes to dance. *European Physical Education Review* 7(2): 117–136.

San Francisco Ballet website. Principals. Accessed December 7, 2014. https://www.sfballet.org/company/dancers/principals.

Sax, J. 2006. *Why gender matters: What parents and teachers need to know about the emerging science of sex differences*. New York: Broadway.

Schaffman, K. 2001. From the margins to the mainstream: Contact improvisation and the commodification of touch. PhD diss., University of California at Riverside, 2001. *Dissertation Abstracts International* 62(7): 2270.

Schaumann, M. 2010. Ripe with meaning: The pregnant body in contemporary dance. MFA thesis, University of Utah. Abstract in ProQuest, UMI Dissertations Publishing, publ. nr. 1479564, 2010.

Schloss, J. G. 2009. *Foundation: B-boys, b-girls, and hip hop culture in New York*. New York: Oxford University Press.

Schupp, K. 2006. The culture of dance competitions. Paper presented at the International Conference of the Congress of Research in Dance, Tempe, AZ, November 2–5.

———. 2011. Informed decisions: Dance improvisation and responsible citizenship. *Journal of Dance Education* 11(1): 22–29.

Schwartz, P. 1994. Discontinuities and transitions in dance education: From the recital studio to the college stage. *Impulse* 1994(2): 232–240.

Scull, M. 2013. The staged self: Embodiment, gender, and relationships among male strippers. PhD diss., Indiana University. Abstract in ProQuest, UMI Dissertations Publishing, publ. nr. 3610232, 2013.
Sendak, M. 1963. *Where the wild things are.* New York: Harper & Row.
Shapiro, S. 1998. Toward transformative teachers: Critical and feminist perspectives in dance education. In *Dance, power, and difference: Critical and feminist perspectives on dance education*, edited by S. Shapiro, 7–21. Champaign, IL: Human Kinetics.
———. 2004. Recovering girlhood: A pedagogy of embodiment. *Journal of Dance Education* 4(1): 35–36.
Sheets-Johnstone, M. 1979. *The phenomenology of dance.* 2nd ed. London: Dance Books.
———. 2009. "Man has always danced": Forays into an art largely forgotten by philosophers. In *The corporeal turn: An interdisciplinary reader*, 306–327. Charlottesville, VA: Imprint Academic,.
Shen, B., A. Chen, H. Tolley, and K. Serabis. 2003. Gender and interest-based motivation in learning dance. *Journal of Teaching in Physical Education* 22: 396–409.
Singleton, Jr., R. A., and J. Vacca. 2007. Interpersonal competition in friendships. *Sex Roles* 57: 617–627.
Smith, C. 1998. On authoritarianism in the dance classroom. In *Dance, power, and difference: Critical and feminist perspectives on dance education*, edited by S. Shapiro, 123–146. Champaign, IL: Human Kinetics.
Spurgeon, D. 1999. The men's movement. Paper presented at Congress on Research in Dance Pomona College, December.
Stafford, B. 2001. *Visual analogy: Consciousness as the art of connecting.* Chicago: University of Chicago Press.
Stanley, D., E. Phelps, and M. Banaji. 2008. The neural basis of implicit attitudes. *Current Directions in Psychological Science* 17(2): 164–170.
Steiner, W. 1995. *The scandal of pleasure.* Chicago: University of Chicago Press.
Stern, R. D. 1994. *1994-95 Dance Magazine college guide.* New York: McFadden Communications.
Stinson, S. 1998a. Places where I've been: Reflections on issues of gender in dance education, research, and administration. *Choreography and Dance* 5(1): 117–127.
———. 1998b. Seeking a feminist pedagogy for children's dance. In *Dance, power, and difference: Critical and feminist perspectives on dance education*, edited by S. Shapiro, 23–47. Champaign, IL: Human Kinetics.
———. 2001. Voices from adolescent males. *DACI in Print*, November, 2: 4–6.
———. 2005. The hidden curriculum of gender in dance education. *Journal of Dance Education* 5(2): 51–57.
Stinson, S., D. Blumenfeld-Jones, and J. Van Dyke. 1990. Voices of young women dance students: An interpretive study of meaning in dance. *Dance Research Journal* 22(2): 13–22.
Stoneley, P. 2007. *A queer history of the ballet.* New York and London: Routledge.
Taschuk, H. 2009. Dance is not a four-letter word! Motivating teenage boys to dance. *Physical and Health Education Journal* 75(2): 35–37.

Thomas, H. 2003. *The body, dance and cultural theory.* New York: Palgrave Macmillan.
Tikkun, K. 2010. Embodiment beyond the binary: Sean Dorsey and the transgender queer presence in contemporary concert dance. MFA thesis, University of California, Irvine. Abstract in ProQuest, UMI Dissertations Publishing, publ. nr. 1476753, 2010.
Tomko, L. 1999. *Dancing class: Gender, ethnicity, and social divides in American dance 1890–1920.* Bloomington: Indiana University Press.
——. 2007. Dido's otherness: Choreographing race and gender in the ballet d'action. In *Dance Discourses: Keywords in Dance Research*, edited by S. Franco and M. Nordera, 121–130. New York: Routledge.
Torp, L. 1986. Hip hop dances: Their adoption and function among boys in Denmark from 1983–1984. *Yearbook for Traditional Music* 18: 29–36.
Trautner, M. N. 2005. Doing gender, doing class: The performance of sexuality in exotic dance clubs. *Gender & Society* 19(6): 771–788.
Tzioumakis, Y., and S. Lincoln, eds. 2013. *The time of our lives: Dirty Dancing and popular culture.* Detroit, MI: Wayne State University Press.
Underwood, M. 2003. *Social aggression among girls.* New York: Guilford Press.
Van Aken, K. 2006. Race and gender in the Broadway chorus. PhD diss., University of Pittsburgh. Abstract in ProQuest, UMI Dissertations Publishing, publ. nr. 3255756, 2006.
Van Dyke, J. 1992. *Modern dance in a postmodern world: An analysis of federal arts funding and its impact on the field of modern dance.* Reston, VA: American Alliance for Health, Physical Education, Recreation, and Dance.
——. 1996. Gender and success in the American dance world. *Women's Studies International Forum* 19(5): 535–543.
van Manen, M. 2014. *Phenomenology of practice: Meaning-giving methods in phenomenological research and writing.* Walnut Creek, CA: Left Coast Press.
Warburton, T. 2009. Of boys and girls. *Research in Dance Education* 10(2): 145–148.
Watson, D. C. 2012. Gender differences in gossip and friendship. *Sex Roles* 67:494–502.
Way, N. 2013. Boys' friendships during adolescence: Intimacy, desire, and loss. *Journal of Research on Adolescence* 23:201–13.
Weisbrod, A. A. 2010. Competition dance: Redefining dance in the United States. PhD diss., University of California, Riverside.
Weitz, R., ed. 2010. *The politics of women's bodies: Sexuality, appearance, and behavior.* 3rd ed. New York: Oxford University Press.
West, C. S. 2005. Black bodies in dance education: Charting new a new pedagogical paradigm to eliminate gendered and hypersexualized assumptions. *Journal of Dance Education* 5(2): 64–69.
Williams, D. 2003. Examining psychosocial issues of adolescent male dancers. PhD diss., Marywood University.
Willis, C. 1995. Factors that affect dance programs. *Journal of Physical Education, Recreation and Dance* 66(4): 58–63.
Wolf-Wendel, L., and J. Ward. 2014. Academic mothers: Exploring disciplinary perspectives. *Innovations in Higher Education* 40(1): 19–35. DOI 10.1007/s10755-014-9293-4.

Wollins, J. 2014. *Dance competitions: Are you ready?* Waldorf, MD: Starpower Talent Competition.

Wulff, H. 2008. Ethereal expression: Paradoxes of ballet as a global physical culture. *Ethnography* 9(4): 518–535. DOI: 10.1177/1466138108096990

Young, I. 2005. *On female body experience: "Throwing like a girl" and other essays.* Oxford: Oxford University Press.

Zwirn, S. G. 2006. Artist or art teacher: The role of gender in identity formation and career choice. *Teaching Artist Journal* 4(3): 167–175.

Contributors

Gareth Belling, MFA, is an Australian choreographer who danced with Queensland Ballet from 2002 to 2012. Since 2005, he has created works for Queensland Ballet, Collusion, Expressions Dance Company, and others. Now an active independent dance maker, he created for Queensland Ballet's 2013 *Elegance* and 2014 *Dance Dialogues* seasons and traveled to China and Hong Kong on an Australia China Council research scholarship. He most recently premiered his new evening-length chamber ballet *Desirelines* with Collusion in the 2015 Brisbane Festival.

Karen Bond, PhD, is director of the NDEO/Temple University Center for Research in Dance Education, Boyer College of Music and Dance, Temple University. She teaches graduate courses on experiential research methodologies (phenomenology, hermeneutics, ethnography, autobiography) and educational inquiry. A recipient of national and international research awards, she has an abiding interest in meanings of dance and dancing for people of all ages, genders, and abilities.

Carolyn Hebert has an MA in Dance from York University in Toronto, Canada, and is currently pursuing her PhD in education with studies in teaching and learning at the University of Ottawa. Her phenomenological research focuses on students' experiences of gender in competitive dance. She is also a competitive dance teacher and choreographer specializing in jazz and tap dance.

Eliza Larson, MFA, is an independent dance artist and writer based in Portland, Oregon. She co-directs the Mountain Empire Performance Collective, a long-distance dance company, and currently performs and teaches throughout the Pacific Northwest. In addition to her research on gender and dance, she has also published articles about creative process and long-distance dance making. She is the author of *Terpsichore's Deck*—a set of fifty-two choreographic ideas and principles in playing-card format and is co-curator of the Summer/Fall 2016 *Contact Quarterly Special Folio*.

Pamela S. Musil, MA, is professor in the Department of Dance at Brigham Young University where she teaches dance education and dance science courses and serves as the contemporary dance administrator and associate chair of the department. Research interests include gender-related issues of dancers, with particular focus on matters pertaining to women.

Wendy Oliver, EdD, MFA, is professor and chair in the Department of Theatre, Dance, and Film at Providence College, where she teaches dance and women's studies. She has published articles focused on women's body image in dance and is currently researching feminist pedagogy in dance. She is editor-in-chief of *Journal of Dance Education* and recently coedited the book *Jazz Dance: A History of the Roots and Branches*.

Katherine Polasek, PhD, is associate professor in the Kinesiology Department at the State University of New York at Cortland. Her research focuses primarily on gender and sport. More specifically, Polasek is interested in the ways in which gender roles impact people's experiences in sport and physical activity.

Doug Risner, PhD, MFA, is distinguished professor of dance at Wayne State University in Detroit, Michigan, and conducts research on the sociology of dance training and education, curriculum theory and policy, social foundations of dance pedagogy, gender in dance, and online learning and web-based curriculum design. His publications include *Stigma and Perseverance in the Lives of Boys Who Dance* and *Gender, Sexuality and Identity: Critical Issues in Dance Education*. Risner is editor emeritus of the *Journal of Dance Education* and associate editor of the international journal *Research in Dance Education*.

Emily Roper, PhD, is associate professor in the Department of Kinesiology at Sam Houston State University. Roper's scholarship is interdisciplinary, situated at the intersection of sport psychology, gender studies, and cultural studies. Her research centers on the ways gender shapes experiences, cultural meanings, and societal structures in sport and exercise contexts.

Karen Schupp, MFA, is assistant professor in the Herberger Institute School of Film, Dance and Theatre at Arizona State University and the author of *Studying Dance: A Guide to Campus and Beyond*. Her scholarly research addresses innovative pedagogical practices and curricula in postsecondary dance education. Currently, she is examining dance competition culture using a transdisciplinary approach that combines creative practices with qualitative research methodologies. Schupp is also an associate editor of the *Journal of Dance Education*.

Jan Van Dyke was professor emerita on the UNC Greensboro dance faculty where she was department head from 2006 to 2011. Van Dyke formerly directed a studio and company in Washington, DC, for eight years, touring nationally with her company and as a solo artist. She also directed the Jan Van Dyke Dance Group and cofounded and produced the NC Dance Festival. In 2008 she received the *Dance Teacher Magazine* Award for Higher Education; she also published on gender equity in dance.

Index

Page numbers in *italics* indicate tables.

Aalten, Anna, 12
Acosta, Niv, 17
Action research, 3, 18, 62–63, 136
Adolescent dancers, 18, 76–77, 95
Agency of the dancer, 3, 6, 60, 65, 69, 71, 137, 145, 146, 149, 151
Allan, Maud, 13
Alterowitz, Gretchen, 62
American Dance Festival (ADF), 18, 23, 25, 27, 29, 40, 43, 51–56, 59
Androgynous, 16
Appearance norms, 82–84, *84*
Arkin, Lisa, 13
Artistic directors, 18, 23–24, 37, 39–41, 43, 75, 117, 177

Ballet dancers, 3, 12, 44, 129
Bates Dance Festival, 28–29
Biology and gender, 33–34, 35–36, 149, 151, 157n9
Black studies, 4
Body image, xi, 6, 15, 79
Bond, Karen, 8, 19, 135, 137
Bourne, Matthew, 11, 61
Boys in dance, 83, 92, 97, 105, 181; as special, 82, 89–91, *91*, 97, 103, 132, 159
Boys-only training, 18, 97–101, 105, 108–13, 153
Boys' vs. girls' movement styles, 15, 112
Brenner, Janis, 23
Broadway chorus, 14
Brooklyn Academy of Music (BAM), 18, 40, 43, 55, 59
Bullying, 10, 99, 130, 133
Burt, Ramsay, xi, 11, 60, 98
Butler, Judith, 3, 6, 65, 69, 102, 152

Capezio Dance Award, 26, 37
Chandralekha, 6
Chatterjea, Ananya, 5
Choreographers: female, 9, 31, 46, 48, 51–57; gay, 11; lesbian, 11; male, 21, 25, 48, 51–53, 55; queer, 11
Commercial dance, 18, 24, 78–79, 97–99, 106, 109
Competition among male dancers, 123, 128–29, 133
Competitive advantage, 90
Confidence in men vs. women, 8, 35–37, 96
Contact improvisation, 8, 78
Contemporary ballet, 12, 18, 44, *49*, 53, 60–62, 64, 67, 69, 73, 75
Croft, Clare, 12, 62
Cross-category friendships, 119, 134
Curriculum, 7, 34–35, 80, 98–100, 103, 136, 153, 156n3, 177, 182

Daly, Ann, 4–5, 64, 153
Dance: administration, 9, 19, 160, 168, 174, 176–177; clubs, 11, 15, 178; competitions, 3, 76–79, 81–84, *84*, 87, 89–91, *91*,

Dance—*continued*
  93–96, 142; and family, 19, 102, 116, 120, 124, 127, 130, 139, 149, 152, 173, 177, 183; festivals, 9, 18, 23, 25, 27–29, 40, 43, 45, 47–54, 54, 56, 58; films, 6, 13–14, 32; in higher education, 9, 17, 19, 158–61, 166, 173, 175–76, 178–80; as macho, 98; and play, 139, 142–43, 150, 153–155; in public schools, 104, 123, 155; studios, 6, 9–10, 17–19, 24–25, 27–28, 37–39, 62, 76, 79–80, 89, 95, 97–106, 109–10, 113–14, 127, 135, 137, 139, 142, 146, 153, 181
  Dance genres: ballet, 3–6, 9–15, 18, 21, 23–26, 32, 43–45, 47, 49–50, 50, 52–53, 53, 56, 60–71, 73–76, 78, 89, 95, 97–98, 100, 103–5, 107, 115, 121, 123, 127, 129–30, 133, 141–42, 144–45, 148, 150, 153–54, 174; ballroom, 11, 14, 16; belly, 15, 145; popular, xii, 9, 11, 14–15; recreational, 4, 14, 99–100, 110; religious, 14–15; social, 14, 16, 107; tap, 10, 24, 47, 76, 78, 97–98, 100
Dance Magazine Awards, 27
Dance/NYC, 23, 40–41, 58
Dance/NYC's Census of NYC's Dancemakers, 23, 40–41, 58
Dancing with the Stars, 14
Davies, Siobhan, 12
Dawson, David, 61
Defensive heterosexuality, 132
Dirty Dancing, 14
Display of ballerina by partner, 64, 68, 71, 73
Duncan, Isadora, 13, 32, 58

Earnings in dance, 22, 40
Emergence of male leadership in modern dance, 25, 33, 174, 183
Equity in dance, 9, 18, 39, 59; in concert dance, 17
Estrogen and testosterone levels, 33–34
Ethnic subjectivities, 15
Ethnographic study, 12, 99
Expressive content, 89

Feminine movement, 87, 92, 107, 141
Feminist pedagogy, 5
Feminist theory, 3–4, 6
Financial success, 38
Fine, Cordelia, 1, 138, 151–52, 156
Fisher, Jennifer, 10, 13, 103
Foster, Susan, 78–79, 92–93
Foucault, Michel, 80, 94
Friendships among dancers, 18, 115–21, 123–25, 128, 130–31, 133–34
Funding opportunities, xi, 3, 18, 21–22, 29–30, 32, 37, 40, 57, 59n1

Gay male dancers, 11, 95, 120, 131, 134
Gender: bias, 7, 22, 30, 44, 47, 178–79; binary/non-binary, 8–9, 19, 92, 106, 149, 152; in the dance studio, 17–18; differences in boys and girls, 138–56; differences in men and women, 64, 129, 139, 163–67, 170–72, 180; discrimination, xi, 17, 19, 22; distribution, 23, 41–42, 52, 55, 58; equity, 17–19; equity in concert dance, 8–9, 17–19, 21–38, 39–55; expectations, 37, 76–96, 103, 105, 107, 116–17; expression, 10–11, 16, 19, 62, 88, 91; and funding, 29; gender-neutral, 2, 17, 58, 95, 108, 151; gender order, 2–3; gender studies, xii, 1–3, 7; in higher education, 17; identity, 2, 7, 16, 69, 103; inhibitors, 80, 114, 136, 147; outside the gender binary, 3–4, 16–17, 46; performance of, 3, 91, 96, 106; and professional dance, 24; queer, 1, 4, 11–12, 16–17, 46, 61; social construction of, 6, 8, 10, 78; status, 3; stereotypes, 5, 98–99, 106, 138–39, 141, 146; and teaching, 28
Gender-based techniques, 100
Gendered role models, 10, 104, 113, 168, 175–76, 179
Gender gap index, 32
Gender-neutral: performing, 95, 108; teaching, 17, 58, 95
Gender norms, problems of, 78, 144, 152, 157

Gender Project, The, 23, 39, 59n1
Girls in dance, 7, 81, 90, 180
GLBT Studies, 11
Graham, Martha, 12, 26, 49, 58
Grants, 9, 17–18, 22, 29–32, 37; grant-giving, 21, 30
Grants and awards for dance: Guggenheim Fellowships, 31, 37; Kennedy Center Honors, 26–27, 37; MacArthur Fellows Program, 30–31; National Medal of the Arts, 27; Samuel Scripps American Dance Festival Award, 27, 37
Grinding and gender, 15

Heteronormative, 18, 63, 68, 72–74, 107
Heterosexual desirability, 79, 93
Heterosexual male dancers. *See* Gay male dancers
Heterosexual narrative, 93
Hidden curriculum, 7, 34, 80, 98–99, 103, 153, 182
Higher education: and administrative responsibilities, 165; gender ratios, 176; salaries, 161–62, 165–67; support systems, 180; work-life balance, 161, 171–73, 183; workload, 161–63, 165; work satisfaction, 161
High school dance, 15, 34, 77, 123, 137, 145, 154
Hip-hop dance, 50, 76, 97–102, 104–13
Homophobia, xi, 8–12, 18, 34, 99, 119
Homosexual male dancers. *See* Gay male dancers

"Industrial body," 79, 92–93
Innate differences, 2
Intersex, 16, 46
Intimate Distance, 63, 67, 71, 74

Jacob's Pillow, 9, 18, 40, 43–45, 47–52, 55, 57, 59n1
Jacob's Pillow Dance Festival, 18, 40, 47, 49–51, *49*, 59n1
Jazz technique class, 99, 102, 106

Jewish identity, 13
Johnson, Chris, 62
Judaism, 14, 16
Judges, 77–79, 83, 90, 93–95; judging, 90, 111

Koritz, Amy, 13
Kylian, Jiri, 61–62, 70

Les Noces, 60–61, 63–64, 66–67, 69–75
Liberatory pedagogy, 5
Lock, Edouard, 14

Maggie Allesee National Center for Choreography, 28–29
Male/female interactions, 87, 88, 91, 125, 129, 133
Male friendships among dancers, 117–18, 133
Male gaze, 5
Male privilege, 181, 183
Male teachers, 10, 87–88, 104, 113, 174
Male vs female artistic directors, 18, 23–24, 36–37, 40–43, 75, 177
Male vs female teachers, 10, 23, 29, 37, 87–88, 101, 104, 113, 174
"Marriage Plot," 60, 69
Masculine stereotype, 9
Matachine, 14–15
McLean, Adrienne, 13
Men in dance, 5, 9–11, 23, 41, 99, 120
Men's studies, 4, 7
Mixed-gender class, 110, 112
Modern dance, 12–15, 23–25, 43–44, 51–52, 58, 107; modern dancers, 32, 58, 115, 121, 130, 133
Movement expectations, 82, 85–86, *86*

National Endowment for the Arts (NEA), 18, 21, 27, 29–31
Neo-classical, 71
Neurosexism, 1, 155
Nijinska, Bronislava, 61, 63, 70
Nijinsky, Vaslav, 12

Ovalle, Priscilla, 6

Page, Ruth, 12
Partnering (male/female), 18, 62, 64–65, 68–71, 78, 120
Pedagogy of embodiment, 5
Phenomenology, 63, 136
Popular culture studies, 4
Pyle, Katy, 62

Queer studies, xii, 1, 16, 46
Queer theory, 4, 11, 16

Race, 4–6, 14–16, 74, 116–17, 135, 177; racism, 4
Ratio of male to female dancers, 21–23, 25–28, 25, 31–32, 36–37, 41, 136
Rebeginnings, 63, 65, 67–69, 71, 74
Regendering, 2, 18, 60–66, 68, 71, 74–75
Relational-cultural theory, 18, 115
Research in dance education, 7
Risner, Doug, xi, 4, 9, 19, 34, 80, 93, 104, 120, 130–32, 161, 181–82
Ritenburg, Heather, 13

Salaries, 34, 161–62, 165–67; salary negotiations, 35
Sean Dorsey Dance, 11, 16–17
Sexism, 4, 8, 11

Sexual dimorphism, 65–66, 71
Sexuality in hip-hop, 107
Shapiro, Sherry, 5
Shaw, JoAnna Mendl, 23, 39
Shawn, Ted, 44, 47–49, 49
Shay, Anthony, 10
Sheets-Johnstone, Maxine, 65, 153
Social justice, 5, 7
Somatic pedagogy, 95
So You Think You Can Dance, 89, 98
Sport culture, 120
State funding, North Carolina, 31
Status quo, 1, 11, 19, 138, 181
Stinson, Sue, 9, 79, 93, 98, 153
Strip club, 15

Transgendered, 4, 11, 16–17, 46, 132

Unequal treatment, 90

Visual artists and gender, 32–33, 37

Western culture, 10, 17
Whelan, Wendy, 12, 49
Women's bodies, 6, 13, 15
Women's studies, xi, 1

Zollar, Jawole Willa Jo, 6

www.ingramcontent.com/pod-product-compliance
Lightning Source LLC
Chambersburg PA
CBHW031435160426
43195CB00010BB/746